# Twelve Steps of Adult Children

# Workbook

*On the Cover:*

*The front cover of the ACA workbook depicts the Laundry List Tree, which represents the traits of an adult child. The tree also shows the distinction between the traits which are learned in childhood and the defects of character that develop later in life. The Laundry List Traits represent the limbs while the character defects are the fruit.*

*The back cover depicts the Recovery Tree and the possible results to be realized by working through the ACA Twelve Steps. With recovery, we integrate many of the Laundry List traits, while removing many of the defects of character.*

Approved by the 2008 ACA Annual Business Conference

Twelve Steps of Adult Children
(Alcoholic / Dysfunctional Families)
Workbook

ISBN 978-0-9789797-1-3 Spiral Bound
ISBN 978-1-944840-07-5 Softcover

Printed in the United States of America

17 18 19  24 23 22

# "Adult Child"

## What is an Adult Child?

"The concept of Adult Child came from the Alateens who began the Hope for Adult Children of Alcoholics meeting. The original members of our fellowship, who were over eighteen years old, were adults; but as children they grew up in alcoholic homes. Adult Child also means that when confronted, we regress to a stage in our childhood." ACA History—an interview with Tony A., 1992.

*Editor's Note: More than a decade has passed since one of our primary founders, Tony A., was interviewed on the topic of the fellowship that he helped found with Alateen members in late 1977 and 1978. For this book we will use Tony's words as the foundation to define the adult child personality. An adult child is someone who responds to adult situations with self-doubt, self-blame or a sense of being wrong or inferior—all learned from stages of childhood. Without help, we unknowingly operate with ineffective thoughts and judgments learned in childhood. The regression can be subtle, but it is there sabotaging our decisions and relationships.*

Note: Both of these items are from the introductory material of the ACA Fellowship Text (Steps and Traditions Book).

This workbook is a companion book for Chapter Seven of the ACA Fellowship Text. Chapter Seven is the Twelve Steps chapter in the ACA book.

# The "Laundry List"
## (14 Characteristics of an Adult Child)

These are characteristics we seem to have in common due to being brought up in an alcoholic household.

1. We became isolated and afraid of people and authority figures.

2. We became approval seekers and lost our identity in the process.

3. We are frightened by angry people and any personal criticism.

4. We either become alcoholics, marry them, or both, or find another compulsive personality such as a workaholic to fulfill our sick abandonment needs.

5. We live life from the viewpoint of victims and are attracted by that weakness in our love and friendship relationships.

6. We have an overdeveloped sense of responsibility and it is easier for us to be concerned with others rather than ourselves; this enables us not to look too closely at our own faults, etc.

7. We get guilt feelings when we stand up for ourselves instead of giving in to others.

8. We became addicted to excitement.

9. We confuse love and pity and tend to "love" people we can "pity" and "rescue."

10. We have "stuffed" our feelings from our traumatic childhoods and have lost the ability to feel or express our feelings because it hurts so much (denial).

11. We judge ourselves harshly and have a very low sense of self-esteem.

12. We are dependent personalities who are terrified of abandonment and will do anything to hold on to a relationship in order not to experience painful abandonment feelings which we received from living with sick people who were never there emotionally for us.

13. Alcoholism is a family disease and we became para-alcoholics and took on the characteristics of that disease even though we did not pick up the drink.

14. Para-alcoholics are reactors rather than actors.

*– Tony A., 1978*

# ACA Twelve Steps

1. We admitted we were powerless over the effects of alcoholism or other family dysfunction, that our lives had become unmanageable.

2. Came to believe that a Power greater than ourselves could restore us to sanity.

3. Made a decision to turn our will and our lives over to the care of God as we understand God.

4. Made a searching and fearless moral inventory of ourselves.

5. Admitted to God, to ourselves, and to another human being the exact nature of our wrongs.

6. Were entirely ready to have God remove all these defects of character.

7. Humbly asked God to remove our shortcomings.

8. Made a list of all persons we had harmed and became willing to make amends to them all.

9. Made direct amends to such people wherever possible, except when to do so would injure them or others.

10. Continued to take personal inventory and, when we were wrong, promptly admitted it.

11. Sought through prayer and meditation to improve our conscious contact with God, as we understand God, praying only for knowledge of God's will for us and the power to carry that out.

12. Having had a spiritual awakening as the result of these steps, we tried to carry this message to others who still suffer, and to practice these principles in all our affairs.

The Twelve Steps are reprinted and adapted with permission from the original Twelve Steps of Alcoholics Anonymous.

# The Solution

The solution is to become your own loving parent. As ACA becomes a safe place for you, you will find freedom to express all the hurts and fears that you have kept inside and to free yourself from the shame and blame that are carry-overs from the past. You will become an adult who is imprisoned no longer by childhood reactions. You will recover the child within you, learning to love and accept yourself.

The healing begins when we risk moving out of isolation. Feelings and buried memories will return. By gradually releasing the burden of unexpressed grief, we slowly move out of the past. We learn to reparent ourselves with gentleness, humor, love and respect. This process allows us to see our biological parents as the instruments of our existence. Our actual parent is a Higher Power whom some of us choose to call God. Although we had alcoholic or dysfunctional parents, our Higher Power gave us the Twelve Steps of Recovery.

This is the action and work that heals us: we use the Steps; we use the meetings; we use the telephone. We share our experience, strength, and hope with each other. We learn to restructure our sick thinking one day at a time. When we release our parents from responsibility for our actions today, we become free to make healthful decisions as actors, not reactors. We progress from hurting, to healing, to helping. We awaken to a sense of wholeness we never knew was possible.

By attending these meetings on a regular basis, you will come to see parental alcoholism or family dysfunction for what it is: a disease that infected you as a child and continues to affect you as an adult. You will learn to keep the focus on yourself in the here and now. You will take responsibility for your own life and supply your own parenting.

You will not do this alone. Look around you and you will see others who know how you feel. We will love and encourage you no matter what. We ask you to accept us just as we accept you.

This is a spiritual program based on action coming from love. We are sure that as the love grows inside you, you will see beautiful changes in all your relationships, especially with God, yourself, and your parents.

# The ACA Promises

1. We will discover our real identities by loving and accepting ourselves.

2. Our self-esteem will increase as we give ourselves approval on a daily basis.

3. Fear of authority figures and the need to "people-please" will leave us.

4. Our ability to share intimacy will grow inside us.

5. As we face our abandonment issues, we will be attracted by strengths and become more tolerant of weaknesses.

6. We will enjoy feeling stable, peaceful, and financially secure.

7. We will learn how to play and have fun in our lives.

8. We will choose to love people who can love and be responsible for themselves.

9. Healthy boundaries and limits will become easier for us to set.

10. Fears of failure and success will leave us, as we intuitively make healthier choices.

11. With help from our ACA support group, we will slowly release our dysfunctional behaviors.

12. Gradually, with our Higher Power's help, we will learn to expect the best and get it.

# How the ACA Twelve Step Workbook Was Developed

The ACA Twelve Step workbook was developed during a two-year period, beginning in 2005. As part of the development and input process, ACA groups across the United States read and used the workbook in small groups and in one-on-one recovery between a sponsor and sponsee. These working groups submitted input and comments that shaped the tone, focus, and detail of this workbook.

This workbook is a reformatted version of Chapter Seven from the ACA Fellowship Text (ACA "big book"). Chapter Seven and this workbook are very similar; however, the workbook has questions at the end of Steps One, Two, and Three and additional writing assignments.

Twelve Steps of Adult Children is designed as a Step-study book and stand alone piece of literature. It can serve as the main piece of literature for Twelve Step discussions at an ACA meeting. The workbook also is designed to be used by ACA members wanting to work the ACA Twelve Steps with a sponsor. Along with the writing assignments, there are worksheets for the Twelve Steps in addition to questions that help unlock clarity about our childhood experiences and our new path of recovery. For example, Step Four contains 35 pages with detailed writing and 12 workbook items on shame, abandonment, PTSD, feelings, and sexual abuse history. The ACA workbook also addresses the topics of grief and integration in addition to the Twelve Steps.

With some modification the workbook can be used by a group of ACAs wishing to work the Steps together during a 12-week to 16-week period.

## 2005 Annual Business Conference of ACA

The 2005 Annual Business Conference of Adult Children of Alcoholics approved the concept of a Twelve Step workbook that would accompany the ACA Fellowship Text. This workbook is specific to the ACA experience of working and living the Twelve Steps.

# What Does ACA Recovery Look Like?

By working the Twelve Steps of ACA and by attending meetings regularly, we begin to realize that ACA recovery involves emotional sobriety*. That is what ACA recovery looks like. But what is emotional sobriety?

To understand emotional sobriety, we must first understand emotional intoxication, which is also known as para-alcoholism. Para-alcoholism represents the mannerisms and behaviors we developed by living with an alcoholic or dysfunctional parent. As children, we took on the fear and denial of the alcoholic or nondrinking parent without taking a drink.

Emotional intoxication can be characterized by obsession and unhealthy dependence. There also can be compulsion. Even without drugs and alcohol, we can be "drunk" on fear, excitement or pain. We can also be drunk on arguing, gossip, or self-imposed isolation.

In essence the Laundry List, the 14 traits of an adult child, offers a textbook example of the behaviors and attitudes that characterize an emotionally intoxicated person. We fear authority figures and judge ourselves harshly while being terrified of abandonment. Without help, we seek out others to reenact our family dynamics. We can recreate our family dysfunction at home and on the job indefinitely until we find ACA. This means that our adult relationships resemble the template relationship we developed as children to survive an alcoholic or otherwise dysfunctional home. We find others to create chaos, conflict, or unsafe relationships.

Emotional sobriety involves a changed relationship with self and others. We measure emotional sobriety by the level of honesty, mutual respect, and the acceptability of feelings in our relationships. If our relationships are still manipulative and controlling, we are not emotionally sober no matter what we tell ourselves about our recovery program. Emotional sobriety means that we are involved in changed relationships that are safe and honest. We feel a nearness to our Higher Power. We cultivate emotional sobriety through the Twelve Steps and through association with other recovering adult children.

---

*Emotional sobriety was formally introduced to the ACA fellowship through the Identity Papers. The 1986 paper, "Finding Wholeness Through Separation: The Paradox of Independence," shows the genesis of emotional sobriety. The possibility of emotional sobriety is created through the broadening and deepening of the Steps and Traditions.

# Part I

# ACA Twelve Steps

*T*he pathway to emotional sobriety that endures time is through the Twelve Steps of ACA. This is the heart of the Adult Children of Alcoholics program. Adapted from the time-proven Steps of Alcoholics Anonymous, the Twelve Steps are precision tools that work. The ACA Steps clarify and help resolve a childhood of neglect, abuse, or rejection. With more than 30 years of experience, ACA is a proven program that offers a way out of confusion. The program brings clarity and sanity in measures we always hoped for, but usually could not believe existed as we grew up in dysfunctional homes.

Since their original publication by AA in 1939, the Twelve Steps have relieved the suffering of millions of alcoholics, addicts, codependents, food addicts, sex addicts, and many more obsessive-compulsive types. The Steps, and their various adaptations, have brought sure hope and a better way of life to those who desire change. In ACA, the Twelve Steps also bring recovery to our members who were not raised with addiction in the home. Our experience shows that these ACA members internalized the same abandonment and shame as children brought up in alcoholism or other addictions.

Beginning with Step One, we address denial, which can involve simply refusing to admit that abuse or neglect occurred in our childhood. Denial also includes trivializing behavior or remarks that were obviously harmful to us. If we admit that harmful behavior occurred, we can still be in denial if we fail to acknowledge the effects of the harm in our lives. Additionally, we are practicing denial if we attempt to explain away the behavior or to offer excuses for our family. By breaking through our denial, we seek a full remembrance. We find our loss and learn our story. With help and acceptance, we recognize the false identity we had to develop to survive family dysfunction.

In ACA, we learn to focus on ourselves and find our real identity. We must be willing to work the Twelve Steps so we can grow emotionally and spiritually. These are the Steps we work to address growing up in a dysfunctional family.

1. We admitted we were powerless over the effects of alcoholism or other family dysfunction; that our lives had become unmanageable.

2. Came to believe that a Power greater than ourselves could restore us to sanity.

3. Made a decision to turn our will and our lives over to the care of God as we understand God.

4. Made a searching and fearless moral inventory of ourselves.

5. Admitted to God, to ourselves, and to another human being the exact nature of our wrongs.

6. Were entirely ready to have God remove all these defects of character.

7. Humbly asked God to remove our shortcomings.

8. Made a list of all persons we had harmed and became willing to make amends to them all.

9. Made direct amends to such people wherever possible, except when to do so would injure them or others.

10. Continued to take personal inventory and when we were wrong promptly admitted it.

11. Sought through prayer and meditation to improve our conscious contact with God, as we understand God, praying only for knowledge of God's will for us and the power to carry that out.

12. Having had a spiritual awakening as the result of these Steps, we tried to carry this message to others who still suffer, and to practice these principles in all our affairs.

*The Twelve Steps are simple but not always easy; however, they work if a person truly wants to change and can hang on while change occurs. The Steps sometimes work even if a person picks at them like a finicky child forking at a lump of unwanted spinach. Such half measures often create the personal discomfort that motivates the adult child into greater action and personal growth.*

*By adapting AA's Steps, ACA is adding its flavor to the Steps while keeping intact the original intent of an admission of powerlessness followed by surrender. Such surrender is followed by a review of spiritual beliefs, self-inventory, making amends, and seeking conscious contact with a Higher Power. We develop a genuine attitude to live in love and service to ourselves and others.*

*While ACA adapted the AA Steps with few word changes, our experience shows that the adaptation has unique considerations. Because of our inherent sense of being flawed or unlovable, the adult child must be reminded that he or she has worth. We have worth and are acceptable, regardless of mistakes made or accomplishments achieved or not achieved. As adult children we are a traumatized group of adults, who can revert to self-doubt when making errors or sensing disapproval by others. No adaptation of the Twelve Steps for adult child purposes will be fully successful unless it emphasizes self-love. We are God's children despite mistakes made. Through such affirmations and Twelve Step work, we come to believe in our self-worth. We learn to tell ourselves that we are human and have something to offer the world. We face our mistakes and the opinions of others with confidence. In ACA, we get to say who we are, instead of a drunk or dysfunctional parent saying who we are not. This is the great fact for us.*

*We have paid our dues with the countless cursings, threats, and subtle neglectful acts we have endured as children. We stand now as adults, not complaining, but as people seeking to feel and be. We have earned it. This is our claiming of the Twelve Steps and their rewards.*

Our solution appeals to cultures across the globe. Our members practice ACA recovery in Europe, Asia, Pacific Islands, and the Middle East in addition to North and South America. We have learned that children anywhere exposed to shame and abandonment develop the same soul wound. When given an option as adults, many choose ACA's way of life. The ACA program is a proven way of life that fulfills its members emotionally and spiritually.

The term "adult child" does not mean that we live in the past or that we are infantile in our thinking and actions. The term means that we meet the demands of adult life with survival techniques learned as children. Before finding recovery, we suppressed our feelings and were overly responsible. We tried to anticipate the needs of others and meet those needs so we would not be abandoned. We tried to be flexible or supportive of others as we denied our own needs. We monitored our relationships for any sign of disapproval. We tried to be perfect so we would be loved and never left alone. Or we isolated ourselves and thought we needed no one.

As adults, we have been responsible team players or invisible loners. We are great employees, listeners, planners and party givers, but we respond to adult life with childhood survival traits that leave us feeling unsure of who we are. This is how we survived childhood, and this is how we lived as "adult children."

When faced with working ACA's Twelve Steps, some adult children feel overwhelmed and balk. Others are alarmed and believe they could be encouraged to abandon or confront their families. This is not the purpose of the ACA program. In ACA, we realize that our parents did not have the options that we have in ACA. If we were raised by relatives or grandparents, these people as well did not always have options. Our parents or relatives passed on family dysfunction. We are not minimizing the fact that many of our parents acted hostile, manipulative, or indifferent. Some dysfunctional parents were inebriated and pitiful. We balance our experiences as children with the knowledge that we have a unique chance through ACA to break the cycle of family dysfunction. Even though our families may not seek recovery, we can respect them. We set appropriate boundaries to protect ourselves. We can disentangle our lives from their lives without shutting them out completely.

We ask the adult child considering ACA to look at the program as a way of life that will unfold over time, bringing rich rewards of emotional relief and self-acceptance. There will be transformations and healing grace as well. We suggest that ACA members work the Steps one at a time, avoiding looking ahead and perhaps becoming overwhelmed. In ACA, we learn to slow down, breathe, and ask for help. The Steps work best when we surrender our self-sufficient attitudes and ask for help.

Our experience shows that the Steps are a proven way of life, yielding new meaning and a sense of purpose in one's life. We apply the Steps with willingness and honesty. In addition to addressing dependence and addiction, the Twelve Steps awaken the person to an inner strength that comes with a true connection to his or her Higher Power. We have always had this inner strength. Even when we appeared pitiful and helpless, the strength was there helping us survive until we could find real help. The Twelve Steps bring forth this God-given strength and true choice or discernment. With the Steps and true choice, we can finally breathe deeply and feel joy.

## Making a Beginning

Beginning with Step One the adult child begins to realize, perhaps for the first time, the destructive malady of growing up in an alcoholic or other dysfunctional home. In addition to shame, our families included perfectionism, rage, mental illness, sexual abuse, religious abuse, or illicit drug use. Some parents were hypochondriacs who abused prescriptions and used an endless number of ailments to control others. By working the Steps and attending meetings, we see that we are not unique and that our family is not unique as well. There are millions of people like us. In ACA, we begin to acquire the language we need to describe what happened to us in a manner that has meaning and resonance. Even adult children with years of Twelve Step experience in other programs gain a new awareness of family-of-origin issues by working the ACA Steps.

By working the Twelve Steps with a sponsor or knowledgeable counselor, the adult child realizes the denial and secrecy that were necessary to survive such an upbringing. Denial, which fosters a lack of clarity, is the glue that allows the disease of family dysfunction to thrive. Cloaked in denial, the disease is passed on to the next generation with amazing consistency. The basic language of denial is: "don't talk, don't trust, don't feel."[1]

With Step One we come out of denial and talk about what happened. We bring details to light. Many of us have smelled our parents' drunken breath. We have found hidden whisky bottles and pill bottles. We have cleaned up vomit. We have comforted a frightened brother or sister. The police have been called to our home. Our neighbors talked about our family. We avoided having friends over because we feared how our parents might act in front of them. We have made excuses for our parents, pleaded with our parents and condemned them with no real change. We have hidden illicit drugs and lied to neighbors. We have slept with our clothes on and ready to run. Some of us have thrown water on a mattress accidentally lit by a passed out mother or father. We have burned with shame after being cursed or belittled. We have listened to a parent's promises to change but have seen no lasting results. We have heard our parents curse one another regularly, swapping insults and hurtful claims. We have listened to them rehash the same blame and threats year after year. Nothing changed. We have seen our parents run up great sums of debt to buy affection or happiness. Our utilities have been cut off for nonpayment. We have lied to the collection agency for our parents. We have experienced divorce or heard talk of divorce that never came. Our siblings may have remembered things differently, but we know our own truth. We know what happened and we are breaking our silence.

[1]It Will Never Happen to Me, by Dr. Claudia Black—1981

Families without alcoholism have similar situations. These families abuse the children through the use of intellect, manipulation, or silence. We know our truth.

By working the Steps, the adult child realizes family roles that were required to approximate protection in an unsafe home. We often feared for our safety and took on roles to disarm our parents. Some of us sought to be invisible. The roles which are usually present in alcoholic and dysfunctional homes include "family hero, lost child, scapegoat, and mascot."[2] Some of the roles allowed us to be a parental favorite. As the favorite, we could temporarily dodge harmful behavior that could be shifted to a brother or sister. However, we were harmed by the process as well or when it was our turn to be abused, neglected or rejected. In addition to physical abuse, we were subjected to emotional abuse. The emotional abuse involved belittling comments or hatefulness aimed at our hearts. The abuse left no visible marks, but it is stored in our bodies just the same as slapping and hitting leave marks on the body.

In addition to creating false safety, our childhood roles had other functions. The hero child of a dysfunctional family might seek to make good grades at school. This is the honors student who shows the world that her family values education and is therefore stable. The mascot, typically the youngest of the family, serves as comic relief for dysfunctional homes that leave little room for joy. The lost or invisible child remains silent. The child knows it is not safe to speak. The lost child retreats to his or her room and remains absorbed in reading books or fantasies of living elsewhere. The scapegoat child lives out the parents' prophesy of being a bad or rotten kid. These are the roles that are almost predictable for any family in which dysfunctional parenting is present.

Such survival roles tend to have a hardy life and remain fixed in our personalities long after we have left our unhealthy homes. Adult children finding recovery learn about such dysfunctional roles. They can look at their families and see the roles in effect decades after the children have grown up and left the family. There is the 50-year-old brother still playing the hero. There is the 40-year-old sister, living out the lost child role by avoiding holiday meals and rarely calling home. This is difficult to watch once we find ACA and begin our recovery journey. The adult child in recovery gets the chance to retire his or her role with dignity. We are never too old to work an ACA program and receive its benefits.

In addition to learning about survival roles through the Twelve Steps, many adult children realize they have absorbed generational shame, abandonment, and rage only to grow up and recreate similar families or relationships. They realize they wanted to fix others. Without focused help, many ACAs spend their lives in adult relationships trying to repair their original family. Who hasn't read a story about a child with an ailing parent growing up to be a doctor in an effort to find a cure for the ailing parent? Adult children are no different. We want to heal our drunken or dysfunctional parents by acting good, silent, or by taking care of them. But the "sickness" the adult child attempts to cure in the parent is the disease of dysfunction, which we have no power over.

[2]Roles by Sharon Wegscheider

The ACA Identity Papers identify this behavior as our main problem—a mistaken belief that we could have changed our parents. Additionally, The Problem, read at ACA meetings, underscores our attempts to heal or rescue others. It states: "We confused love with pity, tending to love those we could rescue." Trying to rescue or heal our parents set the course of our lives. Many ACAs grow up believing they have failed in healing their families without realizing it was never their job to do so. As adults, many of us subconsciously attempt to heal our families in our adult relationships by disguised designs. In ACA, we realize we have no power over alcoholism and family dysfunction. We cannot change anyone but ourselves.

At the same time, some of us were so abused or belittled as children that we felt powerless to have any effect on our parents' behavior. The thought of healing or changing them never occurred to us. However, we grew up with the same loss, shame and self-hate as other adult children. Like others, we turned to control in adulthood for a sense of safety.

Without recovery, we, as adult children, intuitively find dysfunctional people and attempt to heal them or cure them based on our upbringing. We confuse love with pity and get unhealthy dependence. ACA experience shows that such behavior dooms relationships. We cannot change anyone. The only person we can change is ourselves, and an adult child rarely changes unless he or she becomes willing to learn a new way to live. The good news is this: There is another way to live.

The ACA fellowship offers hope to any adult child, who can realize he or she has hit a bottom and become willing to attend meetings, work the Twelve Steps, and seek a Higher Power of his or her understanding. There are many types of bottoms in ACA. Some of our members hit a bottom with alcoholism or addiction. Others hit a bottom in codependent relationships that can be just as addictive as drugs. For instance, some adult children become obsessed and develop a compulsion for another person that is similar to the addict's obsession and compulsion for drugs. The "withdrawal" from an addictive, codependent relationship can be just as painful, if not more painful, as an addict's withdrawal from drugs. ACA members know that codependent pain can grip a person's body with an agonizing sense of abandonment. The fear of abandonment can be so powerful that it makes breathing and concentration difficult. Fear of going insane is not uncommon. Some adult children have been struck with anxiety or panic attacks when going through a codependent separation. For many, it is too much to take without help. Codependent pain of this magnitude is actually our childhood terror of abandonment inserting itself into the break up. The intense fear of losing our spouse or partner is really our Inner Child reliving the fear of being unloved or unwanted by our family.

There are many definitions for codependence, but for our purposes, codependence means that we constantly look outside of ourselves for love, affirmation, and attention from people who cannot provide it. At the same time, we believe that we are not truly worthy of love or attention. In our view, codependence is driven by childhood fear and distorted thinking known as para-alcoholism. We choose dependent people who abandon us and lack clarity in their own lives because it matches our childhood experiences. In ACA, we learn to love and affirm ourselves and develop relationships with people who can do the same. We learn that our feelings will not kill us. The program works for those who want it.

ACA membership is defined by a wide variety of people. There is the newcomer looking for a sponsor and learning the family rules of "don't talk, don't trust, and don't feel;" the older ACA member who has worked the Twelve Steps and who sponsors others; the ACA member who has significant experience in other Twelve Step programs, yet lacks an understanding of the Inner Child; and the adult child who has lost focus on the ACA program and needs to return to clarity through the Steps and ACA meetings.

## Powerlessness versus Learned Helplessness

Many adult children struggle with the notion of powerlessness in Step One since powerlessness is all that many of us have known as children; however, the powerlessness that we describe in ACA is different than the learned helplessness we experienced as children. As children we were overrun by parents who unknowingly taught us to feel helpless or to feel less competent. Some parents accidentally undercut our learning ability and suggested we could do nothing right. Or our parents said we should try harder when we had already reached a level of above average. Some of us learned to be helpless or to give up since we could see no way to please our parents or family. Later on in life, we realized we could do things and learn, but we still had areas of learned helplessness, particularly in relationships. We either gave up or increased our attempts to control others. We could be subtle or aggressive in our attempted control.

In teaching us helplessness, our parents clouded this reality by failing to understand what they had done. They taught us to be dependent and then blamed us for being dependent. When we look at our childhood, we can see how our parents undermined our reality by telling us how we should think and feel when we objected to their treatment of us. As children, we were outmatched. Our parents projected their fears, suspicions, and sense of inferiority onto us. We were defenseless against the projections. We absorbed our parents' fear and low self-worth by thinking these feelings originated with us. Our dysfunctional parents often said: "Why can't you get this?" "I am so ashamed of you." "Why do you act like that?" "You must be the dumbest child in the world." Upon hearing such comments, we felt helpless to defend ourselves. We began to believe we could not trust our perceptions. Some of us knew we could not trust our parents as well, but we believed their words without question. We believed what they said about us was truth, when it was not.

With Step One, the adult child realizes that he or she is now an adult and that the powerlessness mentioned in the Step does not engender a denial of feelings or mean that we are helpless. Powerlessness in ACA can mean that we were not responsible for our parents' dysfunctional behavior as children or adults. It means that as adults we are not responsible for going back and "fixing" the family unit. We are not responsible for rescuing, saving, or healing our parents or siblings who remain mired in family dysfunction. We can detach with love and begin the gradual process of learning about boundaries. We live and let live.

While some adult children confuse powerlessness for helplessness, there are others who dismiss the idea of admitting powerlessness as Step One suggests. These adult children believe they are all-knowing, all-sensing, and all-flexible. They secretly feel powerful in their ability to adapt to any situation or group of people they might encounter. These adult children make great salespeople, planners, and instructors. No situation is too challenging, and no group of people is too complex for these adult children to "conquer" with their adaptive behavior. These adult children usually see no need to ask for help in their lives, believing they are self-sufficient and beyond such a need. They feel powerful in their self-sufficient control. They tend to manipulate others for things they want, but find out they are not happy with themselves when their wants are met by others. These adult children rarely stop to think that self-sufficiency is covering up a fear of rejection which they think could come if they ask for help.

Meanwhile, to ask for help and get it might mean that someone would get to know them, and that is too risky. In such cases, self-sufficient power is really a mechanism to ensure isolation and aloneness. These adult children remain in control and are suspicious or indifferent to notions of powerlessness mentioned in Step One. They don't often trust what they hear in ACA meetings, but they adapt to remain in control.

By admitting our powerlessness over alcoholism and dysfunction, we gradually learn to trust our perceptions and feelings. Whether we are self-sufficient or clamoring about appearing helpless, we can learn to trust ourselves and ask for what we need. We let people into our lives. At the same time, the word "boundary" begins to have meaning and creates a reasonable amount of power for us. We stop giving away our power to others and feeling helpless to change. By admitting our powerlessness, we take our first step toward reclaiming personal power, which is critical for healing our fractured identities. If we are compulsively self-reliant, we take our first step toward trust and asking for help.

With Step One, we also begin to realize that we have a choice. Before coming to ACA and finding the solution to family dysfunction, adult children do not have a choice[3]. While we had the illusion of choice as adults, what we really practiced before ACA was control, which predictably fizzled into binges on food, work, sex, gambling, spending, or destructive relationships. It is not uncommon for us to have had two or more addictive or compulsive behaviors occurring at the same time. For example, we have seen adult children in active drug addiction also enmeshed in a loveless relationship while being sexually compulsive with another partner. These addictions and compulsive behaviors can be substituted for one another in addition to occurring simultaneously. Based on our experiences before ACA, we thought we had made bad choices when in reality we were condemned to repeat the same mistakes of our parents through compulsions

[3]Earnie Larsen—Feb. 26, 2005, Las Vegas talk.

or mad dreams of denial. We had no choice, but we judged ourselves without mercy for "choosing" badly.

We can re-experience powerlessness in our daily lives as we try to fix our current relationships based on old ideas of feeling helpless and hopeless. When we realize such powerlessness as an adult we step back, let go, and take a new course of action or take no action. We learn to detach with compassion and to stop trying to repair our family of origin. We also change our current behavior in our current relationships; however, the key words are "slowly" and "gradually" and come from the Twelve Promises of ACA. Promise Eleven states: "With help from our ACA support group, we will slowly release our dysfunctional behaviors." Promise Twelve states: "Gradually, with our Higher Power's help, we learn to expect the best and get it."

## Unmanageability

Like powerlessness, the concept of unmanageability in Step One is often misunderstood by adult children. While some of our families were chaotic and unstable when we were children, many homes seemed manageable and productive. But we learn that productivity does not always equal a manageable, wholesome life. For many of us, what we thought was manageable or desirable in our dysfunctional homes was actually oppressive control.

The unmanageability that we speak of in Step One involves our desire to control others and ourselves while having a sense that we are not capable or effective. While we have moments of control, we usually experience painful episodes of losing control. We feel hurt when confronted by our loved ones for our controlling behavior. They act out in anger or abandonment to disrupt our attempts to control them. We may be momentarily hurt, but we usually blame others for this abandonment. We blame them for not reading our minds or not acting in a manner that we would approve. We run about attempting to control others and situations in an effort to avoid our own unmanageable lives. Control is an attempt to minimize uncertainty and to avoid our own uncomfortable feelings about the past and present. Yet, our unmanageability, fueled by our fear-based control, inevitably creates what we fear the most: abandonment.

Many adult children, whether they are a newcomer or a member who has worked another Twelve Step program, miss this subtle distinction between powerlessness and helplessness. They miss fear-based control appearing as manageability. ACA experience has shown that adult children will cling to controlling behavior and learned helplessness as long as it works for them; however, these learned behaviors can be changed with diligent Step work and regular attendance at ACA meetings.

Lastly, any discussion about ACA powerlessness and unmanageability is incomplete without the disease concept of alcoholism and family dysfunction. When alcoholism or other dysfunction is present in the family, every member of the family is affected. We are affected in body, mind, and spirit. Through the first 18 years of our lives, our families had 6,570 days to shame, belittle, ignore, criticize, or manipulate us during the most formative years of our being. That is 160,000 hours of living in dysfunction with unhealthy parenting. That is 72 seasons of sorrow stored deeply in the tissue of our bodies. The dysfunction is encoded into our souls as the false self. To survive this long exposure to family dysfunction, our minds developed deeply entrenched roles and traits that changed the meaning of words and experiences. Some of us misremembered the damaging nature of the abuse because we depended upon our abusers for food and shelter.

As children, we did not have the option to leave our homes. If our parents slapped us, molested us, or neglected us, we had to live with them. We had to figure out a way to survive. The subconscious survival decisions we made as children involved changing the meaning of words. Because we were vulnerable, we changed the way we perceived the emotional and physical abuse. We feared for our safety or feared we had caused these things to happen. We developed stories that minimized our parents' behavior or which convinced us that we were wrong and deserved their harmful behavior. We came to believe that we deserved to be hit or criticized with brutality. We confused molestation for love because the person molesting us was a relative describing such action as love. Such confused thinking about hitting or touching fueled our denial as adults. The confusion allows many of us to say we had normal childhoods when we have lived through hell.

We never spoke of family secrets. We thought we had forgotten the abuse, but the body and mind remembered. The survival traits we lived by showed a clear path of our terror of abandonment and being shamed. During these years of family dysfunction, our Inner Child or True Self went into hiding and remained heavily fortified under addictions or dependent behavior. This is what we mean when we say the disease of family dysfunction affects us in body, mind, and spirit. The disease survives in the language of denial and is passed on to the next generation through secrets, blame, and confusion.

The disease of family dysfunction is progressive, incurable, and sometimes fatal. The disease becomes worse over time unless treated; however, the malady is often misdiagnosed, causing the adult child to seek remedies that usually fail to bring true relief. Many adult children have taken their own lives or died from complications of drug addiction or physical ailments that can be traced to childhood abuse. These are stark claims, but we have found them to be true in our experience. This is the dire nature of the family disease of dysfunction and its great reach. But there is much hope in ACA and in sharing our pain with other recovering adult children.

We urge patience and gentleness when addressing these areas of our lives. That means we take care of ourselves. We do the Step work and program work necessary to reap the benefits of the ACA Promises.

## Examining Spiritual Beliefs

Moving to Steps Two and Three, many adult children are confronted with the issue of faith and a Higher Power. In our anger at our parents and God, many of us thought we had outgrown or moved past this issue in our lives. Frankly, some of us did not like this part of the ACA program. Being told of the spiritual nature of ACA irritated some of us. We wondered about the need for spirituality in recovery. We must remember that ACA is a spiritual and not religious program. Faith and religious conviction are not requirements for ACA membership. We avoid dogmatism and theological discussions, yet, a Higher Power is a key part of the ACA way of life.

Many adult children have assigned the traits of their dysfunctional parents to God or a Higher Power. If their parents were shaming, vengeful, and inconsistent, then their God tends to be the same. Some adult children describe having a "getcha God." For them, God keeps a record of their behavior and punishes them or "gets them" for making mistakes.

There are many levels of belief among our fellowship members. There are adult children, who are atheist or agnostic, who struggle with the notion of a universal force who will hear their prayers and make a meaningful impact in their lives. Numerous adult children recall praying to God for their parental abuse to stop, but nothing seemed to change. Many of these adult children concluded the Higher Power did not exist. They thought God did not hear their prayers. For these ACA members we ask that they keep an open mind. God, as we understand God, may have bundled up all such prayers from across the world and created ACA.

Other ACAs are staunch believers who cannot seem to allow a Higher Power to work in their lives. They cannot seem to get out of the way. There are also former believers who think they cannot reclaim faith. They feel abandoned by their Higher Power. One purpose of Step Two is to introduce the idea of keeping an open mind on the possibility of a Higher Power who can restore sanity. In some cases, our Higher Power helps us create sanity or wholeness for the first time in our lives.

ACA is a spiritual program that confronts the effects of the disease of dysfunction head on. The disease affects our bodies, minds, and spirits and requires a spiritual solution for lasting impact. Knowing where our perceptions of a Higher Power originated from and if the perceptions are accurate, is critical. We must discern what we believe or do not believe if we are to work Step Two and the remainder of the Steps.

Moving into Step Three, we see the third Step is merely a decision to ask our Higher Power to help us live courageously and sanely on a daily basis. One day at a time, we recover from the disease of family dysfunction. Step Three is underpinned by the ACA Solution, which is read at the opening of most adult child meetings. The ACA Solution is that we become our "own loving parent." Becoming our own loving parent involves seeing our "biological parents as the instruments of our existence." As The Solution states: "Our actual parent is our Higher Power, whom some of us choose to call God."

Working Step Three in ACA means that we realize that our parents brought us into the world. However, we are children of God, seeking to reclaim our true nature or original selves. The Twelve Steps support this journey to the Inner Child or True Self.

Meanwhile, Step Three helps further free us from the generational shame and abuse wrought by dysfunctional parents or caregivers. By realizing that our actual parent is our Higher Power, we complete more of the separation-from-family work. This work is critical so that we can frame the past in its proper perspective while reaching for a brighter future. We gradually realize our painful past can become our greatest asset. We realize we can help others who lack hope and clarity about what happened to them as children. As we learn to tell our story in meetings and in sponsorship, we move from "hurting, to healing, to helping." By practicing Step Three we begin to stand on our own. We are clear on what we believe. We seek God's will with greater clarity. We come to believe that we really are children of God, as we understand God. We come to believe that God hears our prayers. We are less confused on what to pray about. We begin to have true choice.

## Inventory Steps and Realizing Generational Abuse

In Steps Four and Five, we review in detail how we were raised. We remember the messages, situations, and feelings. We also look at how we react and think in relationships as adults. We tell our story to another person and to God, as we understand God.

Like Step One, the Fourth Step of ACA distinguishes our fellowship from other Twelve Step programs. In ACA, we inventory our family system in addition to inventorying our own behavior. Other Twelve Step fellowships tend to limit a review of family dynamics. In ACA we look at our parents' behavior, family roles, rules, messages, abuse, neglect, and how that affects us as adults. We balance the inventory of our family system with a thorough inventory of our own behavior.

Many of us peep ahead to Steps Eight and Nine and sense that we have amends to make to various people, including our parents, who have harmed us as children. Oftentimes this harm is the vulgar act of incest, physical abuse, or mental and emotional abuse by sick parents or caregivers.

It is not the purpose of the Twelve Steps of ACA to place blame on the parents or caregivers; however, the adult child also must not shield the parents during the inventory process.

Our cofounder, Tony A., believed that adult children could take a "blameless" inventory of his or her parents. That means the adult child can name the types of abuse that occurred and the role playing necessary to survive the upbringing; however, with a "blameless" inventory, the adult child also realizes the generational nature of such abuse or neglect. The parents were passing on some form of what was done to them.

In preparing to make amends to our parents, we must develop a gentler manner toward ourselves. ACA's Fourth Step stresses this process. We must balance taking responsibility for misdeeds committed as an adult with the knowledge that our mistakes probably have their origin in the abuse we endured as children. We seek balance. We don't want to use our childhood abuse as an excuse to avoid taking responsibility for our actions as adults. But we also do not want to belittle ourselves for these mistakes or abuses. Adult children can be brutally hard on themselves for making mistakes. We condemn ourselves and rage at ourselves with ease. This serves no good purpose and only means that we have learned to abuse ourselves. No one needs to beat up an adult child. We do it to ourselves long after our parents or relatives have stopped. We need to stop this self-condemning behavior. We can take full responsibility for our actions, knowing that our childhood abuse contributed to our abuses as adults. We also know that we are not blaming anyone for our adult behavior. We are learning to love ourselves. We can do this.

Making amends to parents or caregivers is a personal choice, which should be considered with the help of a sponsor, trusted friend, or informed counselor. These issues surface in detail in Step Four along with the conditions of abuse that we endured as children. While we encourage ACA members to avoid looking ahead in the Steps, we believe it is appropriate here to plant the seeds of common sense for later Steps. For too many years adult children have been sent to make amends to abusive parents without being given greater options. This cannot continue. There are conditions of abuse to consider, which will be discussed in greater detail in this workbook. Our experience shows that there is a way to make amends to abusive or neglectful parents while protecting one's self. We can proceed courageously with this knowledge.

In Step Four, we also shatter the cardinal rules of family dysfunction. The "don't talk" rule that most of us learned as children is broken so that a self-inventory can be fully reached. Breaking this rule began in Step One with the admission of being powerless over the effects of alcoholism and family dysfunction. When we work Steps Four and Five, we also break the rules of "don't trust" and "don't feel" by listing and articulating our life story in a structured manner. We learn to trust the person to whom we tell our story. We feel the feelings that arise by sharing such information. This sharing of our story with our sponsor or informed counselor reveals destructive patterns in our adult lives while illuminating abuses from our childhood. We also begin to see our grief or stored loss lying beneath our decisions to wrong ourselves and others.

In Step Four, the adult child learns to "name" the acts of abandonment, shame, and other forms of abuse practiced by dysfunctional parents. At the same time in Step Four, the adult child lists his or her own defects of character, acts of selfishness, and blame that allowed the adult child to rationalize destructive behavior or reject real solutions.

## Character Defects Versus Laundry List Traits (Common Behaviors)

In Steps Six and Seven we learn the important difference between defects of character and The Laundry List traits developed as children to endure our dysfunctional homes. The main difference is this: adult children tend to feel relief when reading the 14 traits of The Laundry List because we realize we are not unique. However, we can feel shame or dread when hearing a list of defects of character.

Our defects of character can include judgmentalness, slothfulness, and dishonesty. These defects can cause great discomfort to others and ourselves. In other cases defects of character can include what society sees as noble traits, but for us they are stumbling blocks. These defects can include perfectionism, obsessive tidiness, and appearing self-sufficient by avoiding asking others for help. Employers praise the self-starter who keeps a tidy work place and rarely asks for help.

For the most part, our defects of character are different than our Laundry List traits because the traits are rooted in the First Step. The Laundry List traits include fearing authority figures, stuffing our feelings, people-pleasing, and feeling guilty when we ask for what we need. The traits are the effects of growing up in a dysfunctional family. These common behaviors have deep roots and could easily be called survival traits. The Laundry List traits are like branches of a tree, while the defects of character are the fruit. The defects of character can be linked back to one or more traits.

We use Steps Six and Seven to remove the defects of character. However, we take a different approach for the Laundry List behaviors. We attempt to integrate them through gentleness and patience. Our traits have great value to us if we can embrace them and transform them.

Until integration occurs, the traits can cause great despair for the adult child. We seem unable to change them until we get help. The Laundry List traits represent the false self, which is convinced that it is real. The false self disbelieves recovery and the loving nature of a Higher Power. This false self once protected us, but it now has to be retired.

We must be patient with ourselves as we integrate the Laundry List traits in Steps Six and Seven. The traits are deeply anchored because they are the defense system we developed as children under difficult circumstances. We must acknowledge a certain amount of respect for the traits and for ourselves for figuring out how to survive our dysfunctional homes. As children, they were the difference between living and dying in some cases. We survived, but in ACA we want to move beyond mere survival.

The safe harbor we find in ACA meetings is the starting point for transforming our survival traits. We listen to others share how they did it. We learn that the integrated trait of people-pleasing might look like this: we do helpful things for ourselves and accept praise, instead of constantly pleasing others and pushing away compliments. By transforming our people-pleasing manner, we do not stop caring about others. However, we stop going over the line to ensure that we are never abandoned.

Many times the Laundry List survival traits will rebel and assert themselves more clearly as we begin to surrender to a new way of life; however, our experience shows that the traits can be softened if not tempered into usefulness. Some of us seem to make no real progress on changing our survival behaviors until we become entirely willing as Step Six suggests. With more than survival as our goal, we continue to lessen the strength of the traits and gradually lay them down with respect.

# Making Amends

In approaching Step Eight and our amends list, we should have a more balanced perspective of what happened to us as children and what we are responsible for as adults. Without this balanced Step work in the preceding seven Steps, most adult children will take on too much responsibility for their actions as children and adults. Others will ignore the amends process and remain mired in self-pity or protracted guilt that leads to further deterioration of the body and mind. By working the amends steps, Steps Eight and Nine, we are not letting our parents off the hook for their behavior nor are we taking an attitude about our childhood abuse that would excuse or protect our own selfish behavior as adults. We do not allow fear of uncomfortable situations to block us from making amends. ACA experience shows that amends build the character and inner strength that can only be wrought by going through the process.

In making our amends lists in Step Eight, we work closely with our sponsor or counselor to determine the exact nature of our amends. We look at the concepts of forgiveness and self-forgiveness. Many adult children blame themselves for passing on their childhood abuse to their own children. We must understand that we could not have turned out differently as parents. We simply repeated what was done to us because it is all we knew. This is not an excuse but a fact. With this knowledge, we begin to entertain the possibility of self-forgiveness in Step Eight.

Self-forgiveness is an elusive concept for adult children. We ask that the adult child keep an open mind and consider that God has already forgiven the person. God is waiting for the adult child's acceptance of such a blessing. We realize that we are practicing the concept of self-forgiveness when we hear ourselves talking about being gentle with ourselves.

With such an attitude, we learn to protect our emerging Inner Child or True Self when we make amends to parents or relatives who could still be in denial about their family dysfunction. We go into such amends knowing our Inner Child is listening but also knowing we are attempting to correct our damaging behavior as adults. We know we have made mistakes based on bad information from childhood. But we are focusing on our behavior and our need to change. We don't make excuses for our behavior; yet, self-forgiveness gives us a gentler view of who we are and what we are trying to change in our lives. We nurture our Inner Child by forgiving ourselves and turning over our parents and children to God, as we understand God.

Some incest victims have struggled with forgiving an offending parent or caregiver. We urge these adult children to speak with other ACA members to find a solution that works for them. Some parents are so dangerous and sick that the adult child must avoid them to remain safe and sane. Surely we would think twice about asking an incest victim to make amends to a perpetrator father, mother, or other relative. The actual amends may be to protect ourselves and know we have done nothing wrong.

At the same time, many other abused adult children believe that the healing process for them cannot be complete until they forgive their worst offenders. The process is not always simple, but it is possible to forgive a sick parent and find peace of mind. Forgiveness does not mean that the parent's behavior was proper or excusable. It means we learn to live freer lives by discharging old trauma in a safe manner.

In Step Nine, there are a variety of amends for a variety of people and relationships. Some amends require a simple apology while others will require changed behavior that can only occur over time and with Step work, meeting attendance, and the help of a Higher Power. In some amends, we must pay back money we have stolen or squandered. Other amends are "living amends" which will require us to leave people alone. Amends to a deceased parent or friend can involve writing that person a letter. We read the letter out loud to our sponsor or ourselves. We can usually find a way to make an amends if we pray and seek guidance.

## Daily Inventory, Meditation, and Awakening

In Steps Ten, Eleven, and Twelve, we learn to continue our self-inventory process, pray and meditate, and carry the message of hope to adult children while practicing the principles of the Steps in our daily lives. ACA is a program for continued personal growth. The Twelve Steps call the adult child to live the ACA program with a range of feelings and self-confidence. ACA is a design for living that works.

In Step Ten, the adult child learns to appropriately inventory thoughts, actions, and motives with an honesty and gentleness that was not present in our families of origin. Step Ten is where many adult children learn to balance their responses to situations. We confront our black-and-white thinking and realize we have choices. We learn to say "no." We can ask for what we need. We become actors rather than reactors.

Most adult children learned to take their own inventory long before they arrived at ACA. However, these negative inventories were usually nothing more than our critical inner parent judging us harshly. Many adult children doubt themselves, criticize themselves, and feel inadequate without much prompting. Steps leading up to Step Ten can expose the toxic shame and abandonment we endured as children and teens. The shame gave us a negative orientation to the outward and inner world. In our minds, we developed the deeply grooved, self-shaming messages that lived on long after we left our homes. For instance, who could have his house burglarized and feel at fault for the burglary? An adult child. Who could feel guilty for asking someone blocking a doorway to move? An adult child. Step Ten helps us address any negative messages held over from previous Step work.

Step Ten does not mean we will never criticize our behavior again or never apologize for obvious wrongs on our part. However, with Step Ten we hopefully will learn to judge ourselves less harshly and forgive ourselves more readily. With such an attitude, we learn the difference between condemning ourselves unjustly and identifying areas to improve. We see how we took on too much responsibility for others' thoughts and actions. That's what we did as children when we filled in the unspoken sentences that fell on the floor when our parents argued or criticized with an unreasonable manner. We were children taking on too much blame for dysfunction that was not our responsibility. In Step Ten, we unhook from the behavior of others. We learn to focus on our own thoughts and actions with balance and self-love.

In Step Eleven, we learn that spirituality is not reserved for those of the clergy or those of religious teaching or temperament. God, as we understand God, is available to all. We seek through prayer and meditation to improve our conscious contact with a Higher Power. We seek the power we need to live in freedom each day. It has been said that a life of prayer and meditation leads to a life of mental stability or emotional maturity. In ACA, we believe this to be true. The power we find in Step Eleven is the true power from our True Parent, God as we understand God.

There are many methods to meditation and many fine books on the subject. In ACA, we have learned to keep it simple. Many of our members find a quiet place in the morning to meditate, but any time will do. We usually sit in a relaxed, upright position for 10 minutes to an hour. The time varies for each member. Some members, at the beginning of the meditation, take several deep breaths and exhale slowly, repeating an affirming message in their minds. As we concentrate on our breathing and on self-love or serenity, we feel a closer connection with our Higher Power. We feel relaxed and safe. Practice is the key to meditation. Make a start and continue to try.

In Step Twelve, the adult child begins to realize the value of his or her personal story. This realization is one of the key elements of undergoing a spiritual awakening and psychic change that brings integration to our fragmented lives. Our stories are often painful. Common logic would suggest forgetting the past, but our experience speaks otherwise. We are survivors with a voice. We are learning to live with self-love and grace. We have found the value in our stories, and we feel motivated to pass on hope to the still-suffering adult child. By working the Twelve Steps, we come to believe that our story has great spiritual value. We don't live in the past, but we know where we come from and how to find clarity and meaning in life. By the time we reach Step Twelve, we know about the negative messages we have confronted and changed. We also recognize self-forgiveness. We feel more sure of ourselves. In ACA, the adult child finds his or her voice.

In carrying the message of hope in the Twelfth Step, our story is the identification tool that allows us to connect with other adult children and bring hope like no one else can. Something marvelous happens when one adult child talks to another adult child, sharing experience, strength, and hope. Both are helped, and the message of recovery experiences a heartbeat.

By carrying the message of recovery through Step Twelve, the adult child confirms his or her commitment to the recovery process and passes on what was freely given to him or her. When we give back, we help ourselves in addition to helping someone else.

# Part II

# Twelve Steps of Adult Children

The following pages offer an in-depth section, which can serve as a study chapter for ACA meetings or a Twelve Step booklet for the ACA member. The workbook is designed to be read again and again at Step-study meetings. The workbook offers a detailed guide on writing and working ACA's Twelve Steps. With some modification the section can be used by a group of adult children to work the Twelve Steps together over a 12-week to 16-week period. By working the steps in a group setting, you can expect an exciting journey as you allow others into your life and talk openly about your family of origin. This is a risk worth taking. In the group setting, you can also expect differences of opinion, which can be worked out with the principles of honesty, acceptance and unity. These principles keep the Step group safe and focused on the Twelve Step work at hand.*

In addition to workbook items, this section also offers in-depth writing based on ACA principles and experience garnered from a 30-year period. The section includes about 35 shares of ACA members recorded voluntarily at meetings, retreats and by invitation during a 10-year period. Transcribed mostly from tape recordings, the shares represent an array of ACA Twelve Step experience.

The common behaviors mentioned in this workbook are known as the Laundry List traits. The Laundry List is a list of 14 characteristics of an adult child. (The traits are listed in the front of the workbook). ACA founder Tony A. wrote the traits in 1978. The Laundry List serves as the language for The Problem, which is read at the beginning of many ACA meetings. Jack E. is credited with placing the traits in narrative form known as The Problem.

* **Note**: While this workbook can be used as the main piece of literature for an ACA group, some adult children also meet informally and work the Twelve Steps in a group setting outside a regular ACA meeting. If this occurs, each group member should make a verbal pledge to commit to the number of weeks needed to work the Twelve Steps in this setting. Some of these groups ask the members to sign a simple pledge of commitment, however, this is optional. A verbal pledge to show up each week and work the ACA Twelve Steps is a minimal requirement to ensure continuity and the greatest success of these groups.

These groups are not a replacement for regular attendance at ACA meetings. These groups can enhance a person's ACA program, which requires meeting attendance, sharing about childhood experiences, working the Steps, sponsorship, and seeking a Higher Power.

Additionally, these groups should adhere to or attempt to adhere to the principles and traditions of ACA groups. Each participant should agree to practice honesty and courtesy in addition to helping keep the group safe. The principle of anonymity should be honored as well. We avoid gossiping or talking about a person's story to another person. In ACA, we focus on ourselves and live and let live.

# STEP ONE

*We admitted we were powerless over the effects of alcoholism or other family dysfunction, that our lives had become unmanageable.*

## Someone Finally Wrote It Down

*The first time I read the common behaviors of an adult child, I felt like a bell that had been fetched up and rang hard. I was calm on the outside, but I was vibrating on the inside. I could not believe what I was reading. I remember looking over my shoulder to see if someone had been reading my mail and had planted this stuff somehow.*

*I may have rubbed my fingers on the page, trying to feel the words because they seemed so real. The words of judging myself without mercy and being a people-pleaser were describing my thinking and behaving in a language that was clear. I could not deny it. I was cursed harshly and subjected to violence as a kid. I was never listened to. Now, someone who I had never met had written down how I thought and felt without meeting me. Until I found ACA, I had spent my whole life condemning myself and feeling no good. I took drugs and acted out in disgusting ways, feeling lost. I read the traits for the first time 20 years ago. I have been hooked on ACA ever since. The traits and the Twelve Steps have given me a new life and self-love.*

## My Body Is Remembering What Happened

*It took me awhile to understand what I was hearing in ACA meetings. The common behaviors (14 traits) meant a lot, and I got them quickly. But all the talk about being shamed and abandoned seemed to go over my head for many months if not years. I could recall the mechanics of my abuse, which involved hearing my father call my mother vulgar names and being attacked by my father when I was four years old. I even saw blood and teeth fly when my violent dad knocked out men with clubs and pop bottles. But the feelings associated with these events did not register for the longest time. I was so numbed out and so shut down that I could not connect the terror that I must have felt with the recalling of the memory.*

*I got help from a counselor who would slow me down when I recounted a violent episode in my home. It was the difference in telling the story rapidly without feeling and thinking about it as I talked. She said I had post-traumatic stress disorder. I was skeptical, but I knew my memories were violent and not normal. I had a high tolerance level to seeing violence and not feeling. I also got help from another source: movies. I began to notice feelings and tension in my body if a violent movie scene would occur. I don't watch violence, but the few scenes I would see, even on TV, began to trigger what I had not felt in a long time. It happened on God's schedule. I was not ready for this when I came here, but my body is telling me what happened, and I can handle it.*

## The Gift Of The Twelve Steps

*A friend of mine stopped coming to ACA meetings because he thought the Twelve Steps were a continuation of the dysfunctional family system. To him the Twelve Steps were just a list of things to do to get approval and behave acceptably according to someone else's standards. But Alcoholics Anonymous didn't start out with the Steps when AA was founded in 1935. The written Steps came after the first meetings in an attempt to offer suggestions, not rules, of the recovery process.*

*Someone asked the first one hundred sober alcoholics in AA what they did differently that finally broke the deadly hold of alcoholism, a disease that had defied all medical and religious remedies throughout the ages. The group said they discussed the evolutionary process of their recovery, and then AA cofounder Bill W. documented the process used to obtain sobriety. That was the beginning of the suggested Twelve Steps. In reviewing my own recovery process in Adult Children of Alcoholics, I now see how my Higher Power guided me in working the Steps. The gift of the Twelve Steps resulted in my emotional and spiritual sobriety.*

## There Is Nothing Noble In The Struggle

*I have been in situations where the outcome would have been better if I just said, "I can't do that." Instead I took on the impossible, failed, and beat myself up for it. I would go without recreation, sleep, and food to keep myself focused on the task at hand. Relentlessly, I considered different perspectives until I found a way to get the job done.*

*This depleted the energy I needed to survive.*

*I began to withdraw from my family and friends. One day I was sitting on the carpet in my home office looking at piles of paper. I couldn't organize the papers or find the ones I needed. I couldn't get off the floor. I could only cry. I thought my life would never get better, and I wanted to die.*

*My therapist said, "When you learn you can't do it, then you've got a chance. So far you keep finding more energy to keep trying. The best thing for you to do is to fall apart, realize your life is unmanageable, and understand that you can't do it all."*

*When my life got as bad as it could possibly get, I started coming to ACA. I discovered I had taken Step One by saying, "I can't do this anymore. I quit." My life got better from that moment on. I had hit a bottom.*

*While giving all you can is admirable, I have learned in ACA that it's better for me to know my capabilities and limitations. When I can't do something, I need to just let go. When I see my friends struggling now, I don't try to fix their lives for them. When they hit their "bottom" they will let go and reach out for help as I did. I have finally discovered there is nothing noble in the struggle. I surrender.*

## I Couldn't Do It Alone Anymore

*I grew up in what I thought was a normal household. My mother started to work when I entered first grade. With our parents working, my two sisters and I were expected to care for the house. About that time I remember not wanting to go to school and not wanting to leave the house. When I was at school I wanted to go home during my lunchtime to make sure that everything was all right. I thought, "If I do more, my parents will care more about me. I will be good enough to be loved." But I never felt I was good enough.*

*When I grew up, I became a teacher. As one of the more responsible teachers at the school, I was given extra duties and problem children. For a long time I handled the additional responsibilities. My life revolved around school and home ownership. I was important for what I did. I was my job.*

*When I realized I could not keep handling the stress, I spoke up at school. I was ignored or told I was "doing a fine job."*

*I began having panic attacks. When I began tutoring children after school and conferring with parents on report cards, I experienced chest pains and saw my doctor. The following night, I had a huge panic attack and went over to my boyfriend's house.*

*I visited my therapist and said, "I can't do it anymore." He asked me what "it" was. I didn't know. On the drive home it suddenly occurred to me that "it" was life. I could not go on anymore. My life had become unmanageable. Nothing was fun for me. I saw no future. I needed help just taking care of myself and getting meals.*

*The rehabilitation evaluator I went to suggested I attend an ACA meeting, even though alcoholism wasn't a problem in my family. I went to a meeting anyway. It was too soon for me to go to meetings because I was in such poor shape. I picked up some literature and recognized myself in the 14 characteristics (The Problem). If there was help anywhere, I thought, maybe it was in this ACA program. I started attending meetings regularly. I have been very grateful ever since for this program.*

## I Told God How Powerless I Felt

*On my last weekly visit to my parents' house, my mother hadn't been pleased to see me. The people-pleasing, approval seeker she used to know was gone. Any hope that I might meet her needs was also gone. She was sulky, shaming, and negative. Perhaps she was hoping that I would give in and try to fix her.*

*Many years ago I had planned on having kids to fix me and meet my needs, so I could have a sense of wholeness and self-respect, too. My children would have a lust for life that would lift me to realms of happiness rarely experienced by humans. I had planned on being admired by ranks of the "prestigious sane."*

*My mother must have seen me as a boring cold fish that day. I felt sad and trapped but I chose not to fix her. I told God how powerless I felt, and I began repeating the Serenity Prayer. Suddenly my mother lightened up, and with the opportunity to be happy, joyous, and free, so did I. Sanity replaced insanity. Clarity emerged. The next day I fully understood what had happened. I thanked my*

*Higher Power for the miracle. I realized my past attempts at fixing my mother drained me of my precious energy and demoralized my spirit. I no longer believe I can fix her. I did not cause my mother's discontent.*

## Step One Summary

These shares represent the basic spiritual principles of ACA's First Step—powerlessness, unmanageability, surrender, and letting go. Step One requires that we admit that our family is dysfunctional and the dysfunction affects our thinking and behavior as adults. We must admit that we are powerless over the effects of growing up in a dysfunctional home. Our lives are unmanageable regardless of appearances of self-sufficiency. Social standing or compulsive self-reliance does not equal recovery. We must realize that will power or self-determination is no match for the effects of growing up in a sick family. We cannot figure it out on our own. We need help. We must shatter the illusion that we can reason out a painless solution.

The shares also represent the critical separation-from-family work, which is necessary to gain clarity about our lives. Separating from our families means setting healthy boundaries and removing ourselves from abusive situations and family crises, which are common for dysfunctional homes. Many times adult children struggle in their ACA program because they cannot seem to break ties with destructive or manipulative relatives. We cannot grow and find our true inner selves as long as we engage in family dysfunction that is draining and unhealthy.

Separating from our dysfunctional family is a healthy act of defiance. By doing so, we are challenging the authority of the family lie. We are making a statement that we will no longer be loyal to denial and dysfunctional family roles. This can seem frightening, but we have the support of our ACA group.

Many adult children separate from their families with love not abandonment. They need time away to focus on themselves and to disconnect from the gravitational pull of a dysfunctional home. At an appropriate time, we review the relationship we want to have with our families. We will choose to avoid some family members because they are draining or abusive. Other relatives will accept us and encourage us on our new path even though they may not understand or be willing to walk this way with us. ACA can improve our relationship with our families with the knowledge that we do not have to participate in their dysfunction. We are free to live our own lives.

## Hitting Bottom

ACA recovery begins when the adult child gives up, asks for help, and then accepts the help offered. Some adult children call giving up "hitting a bottom."

Hitting a bottom can occur before the adult child attends his first meeting or it can occur after arriving here and beginning the Twelve Step process of recovery. Some ACA members reach a bottom after years in recovery. Hitting a bottom can involve losing everything and becoming homeless, or it can be a feeling of extreme suffocation brought on by our obsessive need to control others. Some ACA bottoms can be a chronic sense of aloneness in which the adult child never feels joy and never really connects with others in a meaningful manner. Many adult children have become literally paralyzed in recovery because of their inability to let go and trust themselves or others.

Other bottoms can involve a compulsion or obsession for another person. The obsession is so maddening that we think we will go insane unless we have this person in our lives. While we are focusing on another person, the pain we are feeling is actually the abandonment rupture from our childhood. Our compulsion for another person is the refeeling of the original rupture from our parents shaming us or abandoning us as children. The soul wound does not get better with pills, drugs, sex, or other forms of diversion. If we survive this compulsion, we tend to repeat it in the next relationship unless we ask for help and accept it. ACA's Steps get at this wound and heal it with a Higher Power's grace.

All bottoms have meaning, and all bottoms can be a starting point for a new way of life. There is hope. Healing is possible.

Surrender means we become willing to do whatever it takes to recover and find peace and serenity in our lives. We admit complete defeat and give up notions that we can "fix" or control someone else. We become willing to attend meetings, work the Twelve Steps, and break through the denial of family dysfunction. Amazingly, an estimated 50 percent of adult children of alcoholics deny or cannot recognize alcoholism among their families. By growing up in a dysfunctional home we become desensitized to the effects of alcoholism, abusive behavior, and lack of trust.

Recovery from the effects of an alcoholic and dysfunctional upbringing is a process, not an event. We need to be patient with ourselves. We need to be honest about our own behavior and the thinking we developed while growing up in our family of origin. If you find yourself in an ACA meeting, it probably means you are here for a reason. You probably are not the only person in your family experiencing difficulties in relationships, on the job, or in other areas of your life. Your family is not the only family that struggles with denial and silently broken hearts. We have found that family dysfunction is a disease the affects every member of the family. In the individual it affects the body, mind, and spirit. The disease of family dysfunction is pervasive and resilient. The disease is progressive. Our relationships become more violent, controlling, or isolating, depending on which path we take. Our "addictiveness" to work, sex, spending, eating, not eating, drugs, and gambling progresses as well, depending on our path.

Moreover, the disease is generational, which means the traits and thoughts you have at this moment have been passed down from generations hence. Relief from the disease occurs when we do Step work, attend Twelve Step meetings, and seek a Higher Power's guidance. By admitting we are powerless over the effects of family dysfunction and that our lives have become unmanageable, we are ready to move onto Step Two.

## Making a Start

When possible, we recommend that you attend 60 meetings in 90 days, get a sponsor, and make a start. For adult children with addiction issues, we recommend that you attend Twelve Step meetings to address those issues as well. While ACA is often the only program for many adult children, ACA is not a replacement for addicts working a program in Alcoholics Anonymous, Narcotics Anonymous, or Cocaine Anonymous.

We also recommend choosing a sponsor. A sponsor is someone in ACA, who attends meetings, works an active ACA program, and is willing to be available in assisting you in your program. The sponsor will not work your program for you, but he or she can offer support, hope and clarity. We strongly suggest getting a sponsor early on. Do not go it alone. Our experience shows that you cannot recover in isolation.

## WORKBOOK SECTION STEP ONE: We admitted we were powerless...

For the workbook items ahead, you will need support and self-honesty. It is suggested that you get a sponsor or spiritual advisor as well before proceeding. Many adult children also seek out a knowledgeable counselor to offer added emotional support as they begin the exciting work of ACA Twelve Step work. We also offer a word of caution here. Some of the issues raised by ACA step work and attendance at meetings can raise disturbing memories of some of the most atrocious abuse. This could require professional help to be dealt with safely and effectively. We encourage adult children with these issues to seek extra help with their program. In ACA, we do not recommend a particular style or method of counseling; however, in choosing a knowledgeable counselor, you have the right to ask the therapist if he or she is familiar with ACA or the Twelve Steps. (See Chapter 16 in the ACA Fellowship Text for more information on finding a knowledgeable counselor). Many counselors are familiar with the Twelve Step process while others show a willingness to learn. We recommend visiting with at least three counselors before making a decision. Many therapists will answer your questions on the telephone so this saves time and money.

You will also need a copy of The Laundry List (Problem) and The Solution for the workbook section. Welcome to a new way of life through the ACA Twelve Steps.

## Working Step One in ACA

Many adult children find it helpful to answer specific questions about their alcoholic or dysfunctional upbringing. By doing so we begin to see our denial and the role it played in our family structure. For the adult child, denial can mean that we misremember or "forget" segments of our childhood. We have seen adult children describe their childhoods as "loving" or "insignificant" when in reality the childhood was filled with neglect or horrific acts of mental, emotional, and sexual abuse. Researchers have discovered that many adult children suffer from "trauma bonding" (*The Betrayal Bond* by Patrick Carnes, Ph.D., 1997). Trauma bond means that children and adults often form a bond with perpetrating parents, pedophile priests or within a codependent relationship based on a violation of trust by the abuser. While this concept has been controversial in some circles, many of our members have found meaning and peace with their memories by applying this concept.

When parents are abusive, the theory states that the child is forced to bond to that parent because the child is dependent on the adult for survival. The child must deny or develop a distorted remembrance of the abuse, which is often beatings, incest, or lacerating cursings. As an adult, the person says he or she has "gaps" in childhood memory or the person "forgets" or misremembers the abuse. In many cases the adult will defend or show loyalty to their main abusers or perpetrator. Before receiving professional help, we have seen many adult children describe an abusive parent as loving and caring when in reality the parent was neglectful and shaming. At the same time, not all gaps in childhood memories are indicative of sexual abuse or childhood trauma. Professional help and common sense are needed in this area. While we want to recover and live in freedom we do not want to wrongly indicate a behavior that may not have happened. Some memories we will never recover fully but healing can occur regardless of whether we recover a memory extant or not.

Blindness to anger within themselves and their parents is one of the most common forms of denial that we see among adult children. We have seen new ACA members express surprise or shock at the suggestion that they might inwardly be angry or that their parents could have been angry. New ACA members often say: "I don't have an angry feeling in me. I am an upbeat person, who never gets angry."

Adult children have difficulty recognizing anger in their parents because of the high level of abuse the adult became comfortable with as a child. Parents who screamed at or threatened the adult child are recalled as parents who could be irritated but never harsh or mean. Parents who were quietly angry are recalled as controlled or loving but rarely shaming or hateful.

Adult children also have difficulty recognizing enmeshment. Enmeshment is a lack of boundaries among family members or between a parent and child. Enmeshed children become enmeshed adults, who live their lives at the direction of a parent or parents. They call the parent daily, plan vacations around the parent's schedule, dutifully watch after the parent, and feel powerless to refuse the parent's wants and demands. The enmeshed adult child often describes the relationship as loving and close when in reality it is stifling and controlling.

In ACA we get to properly name what happened to us without fear of reprisal. As long as we are in denial about what happened in our childhood, we fail to see the effects of family alcoholism or dysfunction in our lives today. The effects are in our thinking and behaving.

We also have no real choice in our lives as long as denial persists. While in denial we practiced rigid control which made us think we were making choices; however true choice is more than control, which leads to codependence, isolation or self-hate.

There are no right or wrong answers to the Step One questions you are about to answer. The ACA program only asks that you be honest in your answers to achieve the greatest personal growth. In addition to the adult raised in an addicted home, these questions also address the adult child raised in homes without addiction. Since our founding in 1978, we have identified additional family types that create adult children who find ACA and identify with the program. These adult children recover from dependence and connect with their Inner Child in ACA. The questions represent primary family types that include: alcoholic/addict parent; hypochondriac parent; sexually abusive parent; militaristic or rigid parent; emotionally ill parent; and perfectionistic parent. There is overlap among these styles of parenting. There are more family types which can include adult children from divorced homes and foster homes. There is also the dysfunctionally religious home. The first six questions will help you identify the parenting style you faced as a child.

## Step One Questions:

1) Who was the alcoholic or addicted parent in my family?

2) Who was the hypochondriac parent or person in my family?

3) Who was the sexually abusive parent or person in my family?

4) Who was the militaristic, rigidly harsh parent or person in my family?

5) Who was the emotionally ill parent or person in my family?

6) Who was the perfectionistic parent or person in my family?

**Note:** You may use a notebook if more space is needed to answer the following questions. If you are using this workbook in a group setting outside a regular ACA meeting, try to answer the questions before the next session of the meeting.

## Powerlessness:

1) How is powerlessness different than helplessness?

2) Do I understand that the effects of family dysfunction mentioned in Step One are the Laundry List traits?

3) List three effects of growing up in an alcoholic, addicted, or dysfunctional home. (Hint: any of the 14 common ACA traits).

4) What was my role growing up in my dysfunctional home: lost child, hero, scapegoat, and rescuer? Other _____.

5) How many of the common ACA traits of an adult child do I identify with in the Laundry List/Problem?

6)  What does "don't talk, don't trust, don't feel" mean?

7)  Am I powerless over the effects of growing up in an addicted or dysfunctional family?

8)  Do I use food, sex, drugs, alcohol, work, gambling or some other addictive behavior to an extreme? Am I powerless over these activities? (Give an example of powerlessness)

9)  Do I think I can change my parents or significant other by acting right, saying the right thing, or being perfect?

10) Do I think I caused my parent's addiction and dysfunction and I have the power to change it or control it?

11) Have I acted like a victim and acted helpless when in reality I was manipulating others to get what I thought I needed? Have I been rescued? (List an example)

12) Have I been driven by a compulsion or obsession for another person that over powers me and causes me to deny my own needs or take care of myself? (If so, detail how you denied your own needs).

## Unmanageable:

1) What is my definition of being unmanageable or having an unmanageable life?

   *EMOTIONS UP AND DOWN. - VERY REACTIVE.*
   *WORKAHOLIC. - MAKING POOR DECISIONS.*

2) Do I think I can still control people, places, and things by acting right, perfect, or otherwise?

   *YES ( STILL WORKING ON IT )*

3) Do I think I have power over other people and can control their actions and thoughts?

   *YES UNFORTUNATELY.*

4) Am I letting the thoughts, feelings and actions of others have power over me? (List an example if applicable).

   *YES, THINK THE WORST FIRST.*

5) Do I allow the feelings or possible reaction of others to control me or to determine my behavior and choices? (List an example).

   *YES, I RUN OFF MY EMOTIONS.*
   *PEOPLE BEING DISAPPOINTED WITH MY WORK.*

6) What does it mean to be codependent?

   *Love another more than myself*

7) Have my relationships created chaos, abuse, or predictable turmoil in my life? (List an example).

   *YES.*

8) Has my behavior and thinking affected my job performance or my ability to relate to others?

   *YES.*

9) What is my ACA "bottom" or bottoming out? Have I hit my bottom?

*THINKING OTHERS BEHAVING WILL MAKE ME HAPPY.*

10) Has an obsession for another person, drugs, gambling, food or sex made my life unmanageable? How?

*— UPSET AT MY SPOUSE OVERWORKING.*

*— DAD BEING AT THE CABIN WORKING BY HIMSELF.*

11) Is my manageable life actually controlling behavior, which I have mislabeled? (List an example).

*YES.*

12) Am I in denial about my controlling behavior?

*NO AND YES.... ITS HARD TO SEE THE BEHAVIOUR.*

13) Can I recover alone?

*NO*

14) Do I relate to other adult children in meetings? How?

*YES. NOT BEING ABLE TO LIVE COMFORTABLE IN THIS WORLD.*

## Denial:

1) Was I forced to depend upon an abusive or neglectful parent for food and shelter?

*YES*

2) Did I ignore my feelings of shame, fear and neglect to survive my childhood?

*YES.*

3) Did I monitor my parents' feelings or moods to determine how I should feel? Was I only happy when my parents were happy and sad when they were sad? (List an example).

*RENTING A FUNNY MOVIE.*

4) Am I honest about how my parents treated me when I was growing up? Did I fear one parent or both parents?

*I FEARED BOTH PARENTS.*

5) Did I fight with my brothers or sisters? Did I resent them? Did I protect them?

*YES. I RESENTED THEM.*

6) Do I say I am close to brothers or sisters but rarely visit them or talk to them?

*WE ARE NOT CLOSE.*

7) Am I afraid to talk about my past because my siblings will challenge me or try to undermine my memories? They have told me to "Get over it."

*I TRY NOT TO THINK ABOUT THEM*

8) Do I minimize my parents' behavior by saying "That was in the past. What is done is done." Or, "I don't look back. It does no good."

*I TEND TO KEEP QUIET.*

## Step One Spiritual Principles: Powerlessness and Surrender:

1) What am I powerless over in Step One?

   - THE PAST AND THE HOPE FOR A BETTER PAST.
   - WIFE, FAMILY, PEOPLE

2) What does surrender mean to me?

   - TO GIVE UP ANY BELIEF THAT I CAN CONTROL THE OUTSIDE WORLD.

3) If I surrender does that mean I will have no choices?

   NO I WILL BE MAKING SLOWER CHOICES VS. QUICK DECISIONS. (HEALTHIER CHOICES)

4) Am I willing to admit my family is dysfunctional?

   YES

5) Am I willing to admit I am powerless over the effects of growing up in a dysfunctional home and that my life is unmanageable?

   YES

**Get into action:** Call your sponsor, an ACA friend or counselor and discuss this section.

## Step One Activities

The activities here involve diagramming your family of origin, reviewing the 14 traits of an adult child, and writing down family messages. There is also an introduction to ACA sponsorship and affirmations.

## Exercise 1—Family History Diagram

We cannot overstate the need for creating an extensive family diagram, which reveals with greater clarity the effects of family dysfunction in our lives today. This is important Step One work.

In this exercise, you will create a diagram of your family of origin by listing your parents, grandparents, aunts, uncles, and other relatives that you can remember or have heard about. By diagramming your family and their personalities, you begin to see the generational nature of addiction and other family dysfunction. The labels that you will use in diagramming your family serve the purpose of helping you find clarity rather than serving as a value judgment. You are not necessarily judging the family. You are looking for patterns and similarities. You are looking for your position in the structure. If done thoroughly, the diagram will demonstrate how you could not have turned out any differently as an adult. If you were raised by addicts, enablers, spenders, and workaholics, you could not have been substantially different as an adult.

You can create a diagram of your family by listing your paternal relatives on one side of the chart and your maternal relatives across from them. A sample diagram is provided on page 36. For more space, you can duplicate this diagram on notebook paper. As you fill in the diagram, refer to the labels on the following page.

## Family Diagram Labels

Think about your experiences or what you have heard about each relative in connection with addiction, religion, relationships, food, sex, work, etc. Place the name of each relative in the diagram with the label which best describes him or her.

Relatives can have one or more of the following labels:

- alcoholic/addict  *SISTER , BROTHER*
- used alcohol/drugs  *SISTER, BROTHER*
- enabler  *PARENTS*
- religious
- worked a lot (workaholic)  *WIFE.*
- undependable, does not follow through  *MOM/DAD.*
- heavy debt (always borrowing money) or big spender (flashy clothes)  *SISTER*
- worried a lot (neurotic)
- perfectionistic (high strung)
- harsh, always critical, verbally abusive
- chronically ill, hypochondriac
- pill popper (always taking something)
- great cook (always thought of herself last)
- obese sibling/relative  *MCDONALDS.*
- emotionally ill  *MOM.*
- sickly child, too sensitive
- always had her face in a mirror (thought she was better than others)
- ladies man, player, gigolo, skirt chaser
- sexually aggressive, not safe
- violent, slapped others, pinched, threatened, glorified fighting
- grabbed or wrestled inappropriately
- thief, bogus check writer, inmate
- argumentative (will not be quiet, keeps arguments going)  *SISTER*
- people-pleaser  *SISTER*
- martyr  *SISTER MOM DAD*
- loner  *JEFF*

# *Family History Diagram*

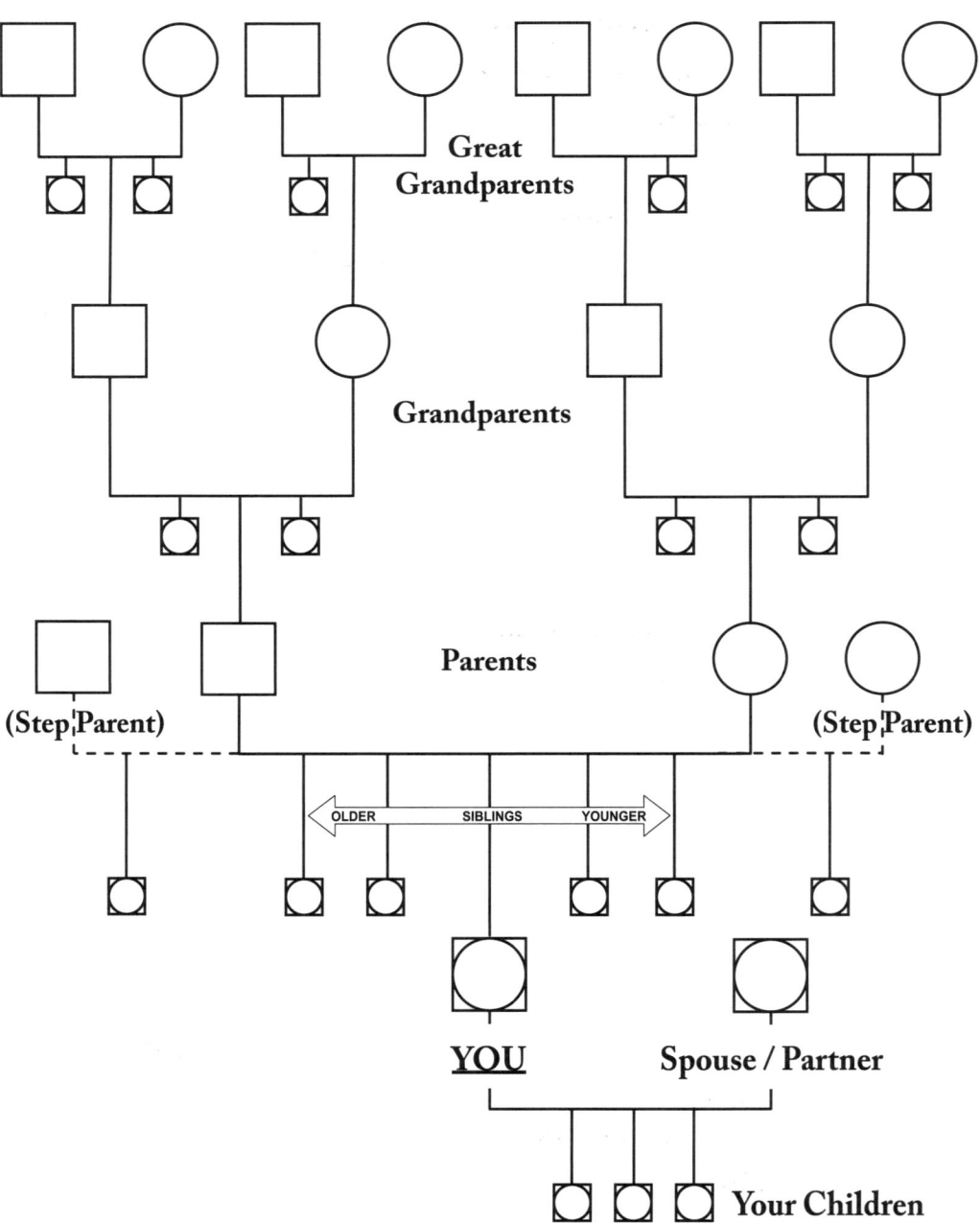

## Getting a different view of the family

After filling in the family diagram, look at the overall layout of your family. Look for patterns of addiction, codependency, or other dysfunction from the grandparents to the grandchildren. Look at the grandparents at the top of the diagram and the youngest grandchild at the bottom. Any similarities?

Where are the lost children, the scapegoats, black sheep, and heroes? What is your role in the structure?

Look at your position in the structure and notice all the personalities around you. This diagram represents the generational nature of the disease of family dysfunction.

## Exercise 2—The family "story line" and labeling

a)  **Childhood labels**

Parents or our siblings give us a label, which can stay with us for a lifetime. Labels can include: "stupid idiot," "lazy brat," "fool," "glutton," "know-it-all," "selfish," "big mouth," "evil," "disgusting," "filthy brat," "liar," and "loser."

Others labels are: "daddy's little girl", "mom's favorite", and "special."

Beyond the home, some ACA members have been labeled as "slow learners" by a school official and placed in special education classes. Many times our school work was affected by the abuse in our homes, but we were classified as learning disabled or with having an attention deficit. But we were not less intelligent or slow. An important part of your recovery involves identifying your labels and making plans to retire them. Write down your labels from childhood.

My labels are:

1)  DISAPPOINTMENT,    SELFISH

2)  LAZY

3)  WANT EASY MONEY (GET RICH QUICK)

Next, write down your labels on a small slip of paper and talk to your sponsor or counselor about them. Try to avoid blaming your parents, but realize the labels probably originated with them or a relative. Avoiding blame does not mean that your anger or sense of shame about the labels are wrong. It is normal to have these feelings, but it is important to stay focused on the process of recovery.

After talking about the labels, walk into the restroom and flush them away. The labels are gone. You get to say who you are in ACA.

b)  **The family "story line" versus the family "reality."**

Almost every dysfunctional family has a family story line and a family reality.

The family story line is the sentence or phrase we use to describe our family to outsiders.

For instance, a member of the Smith family might say: "The Smiths work hard, pay their bills, don't steal, and help others." Or, "The Smiths are enterprising go-getters, who make their own luck. We stick together."

The family reality is different and is rarely spoken within the family much less outside the family. The Smith reality might be: "Father drinks, argues with mother, and scares us with threats of violence." Or, "Mother secretly takes pills and is 'asleep' so I have to take care of my sisters and show affection to dad."

What is your family story line?

What is the reality of the family?

c)  **Family messages**

Try to list 10 messages, phrases, words or sentences your parents said to you about your intelligence, listening ability, your obedience to them, education, gender, sex, truth, love etc.

Examples:

"Dad always said he wanted a son/daughter. I was a girl/boy."

"Why can't you be more like your brother or sister?"

"I am so ashamed of you." "I am so disappointed in you."

"Jose never listens."

"Julie. Men go to college and women marry and keep the home in order."

"Latoya. Go to college but hold a job and be a mother, wife, lover, listener, cook, planner, and keep a clean house."

"Aaron is dumb as a rock. He won't ever amount to much."

"I am touching you like this because it's my love for you. It is our secret."

1)

2)

3)

4)

5)

6)

7)

8)

9)

10)

**d)** This exercise is similar to "c" previously; however this list deals with messages, phrases, words or sentences your family said about topics such as work, addiction, religion, education, sex, truth, love and other races. Some of these messages may reveal family prejudices. The examples of this exercise are not meant to demean any race or group.

Examples:

"Stay away from that group because _____."

"Get an education no matter what."

"After all I have done for you, you are so ungrateful and selfish."

"My mother always worried and predicted catastrophe."

"Father said children should be seen and not heard."

"They said grandfather took a drink of whisky once in awhile."

"Aunt Joan went away for an operation that no one talks about."

Try to list 10 of your own examples:

1)

2)

3)

4)

5)

6)



7)



8)



9)



10)


## Exercise 3—Identifying the number of ACA traits in your life.

In this next Step One activity, turn to the Laundry List (Problem) in the front of this workbook and circle the number of traits of an adult child you identify with. Next, think of examples of how you depend on these traits.

## Exercise 4—ACA Sponsorship

In this Step One activity, begin thinking about choosing someone to sponsor or mentor you through ACA's Twelve Steps. There is extensive information and experience on sponsorship in Chapter 11 of the ACA Fellowship Text (Steps and Traditions Book). ACA also has a pamphlet that details the development of ACA's style of sponsorship. In ACA, we practice a "fellow traveler" model of mentoring and sponsoring. A sponsor is someone who has worked the ACA steps and attends ACA meetings. If he or she attends another program for addiction issues, the sponsor has achieved sobriety in that program. The ACA sponsor is available to share his or her experience, strength and hope in working the ACA program.

## Step One ACA affirmation–meditation exercise:

This affirmation exercise can help you connect the dots between the preceding questions you have answered with the new knowledge you are learning about yourself and your family. These affirmations will help you verbalize a new direction in your life away from dependence and toward a true freedom. There is power in these affirmations. If practiced regularly, they bring clarity to our thoughts while pointing to the truth we are now embracing in ACA.

To prepare to meditate on these affirmations, many adult children find a quiet place and turn off cell phones, televisions or other distracting devices. Sitting in a relaxed condition, they breathe in and out slowly five to 10 times, letting their bodies relax. Glancing at the affirmations, they repeat each one slowly, thinking about each sentence before moving to the next affirmation. After reading the affirmations, continue breathing gently and close your eyes for the meditation time you have allowed. Let thoughts arise that will.

These affirmations can also be taken with you by jotting them down on notebook paper or entering them into your computer. Some ACA members tape the affirmations to a bedroom mirror and repeat them while dressing for the day.

### Affirmations:

1) I am powerless over the effects of alcoholism and family dysfunction.

2) I am powerless over the Laundry List traits.

3) My life is unmanageable when I focus on others rather than myself.

4) I did not cause my parents' addiction or dysfunction.

5) My feelings and thoughts are separate from the thoughts of my parents and my family.

6) I can stop trying to heal or to change my family through my current relationships. I can stop trying to change others.

7) I can stop condemning myself without mercy.

8) I am a valuable person.

**How much to tell: A word of caution.**

We conclude this section with a few pointers on how to discuss ACA with those outside the program. As we find acceptance in ACA and as we learn to trust others and share our story, many of us feel the urge to tell our family members about our lives and our past deeds. Feeling excited at having found ACA, some of us have told too much of our experiences to family members or friends. They could not handle such details with the acceptance found in ACA. We felt hurt when the person misunderstood us or minimized our new-found recovery. While we do not want to keep secrets or hide our past, we must think about what we are about to say and our motives for saying it. That means that there will be a time to talk to our family and friends about ACA. We will know how much of our story to tell our family and friends at that time. But in the beginning, we usually keep our most intimate sharing for ACA meetings and for our sponsor or counselor.

## STEP ONE SPIRITUAL PRINCIPLES:

### Powerlessness and Surrender

# STEP TWO

*Came to believe that a Power greater than ourselves could restore us to sanity.*

## He Learned That Unhealthy Dependence Is Progressive and Powerful

*I am here to tell you that being dependent on others in an unhealthy manner is cunning and patient. After more than 18 years of working the Twelve Steps I thought I could handle a relationship with a woman who I knew was probably a romance addict. The insane obsession I developed trying to rescue and then fix this woman pushed me close to insanity.*

*In the beginning we had so much fun. I bought flowers and chocolates. She drank wine and regaled me with stories from her homeland in Europe. We even wrote poetry to one another.*

*The craziness began when I realized we had different ideas of honesty. As an ACA member I wrongly assumed that most people practiced honesty or attempted honesty. Wrong. But by the time I found out, I was too far in. For the next six months I lived in a dependent, obsessive hell. I felt like I was losing my soul each time I compromised one of my program values for this person. When I finally made the decision to break free, I writhed on the floor with emotional pain that I almost could not bear. It is only by prayer, Step Two, and the help of two sponsors that I am here and sane today. I can tell you that dependency is patient, dormant, and progressive. And powerful.*

## I Was a Bible Teacher But Found a Higher Power Through ACA

*When I first read, "a Power greater than ourselves could restore us to sanity," I thought, "I'm not crazy!" I went to church regularly. I knew I was a good person. I even had a personal reawakening of my faith. Nevertheless, I was miserable for many, many years. There was a void within me I just couldn't fill. I am a Bible teacher and did many wonderful things for God, but I still needed to understand why I had been physically and sexually abused.*

*I was invited to go with a friend to a Twelve Step meeting. I thought the people were odd. I thought they all needed to go to church to find God in a hurry. As I continued to attend those meetings, I learned it wasn't God who was missing. When I got honest with myself, I realized I went to God many times, but I was dishonest. I wanted Him to help me, but I wore a mask of perfectionism. I realized I was not allowing God, as I understand God, to help me. I was telling my Higher Power what to do. I was a little god myself, controlling and abusive. My behavior was insane.*

*Eight years ago I confessed to my husband and my children that I was a fraud because I had hidden my feelings from them. One of my sons said, "Mom, I thought you had the perfect marriage." I had religion, but I had no Higher Power. Now God, as I understand God, teaches me that I'm not a god, that I cannot control anybody or anything, and that I cannot change anybody except myself.*

## Seeing Sanity for the First Time

When I first read Step Two, the notion of being restored to sanity confused me somewhat. Yet, I remained quiet and continued to work the Step and got some benefits anyway. I agreed that the insanity I practiced as an adult child in drug addiction and compulsive behaviors had actually been accepted by me as sane behavior. Being a people-pleasing male, my denial allowed me to act irresponsibly. Sometimes, I acted dangerously without comprehending another way to live.

As I remained in the program and studied the Steps, it slowly dawned on me that I had never really known sanity to begin with. My family-of-origin, with its cursings, belittlement, and threats of abuse, was not an atmosphere that would produce a healthy person with a sane view of life. My distorted view of sanity was not totally insane, but it was not sane either. By working Step Two, I first found clarity and then sanity. I gained clarity about the level of abuse I had grown accustomed to. With such clarity, I glimpsed real sanity for the first time. I realize today that I have a choice of handling situations in an insane manner such as cursing, shaming, and blaming, or a sane manner with feelings, prayer, and asking for help. I am being restored to clarity, and I am finding sanity for the first time as well.

## When I Lost Myself My Higher Power Took Over

It felt to me as if members of my family were spinning around me faster and faster. My mother's Alzheimer's disease was substantially worse. Her boyfriend was battering her. My mentally disabled younger sister was dying of breast cancer and needed to move into a different board-and-care facility.

In my professional life, I could hardly figure out what to do each day. I was not sleeping well. I would wake up and think about death, not suicide, but what it felt like to be dead and still feel pain. I was acting out violently. I stopped being able to do anything for anybody. I couldn't deal with my mother's situation or my sister's cancer. My husband would no longer tolerate my violence. I had an emotional breakdown.

I truly hoped a Higher Power didn't exist, because if He did, I would be judged, and I would be going to hell, I thought.

My therapist said, "Just let go. If you can't do anything, don't do anything." My husband told me, "You've had a breakdown. Leave this to someone else."

I did little things to help my family, but I had to let go of the big situations concerning my mother and my sister. Immediately my mother was accepted into a convalescent hospital where she will be safe. My sister was placed in a home where she will be comfortable as her cancer progresses. God took care of my family problems; I just did what I could do and let go. My Higher Power took over. I lost myself completely, and He took care of the problems I couldn't.

## I Came To Believe

*I'm glad Step Two says, "Came to believe…" I am not on good terms with God. There have been times when I believed in God and times when I wasn't sure there was a Higher Power. As to the last part of the Step, "restoring us to sanity," I don't feel insane. I have, however, made an insane world for myself. For a long time I continued the insane pace as if it were normal. Eventually I became overwhelmed and couldn't meet the demands I placed on myself. Then I did only absolutely necessary things. I got up to use the bathroom. I got up to eat.*

*I have seen some miracles that people in this program talk about, the coincidences that happen too often to be ascribed to chance. In the beginning I thought, "Gee, how did that happen? Wasn't that good planning?" That's when I came to actually believe in a Greater Power who was watching over me.*

*I still have a long way to go on Step Two. Tonight, for the first time, I heard the phrase "came to believe." I felt awful that I couldn't do Step Two because I didn't really believe in a Higher Power. I thought that meant I couldn't do the rest of the Steps since they all rested on this one, so I could never hope to recover. Gradually I am coming to believe there is something that can help direct my life. This I can do.*

## I Am Listening

*There just has to be a Higher Power to my way of thinking if there is any logic in the world. Over the last month, I have been able to simply be present during moments of quiet reflection. I have not experienced any program miracles yet, but I've come to believe my life can be restored to sanity. I have come to believe in a Higher Power. In my recovery I don't expect or require immediate, dramatic changes or improvements in my profession, my relationships, or my emotional health. I'm not trying to keep myself busy. I'm not trying to suppress or medicate my pain. This is new for me.*

*Today doesn't feel quite as unnatural as it did when I first began to deal with Step Two. I'm simply asking God to let me know He exists somehow. I've become receptive to having a little faith.*

## Step Two Summary

These shares illustrate the confusion we have had when it comes to the topic of a Higher Power. Before finding ACA, many of us believe that a Higher Power is indifferent, fake, punishing, or reserved for the true believers of the world. Step Two helps us revisit our earliest messages about a Higher Power to find out what is true for us. We make this journey with an open mind.

A few of these shares detail the insanity or flawed thinking of adult children. The insanity we speak of in Step Two refers to our continued efforts beyond all reason to heal or fix our family of origin through our current relationships. We can reenact our sick family system through our current relationships in the home or at work.

In an attempt to heal our dysfunctional family from the past, many of us set ourselves up as a Higher Power in our current relationships. We played God by being all-knowing or being all-flexible to control or manipulate others. We wrongly believed we solved the problems from our birth family by keeping our own homes in order. We may have even eliminated alcohol or other dysfunction from our home. Our children, who often act out in addiction or aggression, give us a clue to our failing. We unintentionally passed on our family insanity or distorted thinking.

Similar themes arise for the adult child who moves away from a dysfunctional family to find a better life and sanity. Yet, the dysfunction followed us into our lives away from our dysfunctional homes. The thought never dawned on us that we had carried the disease with us in the form of persistent fear and distorted thinking. This is para-alcoholism as we know it.

Meanwhile, some of us set ourselves up as a "helpless God," which is a creative way to manipulate and control others. Before finding ACA, many of us found power in acting helpless, which is a role we learned as children. This is not to say we did not experience real moments of utter helplessness as children, but as adults many of us used helplessness in a learned manner to stay in control.

In addition to the helpless one, dysfunctional family roles include the hero, lost child, scapegoat, black sheep, and mascot. The roles underline our insanity in our current relationships. For example, if we played the family hero as a child, we tend to play the hero or rescuer as an adult. We insanely knock ourselves out in relationships or in the work place, hoping for affirmation and praise, which we don't believe we deserve. Some of us tolerate unreasonable amounts of abuse or neglect in return for meager amounts of attention. We mask our efforts to control another person by appearing helpful. We often do not believe we deserve happiness. We read self-help books and learn about needs and wants and then state our needs in such a demanding manner that we step on the toes of others. We are baffled when they rebel at our efforts. We feel betrayed, but we try again.

The lost child, as an adult, practices insanity by remaining isolated or refusing to ask for help. The lost child appears to have given up efforts to fix his family of origin. Many lost children practice "relationship anorexia." They avoid relationships because they are terrified of abandonment, which has its roots in the childhood years. Like all adult children, the lost child experiences intense abandonment fear. As an adult, he or she chooses to limit chances for such hurt by avoiding relationships. The fear of change seems greater than the fear of isolation. Without help, the lost child passes on this fear to his or her children.

There are other forms of adult child insanity, isolation, and manipulation that we engage in, which usually leaves us feeling abandoned, angry, or confused. Yet, we try again, repeating the same mistakes. Fueled by fear, our false self discounts real avenues of help. The false self chooses to reapply old thinking and behaving that guarantees the same hurtful results we have always known in our decisions.

Many adult children have a poor concept of sanity because our parents did not give us good examples as children. Boundaries were not clear. Punishment or praise were not consistent. Our parents operated from distorted thinking that clouded reality in the home. Their confused thinking created behavior that was inconsistent or uncaring. We came to believe that this behavior was normal when it was insane by the standards of decency or true parental love.

In one respect, Step Two implies that we had sanity and lost it when in reality we may be learning about sanity for the first time in ACA. A helpful tip in working Step Two involves replacing the word "sanity" with "clarity." By working Step Two, we gain clarity about how our family dysfunction affects us in our lives as adults. We gain clarity about our abandonment and internal shame. Many of us find Step Two sanity through clarity.

We know we are drifting back into dysfunctional insanity or unmanageability when we find ourselves relying on the 14 traits of an adult child in our jobs and relationships. These common ACA traits are a great gauge of flawed thinking and reacting. They include fearing authority figures, people-pleasing, judging ourselves harshly, feeling guilty when we stand up for ourselves, becoming addicted to excitement, and becoming an addict or marrying an addict. We confuse love and pity and tend to "love" people we can rescue. We also can be the rescued. Practicing these traits is a form of insane living.

Another brand of ACA insanity involves self-harm and its various forms. We have seen adult children harm themselves in abusive relationships, with drugs, or with a degrading or dangerous behavior. We have seen some adult children repeatedly endure one dysfunctional relationship after the next, thinking it will get better with each new person. The adult child "falls in love" again and again, ignoring red flags involving the object of his or her affection. When the breakup comes, the adult child experiences intense feelings of abandonment, which are linked to the childhood days of neglect and abandonment.

To avoid the devastating pain of a romantic break up, many adult children harm themselves with drugs, sex, gambling, food, or other destructive activities. Others get lost in reading, working, or spending lavishly. Some will fall into the cycle of making up and breaking up with their lover. Others will select a new partner quickly to lessen the pain of a break up.

Some adult children running from the pain of a relationship will create a situation in which he or she can experience a "shame hit." Like the heroin addict who seeks a hit of heroin, the adult child seeks a "hit" of his or her shame. As odd as it sounds, many of us seem addicted to shame or abandonment. Since we grew up with an orientation to fear, shame, and abandonment, we seek out situations that recreate these feelings in ourselves. This is a shocking claim, but many of us can relate to it. Such activity is akin to the crisis-oriented lifestyle of many newcomers to the various Twelve Step fellowships. A crisis-oriented person feels alive when he is in a crisis he has helped cause. Likewise, many adult children feel alive when they can create shame or abandonment in their lives. Adult children seem to seek the thing they dread the most because it is familiar. This is learned by living in an unhealthy home.

It has been said that "insanity is repeating the same mistake and expecting a different result." That has been our experience. Change does not occur until the adult child does the Step work needed to curb the tendency to reach outside ourselves for love and affirmation. One of the keys to being restored to sanity involves surrendering our need to harm ourselves or to run from our feelings. We must also be honest about our actions and motives. We must name our behavior properly to avoid the delusional thinking that we are "feeling fine" when in reality we are headed for trouble. Such honesty or clarity of thought comes from seeking a Higher Power and by attending ACA meetings. We stop reacting and become actors, choosing a nurturing role in our Higher Power's play rather than a nightmare role in a destructive or unloving relationship.

When we settle down and listen, we begin to realize that the Power that brought us to ACA is still with us today. Where we once thought we found ACA by mistake, we begin to realize that a benevolent Power has been guiding us all along. Discovering this Power is one of the great miracles that many adult children have experienced in working Step Two and the remaining Steps. For some the Higher Power is recognized simply as loving and nurturing. The Higher Power is patient as it seeks to help the adult child find wholeness and integration of a divided self.

## WORKBOOK SECTION STEP TWO: Came to believe . . .

For the workbook feature, you will need support and self honesty. It is suggested that you get a sponsor or spiritual advisor as well before proceeding. We also offer a word of caution here. Some of the issues raised by ACA step work and attendance at meetings can raise disturbing memories of some of the most atrocious abuse and require professional help to be dealt with safely and effectively. We encourage adult children with these issues to seek extra help through counseling or therapy.

## Working Step Two in ACA

In Step One we answered questions about the effects of family dysfunction in our lives today. We also learned that our manageable behavior was perhaps controlling behavior that we had mislabeled. Of all the issues facing adult children, control is an issue that seems to take more time and patience to lessen. As children growing up in dysfunctional and sometimes dangerous homes, we had to stay in control of our emotions and thoughts to survive. To show emotion or make the "wrong" move could mean harm or humiliation. Letting go of control can be terrifying for adult children but it can be done in degrees.

In Step One we saw our denial and the role it played in our family structure. For the adult child, denial can mean that we misremember or "forget" segments of our childhood. We have seen adult children describe their childhoods as "loving" or "insignificant" when in reality the childhood was filled with neglect or horrific acts of mental, emotional and sexual abuse. With

Step Two Clarity, we also now see the effects of family alcoholism or dysfunction affecting our lives today. This hardened denial is the major mechanism by which family dysfunction is passed from generation to generation.

In Step Two we realize that some of our "insanity" is played out in the relationships we have as adults. Most adult children have codependent relationships in which we attempt to get our unmet childhood needs met by people, who are incapable of meeting such needs. There are many definitions for codependency but for us it generally means we look outward for love and security from others; however, we secretly feel incapable of being loved and we never feel completely safe no matter what the other person does for us. The term "codependent" and "adult child" are almost synonymous in definition and behavior types. All adult children become codependent to some degree based on their original soul rupture created by neglectful or abusive parents. The rupture of self is caused by being belittled, not being held, slapped, threatened, diminished, overly criticized, compared to another sibling, mocked by parents and blamed without cause.

There are no right or wrong answers to these Step Two questions. The ACA program only asks that you be honest in your answers to achieve the greatest personal growth.

## Step Two Questions and Directions:

1)  What is my definition of insanity?

2)  Am I recreating my family-of-origin dynamics of fear, excitement and pain in my current relationships? Am I setting up my own abandonment?

3)  Am I reenacting my family system through my current relationships? While this feels "normal," or familiar, is this a form of insanity?

4)  Were my responses to the abuse in my family insanity or a defense mechanism?

5)  Did I daydream or dissociate to escape my family abuse, neglect or indifference?

6) What did my parents say or do to undermine my reality when I complained about abuse or inappropriate behavior?

7) What messages did my parents or relatives use to invalidate my perceptions?

8) Did I numb my feelings or dissociate when my parents cursed, criticized or mistreated me?

9) Do I say I feel insane when in reality I am avoiding naming my feelings?

10) Do I secretly believe I am insane or believe I have an incurable brain disorder?

11) Did my parents abandon me by telling me I was emotionally ill or unstable?

12) Do I feel "crazy" but keep my feelings inside and never talk about such thoughts?

13) Do I act like one person in the privacy of my home and another person in public? (List an example).

14) Was there religious or spiritual abuse in my life? Can I talk about such abuse?

15) Have I injured myself physically or been involved in risky behavior and not realized this could have been an adult child bottom?

16) Do I binge eat, gamble, have sex, take drugs or spend money when I feel upset or unsettled? Do I feel insane doing this?

17) Have I asked my Inner Child or True Self what sanity is?

## Dependence and Codependence:

1) Do I tend to get involved in relationships with an addict or another compulsive personality such as a workaholic or sex addict?

2) Do I mislabel violent and chaotic relationships as "passionate" and "complex?"

3) Do my relationships show a pattern of intensity, indifference and fits and restarts? Is blaming others a theme in my relationship?

4) Do I mask my need to control others by appearing cheerful or helpful?

5) Do I try to get my needs of love and happiness met by people who cannot do enough for me or who cannot meet my expectations?

6) Do I label myself as a "giver" but secretly resent others, who do not return my favors or listen to my advice?

7) Do I choose relationships based on people who are "beneath" me but who I can rescue and make "love me?"

8) Do I find myself in relationships with "dangerous" men or women because I feel alive amid the intensity? Did I ignore how he or she had harmed others by thinking I was "special" and would not be harmed?

9) Do I accept a high level of abuse from someone but don't recognize the abuse?

10) Do I look outside myself for love and affirmation? (List an example).

## Came to Believe:

1) Does my God have similar behavior or features of my parents, i.e., harshness, indifference, distant, judging…, etc.?

2) What do I remember being told about faith, belief, prayer and forgiveness?

3) Do I have a "getcha God," a God who keeps score and punishes me for mistakes?

4) Do I have an austere God, who seems hard to internalize or to approach in prayer?

5) Does God or the Power of the Universe hear my prayers?

6) Does a Higher Power love me?

## Sanity/Higher Power:

1) Do I realize I may be the most sane member of my family because I am seeking recovery?

2) Do I realize I am not unique and that other adult children think and act like me?

3) Can I come to believe that I have had an inner strength all along that helped me survive an abusive childhood?

4) Can I come to believe that a Higher Power has been with me always and helped me survive until I could find ACA?

5) Do I believe I can love myself and ask for help? That I don't have to do this alone?

6) Will I consider the possibility that I can face my emotions with help from my sponsor and ACA friends?


7) Can I come to believe there is hope for me?


## Step Two Spiritual Principles: Openmindedness and Clarity:

## Clarity:

1) Is my behavior as an adult, no matter how bizarre or self-defeating, a response to being raised in an alcoholic or dysfunctional home?


2) Can I believe or be open to the promise of another way to live with clarity in ACA?


3) Am I open to the possibility that being an adult child is a spiritual problem rather than a mental problem?


## Step Two ACA affirmation—meditation exercise:

The affirmation exercise can be done at home, at work or a place of your own choosing. Many adult children find a quiet place and turn off cell phones, televisions or other distracting devices. Sitting in a relaxed condition, they breathe in and out slowly five to 10 times, concentrating on a comfortable spot in front of them. Glancing at the affirmations, they repeat each one slowly before closing their eyes for the meditation. For the best results, don't try to figure out the affirmation as you read it. Simply state it slowly and listen to the words and your voice. These affirmations can also be taken with you by jotting them down on notebook paper. Some ACA members tape them to a mirror at home.

**Affirmations:**

1) By attending ACA meetings and working with my sponsor I am being restored to clarity and sanity.

2) I am understanding the effects of addiction and family dysfunction in my adult life today.

3) I am coming to believe that it was insane to think that I caused my parents' addiction or dysfunction. I was the child. They were the parents.

4) I am not unique.

5) I am not alone.

## ACA Activity:

Ask your Inner Child to draw a picture of his or her Higher Power from the Inner Child's perspective. This is your perception of God before you attached parental behaviors to it. Use crayons, colored pencils, glitter, glue and construction paper. Include labels or depictions of the characteristics of your Higher Power. (For more information on the Inner Child, read Chapter Eight from the ACA Fellowship Text).

## A note to the Atheist or Agnostic:

The ACA program is for you. If you do not believe in God or a Higher Power, select something to be a power greater than yourself so that you can work the ACA program and receive healing results. Example: Your ACA group or therapy group is a power greater than you since it meets regularly, discusses ACA issues and produces progress for its participants. Meanwhile, we ask that you keep an open mind about the spiritual nature of ACA and enjoy the fellowship's acceptance.

## STEP TWO SPIRITUAL PRINCIPLES:

### Openmindedness and Clarity

# STEP THREE

*Made a decision to turn our will and our lives over to the care of God, as we understand God.*

## Let Go. Let God.

*Defining God, as I understood God, took a long time. I didn't believe in a benevolent God. I did believe that everything that could go wrong would go wrong. I know it is unrealistic to think the worst would always happen, but it seemed to happen for me.*

*To recover from my own negativity, I came to ACA. I tried to believe everything wasn't my responsibility. I tried to believe that whatever was going to happen in my life was controlled by some God. This was difficult. I always assumed I was wrong in whatever situation arose. I haven't completely given up all my control, yet. When I encounter obstacles now, I remind myself to "let go, and let God."*

*Eventually, by working the Steps, I turned my will and life completely over to God, as I understand God. My life is, coincidentally, working better. Today, when I am acting compulsively, I take a breather from that activity to moderate my behavior. Sometimes I have to say aloud, "I'm turning this over to God." Today I believe in a force some people call God. This force makes certain that what is supposed to happen does happen. I am letting go of control more easily.*

## Control Made Her Feel Safe

*I have trouble turning my will and my life over to the care of God. It's difficult for me to "let go" because I feel like I'm not being responsible.*

*I didn't listen to my body or my thoughts. I ignored my feelings and reactions for so long because I placed no importance on them. My intense fears are what made me start to listen to my body. My panic, I decided, came from things I didn't want to do. I had to be in control to feel safe. When I make a decision now I try not to torment myself with: "I should have," or "maybe if." I do what I need to do, and then I let go. I stop trying to make things come out the way I want them to.*

*In ACA I'm changing my life. I'm receptive to alternatives. In a sense, I'm turning over my power to this ACA group that is greater than me. I have only just begun my work on Step Three.*

## Compassion, Forgiveness, Love, And Gratitude

*I came to the program after a 7-year relationship ended. When my lover left me, it felt like my whole being left. I experienced more pain than I had ever felt. Every fear I had known was boiling up in me. I wanted to live, but I didn't know how to deal with the pain. I didn't trust God enough to take care of me because I was too busy taking care of everyone else. I finally understood the depths of despair that lead people to commit suicide. I began to understand what ACA means when we say: "We learn to focus on ourselves" so we can get better.*

*The gifts and miracles of life were not what I had thought they were when I tried to control people around me. My agenda was a ticking biological clock. When I felt pain, I compulsively cleaned my house to stop feeling anything. I could see pain in others, but I used it as a cue to try to fix them rather than identify with the pain in empathy and just listen. Only when I surrendered my life and my will did what I know intellectually become real for me. Compassion, forgiveness, love, and gratitude became real as I worked the Steps and surrendered. By turning my will and life over to my Higher Power, I could see examples of these spiritual principles in the lives of others.*

*From forgiveness I learned to love. I had this fantasy about love. I didn't know how to love myself, so I always looked for men to be my gods. I did anything a man told me to do: I changed my hair; I changed my makeup; I changed my clothes; and I behaved in the way he wanted me to behave. I thought marriage and children would fix me. When I left the house and went to work I was a totally different person. I didn't know how to be real. I was a fake. I was abandoning myself. I finally learned that abandoning myself would not take care of my abandonment or rejection issues.*

*The ACA program has brought me the miracle of life. I am able to experience compassion, forgiveness, love, and gratitude, the emotions that make my life worth living. I take responsibility for what I want out of life. I am honest and open with other people. I have had this spiritual awakening.*

## I Found A Voice In My Inner Child

*It was hard to turn my life and my will over to my Higher Power. I didn't hear a big, booming voice. I wondered how I would know what to do for God. Somebody said at a meeting, "If I have a result in mind when I pursue a course of action, then I am doing my own will." That was a good tool for me to use.*

*I also heard about the Inner Child in meetings. I did an exercise once that seemed to connect me with a five-year-old child inside me. The first time I got a sense of doing God's will was when that Inner Child wanted to do something and the critical parent inside my head said, "No, you can't do that." I decided to defy my critical parent again if the opportunity arose. I drove by the supermarket one day when I was on my way to the bank. I wanted to pick up a loaf of bread and some bananas. My critical parent piped up inside my head, "You can't stop. You told the woman at the bank you were coming right over." A child's voice inside my head replied defiantly, "I want to get my bread and bananas now!" I parked my car and got the bread and bananas. As I drove to the bank I worried about what might happen because I didn't do exactly what I said I would do. The woman had gone out to lunch. She had, however, left the paperwork for me. I hadn't inconvenienced her at all.*

*I find it interesting now, that I get to do things I want to do that seem completely illogical. I give myself permission because that's the message God seems to send me about what He wants me to do. He excites my Inner Child. More often than not someone seems to benefit from my Inner Child's yens. I believe this is why I get the messages.*

## "Getcha God" Or Actual Parent

*I struggled a lot with the Third Step because I had confused my violent and shaming father with God. I thought God was a super powerful being living in the far reaches of outer space, keeping score of all my bad thoughts and actions. I had a "getcha God" who I believed would "get me" for my imperfect behavior. I gave up on God and told people I was an agnostic because it sounded cool. I lived my life in an endless cycle of harmful relationships, lost jobs, and lost friends. I could never be a friend, actually. I stopped getting into relationships to stop the pain. I had no choice. I was compulsive and getting more out of control with each passing year.*

*When I came to ACA I saw the Third Step and wanted no part of God. I worked Step One and attended meetings. I tried to keep an open mind, but I was angry at God. The Second Step and The Solution helped me open up my mind more about God. Step Two mentions a Higher Power and asks me to consider the notion of a loving, benevolent force. The Solution says that "our actual parent is a Higher Power, whom some of us choose to call God." It says the Higher Power gave us the Twelve Steps of recovery.*

*Through the years I have come to believe that I am loveable. I have replaced my "getcha God" with the "actual parent" who will never abandon me. My parents were the biological couple bringing me into the world. My actual parent is a God of my understanding. I have a choice today when I put my will and life in the hands of this God. This God listens.*

## Step Three Summary

ACA is a spiritual and not religious program, which means we avoid dogmatism, theological discussions, or grand testimonials about the miracles of God. We are not aligned with any religious, mystical, or spiritual systems of belief; however, we believe it is imperative that the recovering adult child find a Higher Power to help him or her find healing from growing up in a dysfunctional home. We make no apologies for this great fact of our recovery program. But we also understand the struggles that many adult children have had with belief and faith. We are not pushing religion or spiritual beliefs upon anyone. We use the Twelve Steps, professional help, and a Higher Power to reclaim our wholeness. This is the ACA way.

These Step Three shares represent the sovereign right of every adult child to choose the God of his or her understanding. For the first time in our lives we can finally think about what a Higher Power means to us rather than relying on what we have been told. Step Two gave us insight into how many of us came to perceive a punishing or indifferent God. In Step Three we open our minds to new possibilities. Some of us are comfortable with the word "God" for a Higher Power. Others will use Spirit of the Universe, Father of Light, Earth Mother, or the Divine. Some ACA members still investigating their spiritual path choose an ACA group as a power greater than themselves. Whatever we choose to call our Higher Power, we make a decision to turn our will and life over to its care on a daily basis.

We turn over everything without bargaining with God as we understand God. We don't release some things to a Higher Power and hold onto others. If we struggle with turning over our will and life to a Higher Power, we can begin by turning over our self-hate, self-doubt, or fear. We can ask God to take our compulsions, resentments, and learned rage. Some of us will work up to turning over our will and life to the care of God. This is a process that we learn to trust.

These Step Three shares also represent a deep well of hope and patience created by a loving God who has given us a program to restore our lives. It is a well of grace we can return to again and again and dip out self-acceptance, self-assurance, and love. Each time we take Step Three, we drink down God's love. We replenish our Inner Child or True Self. We come to believe that God hears our prayers and loves us always.

ACA's Third Step typifies our spiritual approach to the disease of family dysfunction. In ACA, we view our compulsive thinking and dependent behavior as a spiritual dilemma rather than a mental illness. We have no quarrel with science and medicine, which have made great strides in mapping and studying the brain. Such clinical work is of great importance in understanding human behavior and brain functions. We freely use such clinical labels as depression, panic disorder, bipolar, dissociation, and post-traumatic stress disorder. Some ACA members have been diagnosed as multiple personalities and as schizophrenic.

We do not believe our brains are missing any elements. We start with the premise that we are whole and that we had a normal reaction to an abnormal situation of being raised in a dysfunctional home. Our normal reaction to protect ourselves has created survival traits, compulsions, and self-harming behaviors, which respond to the ACA Steps and spiritual remedies. We are not minimizing the severity of our situation as adult children. The disease of family dysfunction manifests itself in dependency, addiction, and dissociative personalities. The disease can kill. Every day, adult children commit suicide, die in addiction, or die one day at a time in silent isolation, thinking they are hopeless. In ACA, we believe we were born whole and became fragmented in body, mind, and spirit through abandonment and shame. We need help finding a way to return to our miracle state.

Whatever mental diagnosis we may have, we seek a Higher Power in prayer and ACA meetings to relieve our chronic nature of feeling different. We believe God understands the root of mental health labels and freely offers help to those seeking God's love and light. We believe in a spiritual solution for the disease of family dysfunction.

In addition to a deep sense of shame and abandonment, we believe that most of our emotional and mental distress can be traced to our steadfast nature to control. In ACA, we realize that control was the survival trait which kept us safe or alive in our dysfunctional homes. We controlled our thoughts, our voices, and many times our posture to escape detection from an abusive parent or caregiver. We knew our parents were looking for imaginary cues to criticize us or verbally attack us. As adults we continue to control ourselves and our relationships in an unhealthy manner. This brings abandonment or predictable turmoil. We make promises to do better but eventually return to our obsessive need to compulsively arrange, question, worry, dust, wash, lock, unlock, read, or hypervigilantly survey our thoughts and actions to feel safe. But it is never enough. Experience shows there is little hope and little spirituality in homes governed by smothering control.

By making a decision to turn our will and lives over to the care of God as we understand God, we are actually making two decisions. By deciding to ask a Higher Power for guidance in Step Three, we are also deciding to back away from control. We are surrendering our plans to run our own lives on self-will. We are asking God for help, which strikes at the heart of our instinctual reaction to solve problems on our own.

The decision we make in Step Three represents one of our first true choices.

Asking a Higher Power for help is not easy for adult children for many reasons. We knew asking for help as children was risky and could be quashed by parents who would not allow such talk. We were told we were selfish or immature if we asked for help. We were told to be quiet. At other times we were taught to doubt our perception of what was happening. As we grew older, the option of asking for help or thinking we could ask for assistance dissolved. By the time we reached adulthood, most of us avoided asking for help, thinking we were self-sufficient and beyond such needs. This attitude can be a major stumbling block for adult children trying to call upon God to heal the disease of family dysfunction in their lives.

This is the same attitude that often stands in the way of us asking a sponsor for help in working the Twelve Steps. If we are to get better, we have to quit playing God, ask for help, and ride out the uncomfortable emotions that accompany this risk. We play God and avoid asking for help in the strangest ways. Many adult children can play God by being philosophical about the origin of people, the cosmos, and mysticism, but we use this knowledge to avoid getting involved in our own lives. People come to us for our knowledge on spiritual matters, but we may feel phony because we realize we are not getting our own needs met. We only have ourselves to turn to for help. We cling to control. We have become knowledge Gods sealed off from others.

Others can play God and avoid asking for help by appearing agnostic or atheistic. They seem put off by talk of spiritual matters. This does not mean that the views of the agnostic or atheist mean less. These views are respected in ACA. But to use such positions to remain in isolation is a tough path to follow. We must ask for help if we are to break out of isolation and join humanity. We can't just talk about it. We have to let go of control and do it. We make a decision to ask someone to help us and then accept the help once it is offered. We cannot recover alone.

We have to change this attitude of not asking for help if we are to make progress with Step Three and all of the Steps. We understand that simply going to an ACA meeting and sharing our fears and hopes does not immediately produce a desire to ask a Higher Power for help. Many of us still wonder if we deserve help and others wonder if we will be rejected if we take the risk and ask. Other adult children are still angry at God for seemingly not intervening in their abusive or neglectful homes. Still others wonder if a Higher Power exists at all. There is one way to find out. Make an effort and try. There is another way to live.

## Endless Supply

Don't worry about wearing out Step Three. This Step is a bottomless well of hope, which is needed to deal with our fear-based attempts to control ourselves and others. As we work the remainder of the Twelve Steps, we will invariably struggle with control and self-doubt. Such struggles are only natural since we relied on controlling our feelings and emotions to survive in our homes and relationships. Control meant a sense of safety and predictability; however, we surrendered much of our personality and spirit through this manner of living. In Step Three we begin the gradual and gentle process of easing off of stifling control and replacing it with emotional freedom.

Each time we encounter the cliff face of control and feel overwhelmed by steep walls, we must remember we can draw on an endless well of God's grace. The Third Step, coupled with our association with other recovering adult children, is an endless resource of hope and reassurance. We can tap it indefinitely, one day at a time.

Letting go of rigid control is possible in our experience. However, we first must realize what letting go means. Some of us equate letting go to dying or potentially being harmed in a severe manner. Many adult children can be filled with panic at the thought of loosening their grip on an addiction or harmful behavior that they believe keeps them alive or safe. We have seen adult children grip a harmful behavior until the end. Some will die because they cannot find the willingness to let go. Others will let go and live. This is not easy but we can do it—let go—with the help of our Higher Power and our ACA support group.

In Step Three, we are not suggesting that we live without some restraint. We are not suggesting living in anarchy without real choice. To the contrary, by identifying our fears and dependent traits we take several steps away from control. We step toward our Higher Power and true freedom.

In Step Three, we deepen our knowledge of how we have battled with control and with a Higher Power most of our lives. Many adult children hoped for God's grace or intervention, but we never seemed capable of truly letting go and letting God work in our lives. We shamed ourselves for being unable to let go and truly have faith and belief. We thought we were incapable of having meaningful faith. We forgot what many of us heard as children: "God loves us always."

We realize we are letting go of control when our prayers bring a settling effect to our spirit or emotions when we are troubled. We realize we are letting go when we break our isolation and ask another adult child to listen to our fears or hopes. We choose company instead of finding comfort in isolation. We let go of control when we become honest about a troublesome behavior we want to change. We pray and ask for help to be willing to change. We let others share our lives.

## The Gift of Choice

Choice is God's gift for letting go. Many of us practice letting go by drawing a continuum chart and placing it on the refrigerator door. We mark our daily progress along a horizontal line. On some days our control registers to the far end of the continuum and we feel alone and isolated. On other days we let go of control and catch a glimpse of God's will for us. We feel freedom. We learn to discern what events or decisions need greater attention and which items can be ignored. We let go of control by asking for what we need instead of manipulating others for things we really don't want. By letting go of control, we continue on the path to greater choice. With choice, we find out what we like and dislike. We feel less compelled to repeat rituals of control to make it through the day. We choose a new coffee shop, or we enroll in a college course and learn to explore the world around us. We choose to take singing lessons or volunteer for a worthy cause. We get our hands dirty in gardening or we let dust collect on the ledge longer without dusting compulsively. We see the art in spilled milk on the counter top. We learn to listen to our Inner Child and to be spontaneous. These are the choices that stretch out before us. There are countless more, but they are missed if we cling to control.

Before we arrived at ACA, we had no real choice. We were dependent or addicted to drugs, food, sex, or work, without a sense of direction. Most of us were reactors locked into unchangeable behavior. With ACA's spiritual focus on addressing the disease of family dysfunction, we break the cycle. We replace rigidity and fear with hope. We create an opening for change.

We choose to turn our will and lives over to the care of our Higher Power on a daily basis. We realize that the path of greater choice is a spiritual path that begins at denial and no choice and progresses through greater levels of choice to discernment. The level of choice we develop in ACA is proportional to the integrity of our boundaries. The more we let go, the stronger our boundaries become. This is an ACA paradox: Letting go creates stronger boundaries.

## A Word About Religious Abuse

ACA respects all the religions and spiritual belief systems of the world. We make no judgment on which religion is better than the next. Our Third Step opens wide the path of exploration on spiritual matters. We encourage our group members to seek the fullest spiritual life possible to make the greatest gains in recovery.

That said, many of our members have suffered from religious abuse that can include harsh treatment at the hands of well-meaning people. Other adult children have been sexually abused by a priest or other church figure.

While we realize God's love in Step Three, we acknowledge that many adult children have been spiritually abused and struggle with a concept of God in addition to struggling with control. The emotional and spiritual damage created by such acts of betrayal are staggering for some. We urge these ACA members to keep an open mind and to be gentle with themselves as they work the ACA Steps to find a God of their understanding. We believe our best hope is seeking a spiritual solution in concert with other recovering adult children.

Other forms of spiritual abuse include the adults in our lives appearing righteous in public while hateful and abusive behind closed doors. This is yet another conflicting view of God in which the child is confused and believes this to be the actual face of God. However, we must remember what the ACA Solution states: "Our actual parent is a Higher Power whom some of us choose to call God. Although we had alcoholic or dysfunctional parents, our Higher Power gave us the Twelve Steps of Recovery."

The Solution also states that our parents were the biological agents bringing us into the world. A loving God is the actual parent for many of us choosing the ACA way of life.

Finding a God of our understanding is essential for long-term recovery and real, inner change. We cannot shrink from the task of seeking God earnestly, regardless of what we may have been taught about God as children.

ACA is a spiritual program, which offers the power and grace needed to help heal these spiritual and emotional wounds. There is power in the ACA Steps and the fellowship created by such Steps. ACA work, coupled with focused counseling, can help the religiously abused adult child find a way to work Step Three. We can find a way to connect to the True Parent, our God of our understanding.

## WORKBOOK SECTION STEP THREE: Made a decision...

For the workbook feature you will need support and self honesty. It is suggested that you get a sponsor or spiritual advisor as well before proceeding. We also offer a word of caution here. Some of the issues raised by ACA step work and attendance at meetings can raise disturbing memories of some of the most atrocious abuse and require professional help to be dealt with safely and effectively. We encourage adult children with these issues to seek extra help through counseling or therapy.

Many adult children find it helpful to answer specific questions about their alcoholic or dysfunctional upbringing. By doing so we begin to see our denial and the role it played in our family structure. We also see the effects of family alcoholism or dysfunction having an affect in our lives today. In Step Three we realize that we get to choose the God of our understanding. No one can do this for us. As children, we were told who God was or was not. But in ACA we are allowed to question and think about a Higher Power in a reflective manner perhaps for the first time in our lives. We get to choose and describe God or the Spirit of the Universe in our own terms. If you have no concept of God or a Spirit of the Universe, we urge you to keep an open mind. Start from where you are at. For some, the starting point for a faith that arrests the disease of family dysfunction is agnosticism or a question of faith. It is okay to begin your spiritual journey with questions instead of a solid faith or a belief system. Atheists are welcome as well. We have found that many atheists enjoy the gifts of the ACA program and find a power greater than themselves in an ACA group.

## Step Three Questions and Information

1) Did I pray to a Higher Power and never seem to have prayers answered?

2) What was I told about God by my parents, religious leaders and friends? Was I allowed to ask questions?

3) If I drew a picture of God or the Divine Power of the Universe, what would it look like?

4) What was I told about prayer by parents, religious leaders and friends?

5) Was it acceptable for me to be angry at a Higher Power?

6) Did my parents act one way during worshiping services and another way at home?

7) How does my attempt to control others or my emotions interfere with God working in my life? *(Give a specific example.)*

8) What is one area of my life I can begin to think about lessening my control urges?

9) Do I know how to have fun?

## Made a Decision

1) What will happen if I make a decision to turn over my will and life to God as I understand God?

2) Can I talk to another ACA member about how they made a decision to turn over their will and life to a Higher Power?

3) Do I realize that the Higher Power that brought me to ACA is still with me and will never abandon me?

4) Do I realize that God is the actual parent and has been there for me all along?

5) Do I believe that God hears my prayers?

6) Do I understand that I am cared for by God no matter what I have done?

## As we understand God:

1) Can I ask my Higher Power to be there for me no matter what happens?

2) Will I be abandoned by God if I don't work a perfect program of recovery quickly enough?

3) Why does God refuse to reject me or let me go when I feel unimportant or not worthy?

4) Can I ask a Higher Power to help me release my most glaring controlling behaviors?

5) How do I accept God's unconditional love for me?

6) What does reparenting myself have to do with Step Three? Who is the "actual parent?" *(Hint: Read The Solution)*

## Step Three Spiritual Principles: Willingness and Accepting Help:

1) Am I willing to do whatever it takes to work my ACA program and to focus on myself? (What am I willing to do?).

2) What am I surrendering so that I can make ACA a priority in my life?

3) What actions can I take that show that I am surrendering and facing my childhood experiences?

4) Can I begin at the level of willingness? Can I be willing to be willing to surrender?

5) Can I begin by surrendering my self-hate and self-harming behavior?

6) Am I willing to ask for help?

7) Am I willing to accept help if I ask for help?

8) How is asking for help a form of giving up control?

## Step Three ACA affirmation–meditation exercise:

The affirmation exercise can be done at home, at work or a place of your own choosing. Many adult children find a quiet place and turn off cell phones, televisions or other distracting devices. Sitting in a relaxed condition, they breathe in and out slowly five to 10 times, concentrating on a comfortable spot in front of them. Glancing at the affirmations, they repeat each one slowly before closing their eyes for the meditation. For the best results, don't try to figure out the affirmation as you read it. Simply state it slowly and listen to the words and your voice. These affirmations can also be taken with you by jotting them down on notebook paper. Some ACA members tape them to a mirror at home.

## Affirmations: Let Go. Let God

1) I am willing to consider releasing some control in my life.

2) I am willing to call someone when I feel the urge to control another's thoughts or actions.

3) I believe that real choice comes from the God of my understanding rather than my illusions of control and orderliness.

4) I desire real choice and discernment.

5) I surrender my family to God as I understand God.

6) I surrender my self-hate.

## Third Step Prayer

Many ACA members use the Third Step Prayer to formalize their Third Step and to move on to Step Four. Some of us say this prayer with another person. This person can be your sponsor, counselor, spiritual advisor, or close friend. We offer this action for the purpose of learning to ask someone to participate in your new life. Sharing a prayer with another person lets us know we are making a connection to life and others in a meaningful way. Here is the ACA Third Step Prayer.

*God. I am willing to surrender my fears and to place my will and my life in your care one day at a time. Grant me the wisdom to know the difference between the things I can and cannot change. Help me to remember that I can ask for help. I am not alone. Amen.*

### STEP THREE SPIRITUAL PRINCIPLES:
#### Willingness and Accepting Help

# STEP FOUR

*Made a searching and fearless moral inventory of ourselves.*

## A Picture Is Worth A Thousand Words

*There was so much to learn in ACA when I got here. I identified with the common behaviors in counseling and at my first meeting but the talk of a Child Within and shame and abandonment was more than I could understand at first. My ACA counselor understood what I was trying to do. She helped me understand my loss or the pain of my "stuck grief" through the Fourth and Fifth Steps.*

*She used the Twelve Steps, ACA books, feelings exercises, affirmations and one other thing that helped me see my shame and abandonment underneath my experience of being an abused kid. She said that when my father cursed or threatened me that he was shaming me and abandoning me. I didn't understand that until I looked at my childhood pictures that the counselor asked me to bring to a session. I had seen these pictures before, but now I could really see them. There was a picture of me when I was 5 years old. Before I found ACA, the picture meant nothing to me, but my mother always seemed to cherish it. She kept it on the television. My counselor had me hold that picture in a session and look at it without speaking. I could finally see how sensitive and gentle I looked as a child. I never realized how bright my eyes were. My smile was true. After this, shame and abandonment began to mean something. I took my first step toward my Inner Child.*

## The Healing Was In The Balance

*I found ACA when I was just getting sober and clean. I felt insane. I had done things and thought things that made me fear for my sanity. I could not stop these voices in my head that told me I was insane or going insane. When I saw Step Four, I could not accept that I might have good qualities. I was convinced I was becoming evil. I felt like a Jekyll and Hyde. I was calm on the outside but terrified of my thoughts or obsessions on the inside.*

*I avoided relationships because I was afraid I would act out somehow and harm someone. As a teenager, I had committed shameful acts against a younger niece. As a newcomer in ACA, I recalled my behavior. I felt disgusting and wondered if the Steps were a solution for me. I took my best shot at Step Three and started Four. Because I had learned to judge myself harshly, I listed mostly negative actions and thoughts on my first Fourth Step. I waited for judgment. The thought of balancing my Fourth Step by listing positive traits never crossed my mind. The thought of looking at generational shame and parental abandonment was equally off the table in Step Four.*

*A caring counselor looked at my Fourth Step and suggested that I write down 10 positive traits I might have. I almost refused because I sincerely believed that to write out any good qualities would be a lie. In my crazy thinking, I believed honesty was my salvation and to write down a trait I did not believe in would be dishonest. Willingness prevailed, and I did the assignment, which included reading my list of good traits in counseling sessions. I stumbled with the reading, but the effect was profound. Even though I did not believe in the affirmations, I found myself thinking about them often. I did my*

*Fourth Step and Fifth Step and thought that I got little relief. But something happened. After my Fifth Step, I could still judge myself harshly at a mistake, but that affirmation list would pop into my head almost immediately and cause me to pause.*

*That was 20 years ago. I can now list my positive traits in my head and believe them. The affirmations and my other ACA work gave me enough breathing room to give myself a break. I thought all the disgusting things I did started with me, but I had help from generational shame. I thought I was no good, and I found out instead that I have worth.*

## Step Four Is The Shame Buster

*For me, Step Four was the "Shame Buster." I had a pervasive feeling of inadequacy and a sense of being defective. The Fourth Step "busted up" that shame.*

*Having my needs ignored or my vulnerabilities abused as a child created shame. As a child, I was not capable of figuring out that my parents' illness and abusive behavior were the reason for my sense of abandonment and neglect. I thought I was not good enough to deserve the emotional support and care I needed. I survived by being good, perfect, and always right. I behaved in ways I knew would receive approval. I thought if I could be good enough, I'd be safe.*

*I did Step Four by making a list of my good and troublesome behaviors. This helped me look objectively at my strengths and areas to improve. My shame started to dissolve as I started to see myself as I am. I no longer had to defend and rationalize my behavior to cope with shame. Shame is the lie that tells me I am bad. I've done some bad things, and I've done some good things. Step Four allows me to see the actual truth. It tells me I am human. I have strengths and areas to improve. Step Four brought me a measure of self-worth, so I could start to let go of my compulsive need to be perfect, to be right, and to seek approval.*

## The Long and The Short of It

*My inventories need not begin with, "Oh God, what's wrong with me?" I have to own what is good in me, as well as those things that are not. I don't need to bludgeon myself further by focusing only on what is wrong with me. I need to be rigorously honest and thorough in both my short and long inventories. I need to balance my good qualities with areas that trouble me.*

*In addition to the long inventory in Step Four, I use a short inventory to explore daily events. When I cooked oatmeal for my husband one morning, he announced that he used a double boiler when he made oatmeal so the cereal cooked evenly and there was no residue left on the sides of the pan. I glared at him. But instead of echoing one of my mother's retorts—"If you don't like the way I do it, do it yourself!"—I took some slow breaths and looked at the situation more calmly. The analysis was fairly simple. When I was a child, whatever my mother did was important and could not be interrupted. My anger came up when my husband crossed what I thought was a boundary. My fury arose when the rules that applied to my mother did not seem to apply to me as an adult. My cooking got interrupted by my husband. I wanted to respond like my mother, but I applied my recovery. I asked him to get my attention and then ask me if I could take a short break before he began a conversation when I was cooking or doing another activity. He said he would, and he did.*

*My long inventory, Fourth Step, poses questions on all aspects of life. I have done three different inventories to date, once in a Step Study group, once with a sponsor, and once alone. By answering the questions in the inventories I discovered who I was, where I had been, where I was right at that time, and where I was going.*

*Through the various inventories, I discovered I was a real person with likes and dislikes, vices and virtues. In revisiting my family-of-origin, I learned that the shame I carried wasn't mine. It was merely a technique used by a dysfunctional parent to control her world. Using this Fourth Step method, I have grown emotionally and spiritually. I now know how to be the person I want to be.*

## Getting Started on Step Four

In approaching Step Four, many adult children have said: "Why dredge up the past? What is done is done. I am forgetting the past and moving forward."

For these statements, ACA has an answer and a guarantee. Most people don't arrive at ACA's door by mistake. You are here for a reason, so keep an open mind. Our experience tells us that our past can be our greatest asset if we are willing to ask for help and do the work to find out what happened. Even the adult children who can recount abuse or incidents of rejection without working a single Step can benefit from Step Four. Simply recounting the past is not always enough to bring about healing and self-forgiveness. Without knowing the meaning of the abandonment encoded within the past, the adult child is doomed to repeat it. The unexamined past becomes the future of the next generation. Dependence, addiction, and hellish living are passed on to the next generation with amazing accuracy. We ask you to work this Step and all of the Twelve Steps to find your True Self and break the cycle of family dysfunction. If the Steps do not bring relief or clarity to your life, we will refund your old way of life in full. This is the ACA guarantee.

## ACA Relapse

If we skip this Step or Step Five, we risk relapsing into unhealthy dependence and self-harming behavior. An ACA relapse always features a recreation of the fear, self-hate, and abandonment from our childhood. Through relapse, we reenact roles and dependent behavior that we learned from unhealthy parents. A relapse can take many forms, but all ACA relapses have this center point.

One form of an ACA relapse involves an adult child acting out destructively for several weeks with one or more of the survival traits. The traits are known as The Laundry List (Problem) or common behaviors. Another form of relapse could involve remaining in a physically or emotionally abusive relationship without a clear plan to get out. Relapse could also involve practicing self-harming behaviors. The behaviors include alcoholism, binge eating, taking drugs, gambling, or promiscuous sex. When we relapse we can return to a life of fearing authority figures and judging ourselves harshly. We can feel "hung over" emotionally when we engage in unhealthy dependent behavior. We see our boundaries weaken, and we find ourselves manipulating others for what we think we need. At the same time, others in relapse will assert themselves as a controlling authority figure upon children or a spouse. With indignance, we dole out abuse through moments of rage and dishonesty. We might feel remorseful, but we feel powerless to change. When this occurs, we usually have not given ACA or the Steps a fair chance.

Still others may have stopped some of their more destructive behaviors in ACA. Yet, we switch to another compulsion or behavior that is just as damaging. This can be a relapse as well. For all ACA relapses, denial returns in some form, and we find ourselves choosing to use the behaviors detailed in The Laundry List to survive. We forget that we have a choice. We return to one of our dysfunctional family roles. We stop feeling. We usually have stopped attending meetings.

In ACA, we seek "emotional sobriety" by making a commitment to love ourselves and be good to ourselves. We stop harming ourselves by attaining ACA emotional sobriety.

## Reviewing Steps One, Two, and Three

Many of us begin Step Four by reviewing the first three Steps. In Step One, we realize we are powerless over the effects of family dysfunction and that our lives are unmanageable when we try to control others or get our inner needs met by outside sources. We are powerless over the survival traits we developed to live through our upbringing; however, we learn that we can fade or soften some of these common ACA behaviors over time.

In Step Two we learned about coming to believe. We learned that we attached our parents' traits of indifference, shame, or harshness to a Higher Power. We begin to separate the behavior of our parents from God in working Step Two. We begin to see our parents as the couple who gave us life. We also begin to see our Higher Power as the Actual Parent who will not abandon us.

In Step Three we learned that our compulsion to control others and ourselves blocks God's will for us, which is to live in peace with our feelings, creativity, and spirituality. We learn that real choice is God's gift to us for letting go. We learned that our attempts at choice before recovery were actually veiled control. In Step Three, we learned that choice often begins by facing our denial. As we grow in the program, our decisions include true choice that progresses to discernment. We learn to be still and know that God is God.

The difference between a searching and fearless moral inventory in Step Four and the Step One identification of our thinking and behaving involves balance. In Step One, we assessed the effects of an abusive childhood and how that abuse played out in our daily lives through defense traits developed as children. To a degree, we took our parents' inventory. We determined what happened so that we might find clarity on how to proceed in the moment and the future. In Step Four, we will balance our knowledge of the effects of family abuse in our lives with our own troublesome behavior as adults. As adults, we have harmed others. We have made flawed decisions based on our family background and blamed others when they challenged us to change. Many of us committed the same mistakes repeatedly, feeling hopeless to change. We secretly believed we could not change. We could assume the posture of a victim, which we thought helped us escape criticism but which brought a greater sense of helplessness. We sank to greater depths of self-hate and despair. Or we became a martyr, blaming others in detail for their abuse but refusing to accept responsibility for doing recovery work. Many defiant adult children have used their childhood abuse as an excuse to defend outrageously sick behavior and push away suggestions for help. We must find a way to surrender and to become teachable. We must understand that suggestions for help are not criticism or personal attacks.

Many of us have children who will possibly qualify for ACA one day due to transferring our disease of family dysfunction to them. This was not our intention, but it has often happened. We feel ashamed and alarmed at some of the things we have done to ourselves and our children. But we have hope in ACA. With the help of an ACA support group and our sponsor, we can change. We come to believe there is another way to live. If we are diligent in working ACA's Twelve Steps, miracles occur that we could not imagine. Healing and a deeper sense of God's presence are often the result of working Step Four. Our sense of shame is dissolved and that feeling of being unforgiven fades with this Step's freeing power. This freedom grows with the completion of each succeeding Step.

## Blameless

The key word to remember in working ACA's Fourth Step is "blameless." ACA founder Tony A. believed that adult children should take a "searching and blameless inventory of our parents because in essence we had become them." Tony believed that we internalized our parents. We had become them in thinking and action even if we took steps to be different.[†] While we focus primarily on ourselves in Step Four, we have added an inventory of the family to the process. ACA believes that we cannot take a searching and fearless inventory if we leave out the family.

Blame is not the purpose of Step Four or any of ACA's Twelve Steps. However, we can hold our parents and family accountable for their action and inaction. Blameless and accountability are the guideposts that steer us toward a balanced but searching inventory.

We hold our family accountable by naming what happened to us without fear of being ridiculed or disbelieved. In Step Four, we name the threats, the hitting, the inappropriate touching, or whatever else might have happened to us. We talk to our sponsor or spiritual advisor about what happened in our childhood.

We avoid blame because we are aware of the generational nature of family dysfunction. Our parents passed on the seeds of shame and fear given to them. They were once children without a choice. They survived as we survived. While some parents were obviously sadistic or unrepentant, others did the best they could. These parents made a conscious decision to raise their children differently than they were raised. Many of these parents abstained from alcohol, yet passed on problematic fear and shame just the same. Some of these well-meaning parents learned to say affirming statements of love and encouragement. Yet, they still transferred their own self-doubt and lack of self-love in large measures. Many of us are the adult children of these parents. We have acted out with addiction or another self-harming behavior, continuing the disease of family dysfunction.

Nondrinking parents raised in an alcoholic home are essentially unrecovered adult children who unintentionally pass on family dysfunction. These parents are typically a dependent personality driven by the inside drugs of fear, excitement, or anxiety. This is para-alcoholism. It affects the children in the same manner that the alcoholic drinking does if it is present. This means that our nondrinking parents were dependent people driven by a hundred forms of fear and self-doubt. They projected their fear and anxiety onto us with the same damaging effect that alcoholic drinking can have on a child. They passed on addiction or unhealthy dependence without taking a drink.

We avoid blaming the drinking parent as well. The alcoholic suffers from an incurable disease that progressively worsens. The alcoholic is very sick in body and mind. We cannot reach the level of spiritual growth that we are seeking by blaming sick people.

Avoiding blame does not mean that we avoid being angry or disgusted. Many of us feel rage when we talk about the abuse and neglect in our homes. These are normal feelings for the abusive and unhealthy parenting we lived through.

We also avoid sinking into a victim mindset. This mindset can disqualify us from the emotional and spiritual gifts of ACA. If we learn to accurately name what happened to us rather than blaming others for what happened, we find the truer path to healing and self-forgiveness. There is power in naming the exact nature of our abandonment and shame. We move out of the victim role and claim our personal power by taking this path. Step Four gives us a chance to identify what happened and transform our painful childhoods into our most valued asset. When we know what happened to us, we can help other adult children as no one else can, including some of the most dedicated professionals and clergy. We can finally say with humility: "This is what happened to me. This is my story. There is another way to live."

We stress fairness with our parents while holding them accountable for another reason as well. Many of us working Step Four realize we have harmed our own children. We have passed on what was done to us. Many of us have changed our behavior and made amends. However, some of us could one day be the focus of an inventory of our own children arriving at the doors of ACA. This is another reason to take a blameless, yet fair, inventory of the family and parents. If we give fairness, we can hope for fairness.

While we will look at the generational nature of family dysfunction in Step Four, we must remember that the Fourth Step is our inventory. In ACA we learn to face our denial and focus on ourselves. That means we will look at our parents' behavior in conjunction with our own behavior. We keep the focus on ourselves and on efforts to find clarity and be free of family dysfunction. We want to stop trying to heal our family-of-origin through our current relationships. We want to stop isolating and repeating the same patterns that bring about our worst fears of abandonment and self-hate. We want to reclaim our wholeness.

While working Step Four and all of the ACA Steps, we encourage you to nurture yourself. We must balance this probing look at our behavior with gentleness. We must protect our Inner Child or True Self vigorously. At the same time, we cannot let discomfort or fear stop us from getting honest about our own behavior.

## Step Four Worksheets and Assignments

The following worksheets and assignments will help you detail the effects of being raised in a dysfunctional family. The worksheets include an inventory of survival traits, secrets, harms, resentments, sexual abuse, and post-traumatic stress disorder. Most ACA members have some form of PTSD, which is often expressed in our hypervigilance of our surroundings or our acute monitoring of comments or actions of others. This behavior is a carry-over from growing up on guard much of the time.

The spiritual principles of Step Four are self-honesty and courage. We urge you to be honest and thorough, but also to be gentle with yourself during the inventory process. Most adult children have no problem listing their faults and feeling overly responsible for the actions of others. The key is to balance your positive qualities even if you think you have none. You have positive traits. These exercises will help you nurture yourself and balance your defects and your assets.

We recommend that you stay in contact with your sponsor or counselor as you go through these Step Four exercises. Use ACA meetings, the phone, and e-mails to remain centered and focused on what you are doing. Step Four is your chance to detail what happened to you as a child. We go through this process in an atmosphere of love, understanding, and support. That's what is different today compared to when we were children and could not talk, trust, or feel. In Step Four, we get to do all three with the support of ACA and God as we understand God.

## Distinguishing Our Feelings

Before starting your Fourth Step exercises, review the following list of feelings. The definitions describe where and how different feelings are felt in the body. This should be helpful in the exercises ahead.

In addition to stuffing or dissociating from our feelings, some of us have great difficulty understanding feelings and their definitions. Many of us have been shown a long list of feeling words only to stare away, wondering what the words mean. We are confused about feelings because naming and feeling our own feelings is new to us. As children and teens, we based our feelings on our parents' moods and actions. We were hypervigilant to a parent's tone of voice, body language, and gestures. We watched a parent's behavior to determine how we should feel or not feel. By the time we arrive at ACA, many of us do not know that it is okay to have feelings that are different than those of people we care about. In ACA, we learn that it is okay to have our own feelings. If someone we care about is sad or angry, we can empathize with him or her, but we do not always have to feel sad or angry with the person. We can support the person in his or her feelings without having to feel or fix the person's feelings. This is an awakening for us. This is a key step in recognizing our own feelings and learning how to truly support another without unhealthy dependence.

Additionally, our parents or relatives used feeling words in ways that did not match the definition of the words. This inconsistency distorted reality and made identifying our feelings as adults almost impossible. Many times our parents abused us verbally or physically and called it love or care. "I only do this to you because I love you," some parents might say. "Don't feel that way" was another way we were talked out of our feelings or told our feelings did not matter.

Many ACA members speak of "bundling" their feelings before coming to ACA. They describe expressing all their feelings in a bundle or as one indistinguishable feeling. For example, anger, shame, joy or worry are expressed by tears. They speak of crying when they are angry and crying when they feel elated. They talk about their feelings "being all together and indistinguishable."

At the same time, many ACA members tend to deny the existence of feelings or have difficulty identifying feelings at all. They talk of feeling numb inside or being confused by the mere mentioning of feelings. The list below offers a general definition of about a dozen feelings as they pertain to ACA. The definitions come from ACA fellowship experience.

**Loved**—A sense of feeling valued, understood, and heard. Listened to. Feeling safe with another. Warmth in the heart. Lightness of body.

**Fear/Anger**—Fear is usually masked by anger. Fear—pounding heartbeat, dilated pupils, increased breathing, tightened skin, extreme alertness. Anger—tightened jaw, upwelling in the chest, gritted teeth, dilated pupils, angry thoughts.

**Shame or Ashamed**—An intense sense of being faulty, wrong, or inferior at the core of our being. A feeling of being ruptured. A burning feeling in the stomach. A sensation of the body shrinking. Spiraling inward in the stomach or chest or both. Constricted throat. Difficulty in speaking. Heaviness on the chest and difficulty breathing. Feeling glared at by others.

**Guilt**—A sense of unease or regret for a wrongful or neglectful act against another. Different from shame because guilt is usually about something we have done rather than a statement of who we are.

**Amused**—A light feeling of humor or good spirit. Grins and smiles. God's medicine.

**Abandoned**—A sense of loss, being left, pushed out, forgotten, minimized, betrayed, feeling vulnerable. Feeling physically small. A dot. Lost at sea.

**Embarrassed**—An emotion arising from being exposed, caught in the act, confronted, ridiculed. Feeling flushed. Heat or redness in the face. Shortened breath. Involuntary stomach flutters.

**Betrayed**—Similar to abandonment; lied to, being deceived in meaning, feeling fooled, Spiraling inward. Weakness in the limbs. Praying is difficult.

**Satisfied**—A sense of feeling full inside, rested, not worried, trustful thoughts. Being in the moment. Not wandering. Being in the body. Centered to earth. Grounded to earth.

**Hopeful**—An expectation that things will work out, trusting oneself and others, energy level rises. Breathing is easier. Hitting all green lights.

**Inspired**—A sense of hope and wonderment of people and things, colors seem brighter, problems seem to find their right size. More energy in the body. Lightness of foot. Obstacles are secondary to solutions.

**Humiliated**—A sense of having the inner self exposed, abused, or taken away by the act of another or self. Vacuumed out. Void. Soul theft.

**Loss or Grief**—A sense that something has been taken, a longing for feeling, given the answers to life but unsure of the questions. A school yard without children.

**Joy**—A sense of integration of the survival traits/common behaviors. Coming out of the dark night of the soul with sureness of foot. Divided self reunited. Inner peace. Recognizing the True Self within. Knowing you can trust yourself. Seeing light in self and others. Energy and warmth throughout the body.

## Feeling Intensity Scale

In preparation for the Step Four exercises ahead, we introduce a warm-up exercise involving the feelings scale. From the list of feeling words you just read, select three of the words. Rank each feeling on a scale of one to 10, with 10 being the most intense. The feeling can be in the present or from the past. Use various cues to recall the feelings. Think about the scene or location in which the feeling occurred. What was said and how was it said? What occurred? What was the hour of the day or the temperature? What were you wearing?

If you have difficulty identifying feelings, think about a movie that has stirred feelings of sadness, joy, or anger. What was the scene? What happened to cause you to feel?

By working this exercise, one of our members said he felt his childhood aloneness when he visited an abandoned schoolyard. Another member said some feelings could be triggered by colors, smells, and shadows.

**Example of feeling intensity scale:**

Feeling word _____.

*(How the feeling felt in my body)*

_____

1    2    3    4    5    6    7    8    9    10

## Step Four Exercises:

### Exercise 1—Inventory of Laundry List Traits (survival traits)

The following are the 14 traits or common ACA behaviors of an adult child. For this exercise, check the number of traits you identify with below. On the next page, use the Laundry List worksheet to describe how the traits manifested themselves in your life.

**Begin** *(check the traits you identify with)*:

❑   We became isolated and afraid of people and authority figures.

❑   We became approval seekers and lost our identity in the process.

❑   We are frightened by angry people and any personal criticism.

❑   We either become alcoholics or marry them or both or find another compulsive personality such as a workaholic to fulfill our sick abandonment needs.

❑   We live life from the viewpoint of victims and we are attracted by that weakness in our love and friendship relationships.

❑   We have an overdeveloped sense of responsibility and it is easier for us to be concerned with others rather than ourselves; this enables us to not look too closely at our own faults.

❑   We get guilt feelings when we stand up for ourselves instead of giving in to others.

❑   We became addicted to excitement.

❑   We confuse love and pity and tend to "love" people we can "pity" and "rescue."

❑   We have "stuffed" our feelings from our traumatic childhoods and have lost the ability to feel or express our feelings because it hurts so much (Denial).

❑   We judge ourselves harshly and have a very low sense of self-esteem.

❑   We are dependent personalities who are terrified of abandonment and will do anything to hold on to a relationship in order not to experience painful abandonment feelings, which we received from living with sick people who were never there emotionally for us.

❑   Alcoholism is a family disease; we became para-alcoholics and took on the characteristics of that disease even though we did not pick up the drink.

❑   Para-alcoholics are reactors rather than actors.

## Laundry List Worksheet

Using the Laundry List, fill out as many of the columns as you can in the following worksheet. The "event" column is the childhood incident that comes to mind that might have helped create a Laundry List trait. Some traits are developed over time. You are looking for incidents, verbal spats, or conversations in which the parents projected their own sense of self-doubt, fear, and flawed thinking onto you. This is one of the places where para-alcoholism and the transfer of dysfunction occur. Para-alcoholism is the chronic fear and distorted thinking of our family transferred to us. It fuels codependence.

Do not be discouraged if you cannot fill out all of the columns. If you struggle with filling in the columns, get a notepad and write down things your parents said about you, family members, or other people. Keep the notepad with you and write things as you remember them. You can use the feelings list from the previous pages to help with the "how I felt" column.

**Example:**

How the trait of fearing an authority figure might have developed.

| Event | Cause of Event | How I Felt *(feelings word)* | Inner Child Reaction | Type of Trait Developed *(from 14 Traits)* |
|---|---|---|---|---|
| Father yelling at me or blaming me for a mistake. | He said I did not listen. | afraid/physically small | knot in stomach/ breathing difficult | fear of authority figure and criticism |

## Laundry List Worksheet

| Event | Cause of Event | How I Felt<br>*(feelings word)* | Inner Child<br>Reaction | Type<br>of Trait<br>Developed<br>*(from 14 Traits)* |
|---|---|---|---|---|
| | | | | |

## Exercise 2—Family Secrets Inventory

Almost every dysfunctional family has a story or image that family members present to friends and outsiders. For example, "The Rodriguez family believes in education and challenge. We never give up," the family says. Another family says "The Wilson family works hard, and we stick together no matter what comes our way."

Beneath the story line is the reality of the dysfunctional home. There are secrets, inconsistencies, and wrongs that are contrary to the family image. Family denial supports the family image and denies the hidden story. In this exercise, we ask you to list family secrets. The secrets can involve attempts by parents to hide addiction, inappropriate touching, mishandling of money, lying, and infidelity. In some cases, seemingly insignificant events can also be secrets. In the space below, list all memories, incidents, and messages that were considered family secrets or inconsistent with the family image.

_____

_____

_____

_____

_____

_____

_____

_____

## Exercise 3—Shame Inventory

The Big Book of Alcoholics Anonymous states that "Resentment is the number one offender. It destroys more alcoholics than anything else."[†]

In ACA, we believe shame claims the Number One spot. We believe that shame is so potent that a few drops can create a lifetime of lost self. Shame often was on the scene before abandonment, which is perhaps the second most troublesome abuse we have faced as children of unhealthy parenting. Shame and abandonment serve as the fear-based launching pad for an outward search for love and security which we never find in other people, places, or things. Shame blinds us to the fact that love is inside each of us waiting to be discovered.

To shame a child is to abandon the child. A parent can shame and abandon a child without ever leaving the room because a shamed child feels unlovable and alone at a deep level.

Adult children not only feel shame at the molecular level, but we also carry inherent shame. That means most of us carry around a deep sense of inadequacy, embarrassment, or uniqueness without having to interact with another person. We not only feel shame. We believe we "are" shame.

When shamed as an adult, we can literally vibrate with shame as if being struck like a bell. We can feel the shame burning in our stomach and our face. When shamed, we can spiral inward to an unreachable spot. In some cases a shame spiral is so intense that the adult child's vision is distorted and perceptions change. Room lighting can seem more intense or dense and the expressions on people's faces seem over exaggerated. Shame of this nature has accumulated over many years, but it can be lessened and made more bearable in ACA and with God's help.

## Shame List

List incidents in which you felt shamed by your parents or caregiver. In addition to sexual abuse or harsh cursings, shame can come from calm statements by parents about appearance, speech, dress, and mannerisms. Some shame can be uttered in tones of sarcasm, overly critical judgments, and hurtful comments veiled as teasing or jokes.

The difference between appropriate parenting that corrects with love and affirmation, and shame which destroys the spirit, is how you feel about the act or comment. Shame tends to make you feel isolated, inferior, and unwanted. Discipline from loving parents can cause discomfort, but you still believe that you have worth and that you are loved despite your mistakes.

In the space below, list examples of shame. Try to include as many details of the incidents as possible, including your age, where you were, what was said, and how your body reacted to the shame.

_____

_____

_____

_____

_____

_____

_____

## Exercise 4—Abandonment Inventory

Abandonment is the bookend to shame when growing up in a dysfunctional family. Abandonment can be a physical abandonment in which our parents left us with friends, relatives, or day care centers while they practiced their addictions or dependence. Some children have been left alone at home for days while a parent or parents stayed away partying or chasing a loveless relationship. However, abandonment can also involve shaming statements as you learned in the previous exercise. We know of an adult child who cut her finger badly as a child and hid in the bathroom instead of running to her mother for comfort. The little girl intuitively knew that her bleeding finger would bring a harsh and blaming response from her mother, and it did. Instead of comforting the child, the overwhelmed mother howled at her husband and her child as he rushed the girl to the emergency room. The frightened mother shamed the injured child while also abandoning her emotionally.

## Abandonment List

In the space below, list the times you felt abandoned by your parents or caregiver. List your age, the location of the abandonment, and any other details you can remember.

_____

_____

_____

_____

_____

_____

_____

_____

_____

_____

## Exercise 5—Harms Inventory: Generational Transfer

In this exercise, we inventory how we have abandoned or neglected other people in our lives. If we have children, we also look at how our actions and words served as the transfer mechanism for the disease of family dysfunction. This transaction is brokered by what we tell our children. We may hear ourselves saying things to our children that our parents said to us. Our words, flawed thinking, and reactions to life transfer dysfunction to the next generation. This was never our intent. Indeed, many of us swore to be different than our parents. Many of us have said: "It will never happen to me." But it did.

We know in our hearts that we would not have harmed our children purposely. We must remember we are facing our actions with courage and honesty. This is not easy, and we should give ourselves a break. We are not alone here. We have the support of our ACA group, a sponsor, and our Higher Power as we face the consequences of our behavior. The guilt we might experience in this exercise is healthy guilt.

## Harms Worksheet

| Those I have harmed, abandoned, neglected, mistreated | What I did, my behavior | Results, or memory of incident | My memory of having been similarly harmed as a child |
|---|---|---|---|
| | | | |

## Gentleness Break

The ACA Fourth Step involves a balanced look at our family of origin and our own behavior and thoughts. The emotions, events, and self-blame stirred by this Step can seem overwhelming for some. As you work Step Four, we urge you to be rigorously honest, holding nothing back, but we also remind you to be gentle with yourself. Remember you are not alone, and you have not done or thought anything that someone else has not done or thought. You have character assets and abilities that help balance disturbing aspects of your life.

In Step Four, we ask you to balance any shameful or fearful memories that might arise with the knowledge that you have honesty and courage in your life. ACA is not an easy program to work, but your courage is apparent and shows in working this Step and the Twelve Steps of ACA. Adult children have an inner strength that has always been there. That inner strength, which some choose to call a Higher Power or Divine Spirit, is with you now as you face this liberating inventory of your life. We suggest that you remain focused during this process, but take gentleness breaks and stay in contact with your sponsor or counselor. During this break read the Eleventh Promise of the ACA Promises out loud. Also read the ACA Fourth Step Prayer. (You will find the ACA Promises at the front of the workbook).

**Promise Eleven:** "With help from our ACA support group, we will slowly release our dysfunctional behaviors."

## Fourth Step Prayer:

*Divine Creator. Help me to be rigorously honest and to care for myself during this Fourth Step process. Let me practice gentleness and not abandon myself on this spiritual journey. Help me remember that I have attributes, and that I can ask for forgiveness. I am not alone. I can ask for help. Amen.*

## Exercise 6—Stored Anger (Resentment) Inventory

In ACA we want to "lift up" resentment and see what is underneath. We believe resentment is stored anger caused by innumerable losses as a child. Such loss creates grief appearing as depression in addition to creating stored anger. We will cover grief work in Step Five.

Most adult children deny they have anger and therefore deny they are angry. On the other hand, there are some adult children who can explode with anger but never seem to tap the stored anger deep within them. Without naming their childhood loss, they can "recharge" and explode repeatedly, feeling ashamed or confused by their behavior. They really want to change or curb their anger, but they feel powerless to do so.

In the "affects my" column below, losses can include the loss of the sense of safety in the home. There is also the loss of identity and the loss of childhood experiences of learning to play, imagine, and be spontaneous. Many adult children also lost friends due to a dysfunctional parent's behavior. Others had to stop a favorite sport in high school due to a parent's intolerance or nonsupport. The goal of this exercise is to find your anger and lift it up and see the loss beneath it.

## Stored Anger (Resentment) Worksheet

| I resent | The Cause | Affects<br>*(my self worth,<br>friendships,<br>safety, ability to<br>imagine)* | My reaction<br>*(anger, rebellion,<br>withdrawn, passive/<br>aggressive, or other)* | Inner Child's<br>reaction<br>*(don't trust,<br>don't talk,<br>don't feel, or other)* |
|---|---|---|---|---|
| | | | | |

## Exercise 7—Relationships (Romance /Sexual/Friendships) Inventory

As adult children, most of us have used a variety of relationships in an attempt to heal ourselves from the chronic sense of aloneness in our lives. We have used sex, romance and friendships to feel safe or not alone. This sense of aloneness has its roots in abandonment by our family. Until we get help, we continually look outside ourselves for drugs, gambling, sex, work, or people to make us feel whole, but it never works. This is the codependent germ appearing as addictiveness in us.

List your relationship partners, friends and other people you have had relationships with. Watch for patterns that emerge in your relationships. (Note: Some adult children practice relationship "anorexia," which means they avoid relationships to remove any chance of being abandoned or hurt. For these adult children we ask that you inventory the relationships or relationship that brought about this scenario in your life).

## Relationship Worksheet

| Person | What I expected to get | What I got | My dependent behavior | How relationship ended |
|--------|------------------------|------------|-----------------------|------------------------|
|        |                        |            |                       |                        |

## Exercise 8—Sexual Abuse Inventory

This exercise helps some adult children identify sexual abuse. For many incest survivors, this exercise can stir strong memories. We urge you to stay in contact with your counselor or sponsor. It is important to remember that you did not cause the sexual abuse. Many adult children are confused on this issue because they were children when the abuse occurred. They lacked the ability to think objectively about what was happening to them so many children assumed they caused it or asked for it. As adults, these childhood assumptions can linger and undermine the adult's review of what happened. If you were touched, fondled, forced to perform sex acts, asked to perform sex, or watch sex acts as a child, it was not your fault no matter what the circumstance or no matter what was said by the adult or teen abusing you.

Some adult children have grown up to be perpetrators by reenacting what was done to them. These acts can be disturbing and painful to admit, but you are not disqualified from being an ACA member. You are not disqualified from the healing grace of your Higher Power or the acceptance of the ACA fellowship. We ask you to modify this inventory to include these acts; however, we caution you on how much detail you would share in an ACA meeting about such acts. If you are acting out and feel out of control, we ask you to seek professional help.

## Sexual Abuse Worksheet

| Abuser | What happened | My age | Who I told or did not tell | Who got blamed? | How did abuse stop? |
|--------|---------------|--------|----------------------------|-----------------|---------------------|
|        |               |        |                            |                 |                     |

## Gentleness Break

During this gentleness break, read the Twelve Promises of ACA listed at the front of the workbook.

**Affirmation:** *The promises of ACA are for me, and they are being fulfilled in my life. I am discovering my real identity. I am facing shame and uncomfortable feelings without running or acting-out. I have positive attributes that I am discovering. God, as I understand God, hears my prayers. I can ask for help.*

## Exercise 9—Denial Inventory

For ACAs, denial lives in the way we recall the abuse, neglect, or rejection we suffered as children. Denial is the mechanism which protects and helps plant the seed of family dysfunction in the next generation. For help with this exercise, look at some of your descriptions in the worksheets involving sexual abuse, stored anger, and Laundry List traits. There is no need to embellish or understate what happened. (To review categories of denial, turn back to page 1 of this workbook and read the entire page).

Categories you might be in denial about include the manner of punishment used by your parents or how your parents or siblings teased you. Constant arguing by the parents also is a form of abuse that many of us grew accustomed to, but which we do not see as abuse. Many times our parents argued abusively or cursed in front of us without regard to the impact it had on us as children. Their arguing changed us.

You may also be in denial about your behavior as an adult. We ask you to look at your manner of language and actions in dealing with your children, employer, or spouse or partner. What language do you use? What is your tone? What messages do you give other people about their worth? Do you ask for what you need straight out or do you manipulate to get what you want?

The denial worksheet has two exercises. The first one deals with how your parents or relatives treated you. The second involves how you treated others as an adult.

In the first exercise, in the "what happened" column, many ACA members list incest, touching, harsh spankings, and threatening talk, but this column is not limited to these types of events. The worksheet involves unhealthy actions by your parents and how you remembered the incidents. The exercise helps you see how you recall the incident years later. Denial can flourish when we recall a harmful or abusive event without the full details. We can blame ourselves for the abuse or explain it away if we leave out details. If you were abused by a sibling or other relative, include that person's behavior in this exercise. This exercise will help you determine the facts of an event and how it was described later with accuracy or inaccuracy.

# Denial Worksheet: My Parents' Behavior
*(include other relatives)*

| What happened *(facts)* | My age | How I felt about what happened | Parents' message of what happened | How I later described what happened |
|---|---|---|---|---|
| | | | | |

## My Behavior: The Laundry List Reflection

In this worksheet, you are looking at your own hurtful, neglectful or possibly abusive behavior. This is not an easy exercise since most of us would not like to talk about our own neglectful acts. We need God's help with this exercise to avoid condemning ourselves. We must remember that we have inner courage and that we are not evil or beyond recall. Given our dysfunctional upbringing, we must realize we could not have turned out differently. Our behavior as adults was scripted from our childhood. We repeated what was done to us by our parents but there is a big difference between ourselves and our parents. We are facing our shameful actions and abuse with ACA and with a Higher Power. We are owning our behavior with help and prayer.

In this exercise we are looking for the reflections of the Laundry List traits. Most of these common behaviors have a reflection that is just as damaging as the original trait. For example, we have lived as victims, but many of us have victimized others in an attempt to control them or harm them. We have feared authority figures, but we have become authority figures who have been feared. Some of us have been perpetrators, acting against our will. We have perpetrated abuse and abandonment.

In the "what happened" column, list incidents with relatives, co-workers, and spouses or partners. How have you victimized others? How have you been an authority figure? How have you judged others harshly? Do you gossip? Malicious gossip can be a form of perpetration.

# Denial Worksheet: My Behavior

| What happened (facts) | Who was involved (child, spouse, other) | My perception and feeling of what happened | How I later described what happened |
|---|---|---|---|
|  |  |  |  |

## Exercise 10—Post-Traumatic Stress Disorder: Body Work

In ACA, we believe that the disease of family dysfunction affects the adult child in body, mind, and spirit long after the adult has left his or her family of origin. Our bodies are composed of bones, tissue, and a central nervous system connected to our brain. We think it is reasonable to believe that the body remembers much of what it experiences, just as the brain remembers what it has processed and responded to.

Who among us has not performed a certain task for many days or months, but we repeat the same hand motion or same reflex when the task has changed. For instance, if we stored our favorite pair of shoes in a certain area of our closet for many months, then move them, we may reach into that section of the closet before realizing we have moved the shoes to another place. The mind and the body react automatically to a remembered task. The arm is extended into the closet before the mind realizes the shoes are at the other end of the closet. This may happen two or three times before we rewire ourselves to remember the new location of our shoes. The same response holds true for those of us writing checks and making an error by writing out the wrong year after January 1st. Many of us automatically write in the wrong year before realizing it has changed. These are simple examples of stored memory in our minds and bodies.

Medical research reveals that the brain and body are inseparable as we live, breathe, feel, and sense our surroundings as children and adults. As the brain remembers and reacts automatically, so does the body.

Post-traumatic stress disorder involves the mind and body and remembered responses to severe trauma or near trauma. PTSD is a documented disorder that affects adult children in addition to war veterans and victims of traumatic events. PTSD symptoms can include hypervigilance of surroundings, unexplained body sensations, increased heart rate, and being startled easily. In adult children PTSD tends to manifest itself in hypervigilance, compulsive behavior, and hard-to-detect body sensations. It is as if our bodies have "rewired" themselves to protect us from severe harm or severe harm that almost occurred.

Many adult children are skeptical or confused about PTSD, and we understand. We can see how our minds would store memories and adapt with survival traits to live through a dysfunctional upbringing. However, it is difficult to understand that our bodies would remember or store trauma. This skepticism is often underlined by the fact that most adult children are shut down emotionally or "numbed out." We have become adept at shutting down our feelings instantly. It is difficult for us to realize what our body is trying to tell us. We ignore our body or misinterpret its language.

The body's language can take on many forms that include backaches, headaches, stiff necks, tastes in the throat, genital pain or numbness, arm pain, foot pain, or a sense of disorientation when feeling stressed or fearful. Others have sharp or dull sensations in the legs or feel a lump or obstruction in the throat. There can be diarrhea, stomach pain, or flashes of panic. With PTSD work, some ACA members will realize they hold their head a certain way or sleep a certain way. Some adult children realize they cannot sleep facing a doorway while others must check and recheck locks before going to bed or leaving for a trip. Most, if not all, adult children have some degree of PTSD; however, not all such symptoms are indicators of a PTSD incident. Symptoms in the body can be caused by medical conditions, aging, or disease that are not PTSD related.

PTSD caused by battering and incest is typically easier to detect or suspect. Subtle, but just as telling, forms of PTSD are more difficult to recognize. PTSD caused by years of parental neglect and hurtful acts intermixed with moments of nurturing can be tricky to detect and understand.

We know of an adult child who seemed to love canned potatoes. She felt "comfort" just knowing there was a single can of potatoes in her cupboard. As this person began addressing her ACA issues as an adult, she realized that the canned potatoes meant something more than a fondness for a peeled vegetable in a can. She realized, or her body remembered, that canned potatoes were the difference between going hungry or having something to eat when her alcoholic mother went out for days without coming home.

By doing ACA work, she realized that her body remembered the hunger pains brought on by an abandoning mother. As a child, while feeling fearful and hungry when her mother was gone, she found a can of potatoes. She ate the potatoes and felt full. Her hunger left, and she could sleep. At a young age, she felt comforted by the potatoes for two reasons: she solved her immediate problem of hunger, and she knew she did not need her mother to take care of her. She could now take care of herself. She would take care of her sister, too. She learned to drag a chair to the edge of the stove to warm up soup and drag the same chair to the sink to wash dishes. She no longer had to feel hurt or abandoned by a mother she loved and adored. The child could take care of herself and not show her love for her mother because it hurt too badly when her mother left home for days. The canned potatoes represented her introduction to adulthood before she attended her first day of school as a first grader.

This is a subtle example of PTSD buried deep but which produced a real action in the adult child's life. The memory contains PTSD elements of fear, threat to survival, and feeling alone, perhaps destitute. The memory resided in her mind and stomach. As a 30-year-old woman, she shopped for canned potatoes and thought of it as a funny nuance in her life. She was a successful professional, divorced and raising her own daughter without relying on help from her family. However, 25 years after the original incident, this woman's body, her stomach, remembered that hunger pain but transformed it into a comforting memory of canned potatoes with the help of her brain. Through ACA work, she also realized she had a hunger for her mother's love, a hunger she could never completely swallow.

Was this adult child starved by her parents as a child? No. But there were moments of extreme hunger and a feeling of terror when nightfall would come and the house would grow dark without the mother coming home. The child's father was often away as well on business. This adult child missed enough meals that she had to find a way to take care of herself and a sister. There were other acts of neglect and abuse in this woman's life: harsh whippings, threats of beatings, and incest. As an adult, she tended to have enmeshed relationships, focusing on others and feeding them first before she fed herself. She typically placed herself last and lived with an unnamed sense of having little value as a person. When she finally walked away from an abandoning and loveless relationship, she felt like her world had ended. She was sure she was guilty, wrong, and defective. Her own alcoholism, exposed publicly by her own behavior, caused much shame. However, she has found the ACA way of life and realized she has an inner strength and real connection to God. She now reaches into her cupboard for a variety of food to nourish her body and soul.

## A Word of Caution

PTSD work, coupled with ACA meetings and quality counseling, can produce powerful clarity and healing for adult children. Yet, we offer a word of caution. Not all actions or thoughts you had as a child have a deeper meaning. Some do and some do not. Our parents were only human, and they made mistakes. A harsh comment or being left for the afternoon with a babysitter does not equal PTSD or abuse. An occasional swatting on the behind without malice is not always abuse. A parent threatening to leave you at the grocery store to scare you into leaving with them when they have finished shopping may not be traumatic.

However, at the same time, one vicious whipping or battering can be stored in your body and memory for decades. Certainly, incest, rape, and inappropriate touching are trauma by their very nature. Also, a parent who chronically left you in day care or with relatives without returning home for days begins to venture into neglect. From this scenario, you can have cumulative abandonment or a PTSD memory as a child. These memories can produce stress chemicals and brain pathways that underline the formation of stored trauma known as PTSD.

The difference between neglect or abuse, which can produce stored trauma, and a parent being human is usually a matter of degree and longitude. When a parent misses enough birthdays, curses loudly and hotly long enough, and constantly blames the child for normal needs, then you have an area to review.

We ask that you find a qualified professional to help you sort out what you experienced as a child. Listen to your body and write about funny habits or rituals that seem innocent yet persistent.

While counseling is supportive and meaningful, we have found that counseling alone is not always sufficient for lasting internal change. ACAs need a place to sound out their experiences and thoughts among people who give support and lasting meaning to such experiences. Attendance at ACA meetings helps clarify actions and thoughts that seem mundane. Keeping a journal of your daily thoughts and feelings helps as well. Thoughts, actions, and sensations that tend to have a pattern could be the tip of a PTSD iceberg. We urge caution and prudence.

ACA members completing the PTSD exercise have sought helping professionals who have helped them detect and free up stored trauma and neglect. We do not recommend specifics on which type of body work is best. Experience shows that ACA members have received good results from massage (deep tissue), nondominant handwriting exercises, and guided meditation. Guided meditation and nondominant handwriting tend to offer clues on where stored trauma exists while deep-tissue massage often releases that trauma.

We have seen some adult children benefit from deep-tissue massage without knowing the exact location of an old abuse wound. When we speak of trauma we are not limiting the trauma to hitting, slapping, or vulgar acts of incest. Trauma and neglect can occur and be stored by subtle but longitudinal acts of neglect and blame. Parents who never admit being wrong and who heap heavy doses of perfectionistic language and expectations upon their children create stored trauma without lifting a hand. This type of shaming and abandoning behavior produces the fatigue of spirit that can be misdiagnosed as depression or lethargy. We ask that you keep an open mind as you do this worksheet. (p. 101)

This exercise is not meant as a replacement for a diagnosis from a qualified therapist or counselor. If seeking a massage therapist for PTSD or grief work, we suggest that the therapist be educated and experienced in working with trauma survivors if possible. There are issues of touch and boundaries that should be honored.

## Trauma/Neglect Inventory

For the PTSD worksheet, begin by writing down any traumatic or neglectful act you can recall. Was there hitting, cursing, threats, or talk of threat in your home? Were you injured? Write down the area of your body that was injured. These places can hold PTSD triggers.

There are also elements of PTSD not caused by overt trauma. For example, a child growing up in a home with perfectionism and unreasonable expectations can feel anxious turning in a project at work. This is a form of PTSD caused by being undercut by a parent who usually found fault in our housework or schoolwork even when it was above average.

Next, write down PTSD symptoms you might have. They might include headaches, backaches, throat problems, tense shoulders, genital sensations, dull pain, twitches, or numbness. You might also list funny or noticeable habits, rituals, and routines.

As you recall information for this worksheet, think about your posture, breathing, or feelings associated with the items you list. Think about whether you were sitting, standing, or lying down. Was the room lighted or dark? Were you outside? Did you place your hands anywhere or squeeze your eyes shut during the trauma or abuse? Did you rock yourself in a chair after the event? Did you take a walk or hide in your closet after abuse or anticipating abuse?

Try to fill out all the categories in the worksheet, but if you draw a blank, put the worksheet aside for a day or two and return to it. This worksheet is not a replacement for a professional evaluation, but it can help you get started on this important aspect of ACA recovery.

When you have recalled some experiences or memories, fill in the categories of the worksheet with your listed items.

As a hint, write a sentence about a current incident that might have caused you to react a certain way. Using the labels from the PTSD worksheet, label the parts of the sentence as you trace the event back to your childhood if it relates to your childhood. For example: "My body tensed up (symptom), and I felt frightened when I overheard an adult scolding a child (event/trigger). I can recall my parents standing over me and yelling at me when I was young (my reality). My parents said I was a rotten kid (parents' message about what happened). I just always felt like a screw up. I must have been six years old (my age)."

A more subtle example of PTSD might be the symptom of hoarding food or never throwing anything away. For example: "I realize my intoxicated parents rarely fixed us a meal (event). We were hungry a lot growing up (my reality). We never had decent clothes and kids at school laughed at us. I get anxious (sensation) when I think about throwing anything out. My parents said we were a proud family and relied on no one for help (parent's message). I say we were poor due to alcoholism (my reality)."

After identifying the items in the sentences you write about yourself, place them in the worksheet categories where they fit. This exercise will help you see the trigger, your reality, and other important information.

## PTSD Worksheet

| Event or trigger | My age | My reality of what happened | Parents' message of what happened | Symptom or ritual, funny habit | Where stored in my body, type of sensation |
|---|---|---|---|---|---|
|  |  |  |  |  |  |

## Exercise 11—Feelings Exercise

The Step Four feelings list helps adult children build on the feelings exercise at the beginning of this section. This exercise addresses the "don't feel" rule developed while growing up in a dysfunctional family. By talking about our feelings we address the "don't trust" and "don't talk" rules as well.

Many adult children are unsure of their feelings or cannot distinguish feelings, so this exercise helps you get started identifying emotions and becoming more comfortable with using feelings words.

Most adult children are terrified of feelings and believe they cannot withstand them. In ACA, we must remember that we are not alone. Recovery is different than when we were children and had to face the feelings of isolation and despair alone. When feelings arise in ACA, we learn to "sit" with them without acting out. We hug a pillow, lie on the floor and breathe deeply, take a walk, or simply sit still and hang on. Our feelings will not kill us. We can name our feelings and understand them. This is an ACA promise. We learn that we can pick up the phone and call someone to listen to us. Feelings pass. We can survive our feelings.

Many adult children have "frozen" feelings in addition to being confused about feelings. Our feelings are like a great glacier, which appears stationary, but which moves with great force and sureness. Hidden within the glacier are huge boulders that scrape the earth leaving deep scars and ruts. Occasionally, one of these huge rocks works its way up, piercing the icy surface of the glacier. Release occurs.

Addictiveness and unhealthy dependence are often attempts to ignore a frozen mass inside. ACA Step work helps locate trapped feelings and melt the glacier of our soul. At some feelings we shiver, but there is release that brings healing. By claiming our feelings, we step out of the shadowy chill of a glacier into sunlight. We feel the warmth of acceptance in ACA. We are finally home.

Identifying our feelings and talking with others about how we feel is a critical step in breaking the isolation we have lived with for so long.

Talking about our feelings is a risk; however, this is a risk worth taking because the rewards are great. When we let others know about our feelings, we connect with people on a spiritual and equal level instead of a dependent and manipulative level. We learn to not fear our emotions in ACA.

Many adult children learn how to identify and distinguish feelings by practicing the feelings sentence. Select one of the feeling words and complete the sentence. Complete three sentences each day for two weeks and then continue to practice the sentence regularly.

**Example:**

"I feel hopeful when I attend an ACA meeting because I know I am heard."

## Feelings Sentence:

I feel _____ when _____
because _____.

## Word selection:

| | | | | |
|---|---|---|---|---|
| loved | joyful | ashamed | humorous | irritated |
| angry | embarrassed | trusted | betrayed | pleased |
| satisfied | ambivalent | hopeful | inspired | loving |
| frustrated | disappointed | grief | accepted | excited |
| grateful | confident | humiliated | guilty | serene |
| rested | shame | abandoned | pleasure | safe |
| tenacious | thoughtful | playful | fascinated | enthralled |

## Exercise 12—Praise Work

Most adult children constantly seek affirmation but do not truly believe compliments and praise when they come. In this Step Four exercise, we are introducing the practice of praising or affirming ourselves. Most adult children have a praise deficit, which can never be solved by an outside source. Before recovery, we tended to operate with closed feelings and dismissed any affirmation coming our way from others. Or we manipulated others into praising us while we still felt inadequate and inferior. The affirmation work here is more involved than self-esteem work, which tends to be topical in nature in addressing mannerisms, attitudes, and dress. With praise work, we go further inside and confront ourselves about pushing away compliments and sincere attempts by others to affirm us. Because we shut out our parents when we were children, we tend to shut out people as adults. If we were not affirmed or praised as children, we are typically uncomfortable with praise as adults. Ignoring praise or failing to see our accomplishments as adults can help disqualify us from loving relationships.

Learning to accept praise is different than the ACA trait of constantly seeking affirmations. When we constantly seek affirmation, we set ourselves up to live a goal-oriented life. By living such a life, we tend to feel fulfilled only when we complete a project and only when affirmation comes with such tasks. We lack the inner voice to tell ourselves that we are okay when others don't deliver the affirmations that we were seeking.

By learning to praise ourselves and accept praise from others, we are less prone to suffer the debilitating effects of being a people-pleaser. We tend to stand more steady and affirm ourselves when external praise does not come. Our mistakes, while still unsettling, are more tolerable.

In addition to introducing affirmations, this exercise is presented here because it is a balancing exercise. These affirmations will help you understand that you have good qualities as you inventory your past behavior.

## Praise Exercise

Following is a list of 25 assets, which will help balance positive and spiritual qualities while working Step Four. Circle at least 10 attributes even if you do not believe you possess all of them. Because we operate from a praise deficit, we often do not realize the assets we have in our lives. This is the start of the praise work. There will be a praise exercise in the Step Ten daily inventory as well.

| | | | | |
|---|---|---|---|---|
| strong | compassionate | spontaneous | trustworthy | prompt |
| humorous | courteous | creative | tenacious | kind |
| sensitive | talented | loving | judicious | hard working |
| willing | honest | a listener | accepting | a friend |
| intelligent | organized | spiritual | modest | an ACA member |

After circling your assets, sit quietly and say each one by repeating: I am _____ (fill in the affirmation). Hang onto the list to help balance the defects of character that you will find in your Fourth Step inventory. It is essential that you remember that you have positive qualities and spiritual direction in your life. You are not a defective character. You have defects of character.

## STEP FOUR SPIRITUAL PRINCIPLES:

### Self-honesty and Courage

You have finished the Fourth Step outline. Congratulations. You have taken a searching and fearless look at your family-of-origin and your own thoughts and actions. You have also balanced this look with positive traits that include the courage you exhibited by completing this challenging Step. Your journey is still unfolding. You are not alone. Ask for help and accept it.

Set an appointment with your sponsor or counselor to work Step Five: "Admitted to God, to ourselves, and to another human being the exact nature of our wrongs."

**My Fifth Step Date is: Day** _____ **Time** _____

Important Note: Before your Fifth Step date arrives, read all of the section on Step Five and learn about the exact nature of your wrongs. In Step Five, you will also find instructions on what to do when you have finished Step Five. Many ACA members work Steps Six and Seven immediately following their Fifth Step. These instructions in Step Five will guide you through the sequence of Steps Six and Seven.

## A Fifth Step Tool for the ACA Sponsor

The appendix of this workbook has an outline for your sponsor or the person hearing your Fifth Step. This outline helps the sponsor, spiritual advisor, or mentor guide you through Step Five and prepare you for Steps Six and Seven.

# STEP FIVE

*Admitted to God, to ourselves, and to another human being the exact nature of our wrongs.*

## He Expected Condemnation And Got Fairness

*When I did my Fourth and Fifth Steps with an ACA counselor, I had to be reminded to be gentle with myself while also being rigorously honest about how I had harmed others. I started in a Twelve Step program that did not allow you to look at another person's behavior. Looking at family dysfunction was out of the question there. I was told to forgive my parents, which I did, but I was left with a sense of not being whole inside.*

*When I worked the ACA Steps, I got to look at shame, abandonment, and loss in addition to inventorying my own selfish behavior. I got to find out about the exact nature of my abandonment by my parents. They tried to love me and protect me, but in reality they passed on low self-worth and self-hate. I used to say they did the best they could, but now I say they passed on what was given to them—family dysfunction.*

*Being gentle with myself or writing down my assets was odd or even weird at first. My counselor encouraged me, and I continued to do this. After awhile I began to believe that I have good traits as well as areas I can improve. My Fifth Step gave me a balanced look at my life. I wasn't looking for that. I was expecting condemnation, but I got fairness.*

## Exact Nature Of His Wrongs

*I went into Step Five holding back nothing. I figured I had nothing to lose. The best I could do with my life got me to my first Twelve Step meeting 22 years ago. If I got arrested again for DUI, I was going to prison back then. I found sobriety and then I found ACA. My life and the Twelve Steps took on a new meaning that has continued to grow inside of me more than 20 years later.*

*In Step Five I found out the exact nature of my wrongs. For instance, when I stole something, I found out there was a legal wrong and a spiritual wrong. The legal wrong was that my petty theft was against the law. The spiritual wrong meant my theft separated me from my Higher Power. When I stole or acted out with drugs or sex, I was separating myself from my Higher Power and other people.*

*After I took my Fifth Step, I did not feel alone all the time like before. I have had my moments of feeling alone since then, but they are not as powerful. I finally feel like I fit somewhere. I am a member of ACA.*

## The Most Important Lesson: Listening And Trust

*I guess the most important lesson I can take away from Step Five is that I finally trusted someone enough to tell him my story. I finally got to tell someone about all of the thoughts and behaviors I thought made me beyond help.*

*I remember feeling odd about talking about some things, but my sponsor just listened and nodded his head in agreement. Sometimes he talked about an incident that he had done that was similar to mine. He did not judge me. That was a huge relief.*

*I have since sponsored others and listened to their Fifth Steps, and the rewards have been great. I have been able to return the gift of listening to someone and not judging him. This is the heart of ACA in my opinion. We could never do this as children. We could never trust or just have someone listen to us. I thank God every day for this program.*

## She Followed Through With Step Five

*I once thought I could skip admitting the exact nature of my wrongs to God and myself since I seemed to be doing that in writing my Fourth Step inventory. Looking back, I can now see that the Steps separate Step Four and Step Five so there is enough time for real progress to happen. We need time to recall what happened. We also need to talk to a trusted sponsor or counselor about our story.*

*The benefit of Step Five is improving my relationships with my Higher Power as well as myself. I do this through trust and honest communication.*

## She Broke the "Don't Talk" Rule and Found Freedom

*The Fifth Step was by far my most difficult Step. I remember when I grew up my father would explode emotionally, and we'd walk on eggshells. Afterwards, no one would ever talk about the incident. There was never an apology. My father frequently said to me, "No one wants to hear what you have to say. Nothing you have to say is valuable. You're not learning anything when you're talking. Shut up."*

*To ask someone I barely knew to listen to me talk about my problems for even a few minutes was very difficult. To ask them to listen to my entire Fifth Step was much harder. I overcame my father's admonitions when I worked Step Five. My sponsor and I spent two afternoons, for three hours each time. I told her about my character defects, my life, and what I had contributed to my problems. I felt guilty because I made a lot of mistakes, but admitting my mistakes made me feel incredibly free.*

*The Fifth Step process has been very challenging. The reward, however, is freedom from the past.*

## Step Five Summary

By working Step Five we are challenging the three main rules entrenched in our souls as a result of growing up in a dysfunctional home. The rules are: "don't talk, don't trust, and don't feel." Growing up in a dysfunctional family meant not trusting what you were seeing or what your parents said. Abuse was often minimized or blamed on another cause, which resulted in the child not trusting his or her perceptions.

The "don't talk" rule has its origins in homes where children were often told to "shut up" or "be quiet" whenever they attempted to speak or express a thought. Others were ignored under the "don't talk" rule and therefore stopped talking. The "don't talk" rule also means the family does not talk about things that are important such as feelings or spirituality. The rule is also a method of keeping sick family secrets.

The "don't feel" rule of dysfunctional homes often means that feelings were unimportant or too scary to address. Before recovery, we could be accused of being too sensitive or being immature if we expressed feelings in a dysfunctional home. To avoid such ridicule, we usually shut down our emotions. The "don't feel" rule is the rule that underlies our ability to stuff feelings such as fear. Some of us lived in constant fear of being ridiculed, teased, or battered by an abusive parent. By the time we reach recovery, many of us are numb from living with fear. We cannot call the feeling of fear into focus, but it is there, driving our hypervigilance.

In Step Five, we talk about what happened, and we trust another person to hear us without judgment. We feel the feelings that come up with the help of our ACA support group and a sponsor or counselor.

In Step Five, we finally get to talk about what matters rather than denying or filtering what happened. This is a critical step for any adult child hoping to face the effects of a dysfunctional upbringing and to continue to grow in the ACA program.

We know that breaking dysfunctional family rules does not come easy for adult children. These rules are similar to the survival traits we used to live through our childhoods. We learned to trust these rules and use them in our daily lives; however, the rules have outlived their usefulness. They are strangling our lives and our relationships. We have to find another way to live with feelings, trust, and voice.

For some ACAs, the Fifth Step will be the first time they have told anyone some of their most troublesome memories of abuse. We know the courage this will take to move forward with Step Five. We know you will be letting someone into compartments of your mind that you may have thought would remain tightly shut forever. But these are the very secrets and problematic memories that need letting out. You are finally safe to take this action in ACA with a sponsor, trusted counselor, or spiritual leader.

## Avoid Half Measures

To skip over this Step, or to employ half measures in the Steps, has proven disastrous for adult children. By not following through with Step Five, these adult children seem to never grow spiritually in the program. They have exposed painful behavior and secrets in Step Four only to hold onto such pain by not doing a Fifth Step. They are stuck. They have meeting knowledge and ACA knowledge, but they hang onto some of their most painful behaviors. They often sound polished at ACA meetings, but they have not faced their worst fears or secrets.

The clues are there. They continue to reenact the abandonment of their childhoods, or they position themselves for constant chaos or heavy doses of shame. They still feel responsible for their parents' dysfunction on some level.

By avoiding Steps Four or Five, many of these adult children seem to practice greater degrees of dysfunctional control and are cut off from God. Many drop out of meetings never to return. Others attempt to work a program but feel somehow cheated by a Higher Power and ACA. They lead a double life outside the meetings, stopping by ACA occasionally to check in but avoiding the necessary actions to change. Our hearts go out to these suffering adult children. They need to complete the Steps. Step Five shows us the value in following through with the Twelve Steps.

If we skip Step Five, or attempt to somehow minimize it, we may never claim the promises of the ACA program. The Twelve Promises involve learning to live with inner peace and a grateful sense that we have survived an ordeal. We have something to offer the world, but we must put forth effort to claim it. With this effort, we realize how our stories and experiences matter.

In reality, going through Step Five is the easier, softer way compared to codependent living, which brings constant torment or chaos. The emotional and mental effort it takes to run our lives by dysfunctional control or through loveless relationships is enormous.

## Go Through the Pain

There is no way around Steps Four or Five. We must go through them to get to the other side, to find the God of our understanding waiting there with a timeless embrace. This is our experience. Thousands of adult children have completed Step Five and found a peace and serenity not known before. They are waiting for you on the other side of Step Five. They called upon the inner strength which helped them survive a dysfunctional upbringing. They used that inner strength to make it through Step Five with room to spare. You have this inner strength by the very fact you have completed the first four Steps of the program.

Step Five gives us a chance to finally talk about what matters to someone we trust. We give our Fifth Step without grand promises to be perfect or strive for perfection. We tell our story to another person with honesty and sincerity and leave the results to God as we understand God. We can finally give ourselves breathing room to change one day at a time. We claim our humanness and our position in the world.

## Reparenting Ourselves

In addition to breaking dysfunctional family rules, Step Five is another significant step in learning to reparent ourselves and to face the exact nature of our childhood abandonment. This abandonment is linked to the wrongs we have committed against others. We take a balanced look at how we have harmed ourselves and others as well. Reparenting tools include addressing the hypercritical voice in our head that fuels our self-doubt or self-harm. With reparenting, we begin to accept the fact that we have good qualities. The qualities have been understated, but they are there. We fail to see our internal goodness because we tend to focus on a mistaken sense of being flawed or hopelessly wrong. In Step Five, we must be honest about our selfish behavior and claim it. We also must lift our eyes to see our kindness and our love, which is there and which was first. Some ACA members find it difficult to identify or to claim their good qualities, but we have them. Through reparenting, we challenge our inner critic by reminding ourselves of our strong points. By doing so, we realize that we are not as bad as we thought we were nor are we as noble. We have a balance of positive and problematic traits that we are learning to accept or to address.

We approach Step Five with an attitude of self-love and trust that our Higher Power is with us and will not abandon us. We have taken a hard look at ourselves and our family of origin in Step Four. We have held nothing back. We are now preparing to release years of stored grief, shame, and hurtful secrets to God and to someone who understands.

Many ACA members choose their sponsor or counselor to hear their Fifth Step because they have developed trust with this person. It is important that the person hearing the Fifth Step understand what we are trying to do. It is not our job to explain the Fifth Step process or to educate the person about ACA when we sit down to tell our story to him or her. We choose someone we can relate to and who will not pass judgment on our inventory of our lives.

The spiritual principles of Step Five are honesty and trust. We must have self-honesty about the effects of growing up in a dysfunctional home. The effects are our survival traits, which include people-pleasing, becoming addicted or marrying an addict, fearing authority figures, and feeling guilty when we ask for what we need. We often confuse love and pity, and we tend to "love" people we can rescue. We also can be the rescued. We stay in abusive relationships because they resemble how we were raised. We are terrified of abandonment so we tolerate high levels of abuse or neglect as adults. The abuse seems normal.

In Step Five, we must also have self-honesty about those we have harmed, including ourselves.

When looking at the exact nature of our wrongs we must be honest about our motives and designs. We must take ownership of our wrongs without minimizing our errors or exaggerating them. Many adult children commit wrongs against others based on a sense of being defective or unwanted. Driven by an unnamed hurt inside of us, we harm others so that we might feel powerful. Or we recreate the isolation we became comfortable with as children. We harm others, which is wrong, but the exact nature of our wrong is that we have harmed ourselves. In harming another, we usually have acted out on a survival trait. With such behavior, we miss a chance to address our isolation and the feeling of being defective.

The old saying goes: "Hurting people hurt others," and that appears to be true for adult children. The script goes like this: "If I can hurt you before you hurt me then I will feel powerful or in control."

Our inside hurt does not give us the right to harm others, but understanding that pain can begin the process of freeing us from its grip. Realizing such pain is the starting point for change and learning to love ourselves. We listen to our hurt and reparent it toward self-love.

If we minimize our wrongs or fail to see their exact nature, we fall short of the mark of self-honesty in Step Five. Self-honesty does not mean self harm. We want rigorous honesty, but we do not want to abuse ourselves by being rigorously scathing. If we overstate our wrongs and beat ourselves up, we tend to drift into an attitude of martyrdom, or we assume the victim posture.

At the same time, we cannot be too lenient on ourselves for harms committed against others. Being too lenient can lead to an attitude of being "damaged goods" without hope for repair. This can lead to the victim plateau as well and mire us in self-pity or push away the true path to self-discovery in Step Five. The key to rigorous honesty that steers between self-abuse and leniency is this: We become willing to face whatever we have done and then do the footwork to change. We work the Steps, we listen, and we talk to others about our feelings. If the pain of feeling defective or shamed emerges, we sit with it instead of acting out. The pain will pass. We pray, and we seek the truest course with input from our sponsor, counselor, or ACA group members. Our answer will emerge, and we will recognize it.

Step Five is where we embrace a more balanced view of who we are as sons, daughters, citizens, employees, business owners, and spiritual seekers. Since we come from homes that were out of balance with abuse or hypercritical attitudes, it is not easy for us to embrace our positive qualities. But we have such traits as compassion, trust, intelligence, and spirituality. Other positive traits are friendliness, honesty, and tenacity. We are not the disease of family dysfunction, but we have acted on harmful traits developed in that family when we were children. We are facing our behaviors in Step Five and making an honest attempt to change. We can feel good about this effort and our good character no matter what our story reveals.

## Exact Nature

When we look at the exact nature of our wrongs, we see that we have harmed ourselves based on our sense of being unacceptable, inferior, or lost. Further examination of our wrongs reveals there can be both legal and spiritual consequences to our actions. When we break the law there is a legal wrong, but we also see a spiritual separation as well. We separate ourselves from our Higher Power with our behavior. We experience spiritual loss.

Some adult children have committed crimes that have caused them to spend time in prison or lose their family and job. Others have been so caustic or difficult to live with that they end up alone. Still others remain on the job and in relationships but are not connected to life in a meaningful manner. Each of these adult children has committed a wrong and should stand ready to make amends.

But the adult child should also realize that the exact nature of a wrong can also involve loss. That is the secret in understanding Step Five. All of these harmful acts add up to loss. Each time we harmed another person or ourselves, we lost a piece of ourselves. Each time we shamed our own child or spouse, there was loss. Each time we judged ourselves without mercy for common mistakes, there was loss. Each day we remained in an abusive, dependent relationship there was loss.

Before finding ACA, we grew more weary each day, but we continued to try. We were the walking wounded with a smile. We were always on the verge of grief.

## Grief: The Onion and Time

Every adult child has unexpressed grief, which is usually represented by the symptoms of depression, lethargy, or forms of dissociation. The grief that we speak of in ACA is the cumulative loss of childhood. Grief is loss that is stuck beneath denial, willful forgetting, and the fear of being perceived as dramatizing the past. Grief is the built-up defeats, slights, and neglect from childhood. We carry this grief with us as we create careers, raise families, or trudge through life as best as we can. Keeping ourselves busy or focusing on others seems to help us avoid looking at our childhood grief/loss, but it is there. Until we find ACA, we rarely understand the exact nature of our loss or how we can address it. If we sought help before ACA, our childhood loss was usually diagnosed as depression and commonly treated with ineffective methods.

The losses we speak of in ACA include the actions and inaction of our parents or family. Being shamed by our parents or a relative represents the loss of being able to feel whole as a person. Shame tramples a child's natural love and trust and replaces it with malignant self-doubt. With shame, we lose our ability to trust ourselves or others. We feel inherently faulty as a child. As adults, we can have a mistaken sense that something is wrong with us without knowing why. Other childhood loss includes being unfairly criticized by our family or being compared to a brother or sister and coming up short. This represents a loss of feeling valued as a person by our family. When our parents project their own lack of self-worth onto us, we experience loss as well. If our parents have said we are bad, dumb, or inferior, they were actually projecting what they believed about themselves. As children we were defenseless to throw off these projections. This is loss and grief carried into our adult years. These are examples of loss in addition to the early loss of security brought by trauma and neglect.

We introduce grief work in Step Five, realizing that such work is a lifetime journey. Long-time ACA members understand the importance of claiming grief or loss. Many older members will speak of finding their grief by working the Twelve Steps or by sitting alone quietly and feeling the feelings that arise. Experienced ACA members speak of grief with a sense of serenity rather than with sorrow or resentment. They have made peace with their losses and found wholeness. They know that grief exists in every adult child. They know that time will reveal it. Time will heal it.

While grief can be perceptible through writing and talking about our memories, some grief is not always visible. We indirectly address our childhood losses each time we attend an ACA meeting and listen to the experiences of other adult children. We also address our grief each time we work a Tenth Step inventory or practice an Eleventh Step meditation. Our experience shows that grief is there between the lines and the thoughts waiting to be released. Emotional release and meditating on what we have lost are certainly part of addressing grief, but there is more.

With Step Five, we are ready to remove deeper layers of the "onion," which is analogous to our recovery journey. We are removing layers of shame and despair to find our True Selves. We began peeling back layers of the onion in Step One with the admission of being powerless over the effects of family dysfunction. Just as an onion can bring tears, our grief work will help us find our tears.

Our experience shows that grief is often stored in our minds and bodies, waiting to be purged when the time is right. We understand that grief is cumulative, which means all the neglectful and shaming acts of our past are piled up. We had not forgotten them as we had thought. Our bodies remember. Our minds remember. Our Inner Child knows. In addition to addiction or depression, many of our members believe grief helps fuel our compulsive acts of cleaning, perfectionism, sex, binge eating, work, and gambling.

Addressing grief is not self-pity. Self-pity is a refusal to accept real help while clinging to denial and a dead way of life. Seeking our grief is an honest effort to go inward to find the God of our understanding waiting there with release.

To place a foot on the path of grief work, we need a balanced view of who we are and what happened to us. We cannot come to grief work weighing in too heavy as a victim or weighing too light as the hero child. The victim aspect of our personalities can take the road of self-pity and refuse true help. The hero believes he or she has placed childhood abuse in the past and is no longer affected by such memories. We must avoid these two paths if we are to accurately identify and purge our stored grief.

Steps Four and Five give us the balanced view of ourselves sufficient enough to go after stuck emotions and feelings and find our productive tears. Before grief work, our tears were unproductive. Before recovery, many adult children eventually stopped crying because their tears did not bring relief from relentless despair and abandonment. Grief work restores the power of tears. We cry deeply knowing that we are finally safe and that we are finally understood.

By finding our grief, we come to believe on a deeper level that our parents' dysfunction was not our fault. We did not do anything wrong as children to cause their sick behavior. We are not bad, defective, or imperfect. We are human. We are focusing on our lives and moving forward. We want to make things right and to understand who we are.

By addressing our stuck grief with the Steps, we get a better understanding of our assets as individuals and our problematic behavior. We do not take too much responsibility for our family's dysfunction, but we do not shrink from taking responsibility for our own harmful behavior. We are gentle with ourselves, but we don't make excuses for our behavior. We pray, make amends, and continue to change our behavior in the Steps going forward from here. We no longer judge ourselves without mercy, but we are saddened by our losses as children. This is the bittersweet taste of grief work. We also see the losses that our parents must have endured as children. In grief work, we find it easier to have forgiving thoughts of our parents because we begin to have forgiving thoughts of ourselves. We have separated from our family without abandoning our family. We also have found a safe family in ACA.

## What to Expect in Addressing Grief

Grief work can take many forms and can bring some of the greatest rewards of the program. Some grief work involves journaling in which we write about incidents in our life and reflect on the feelings we had at that moment. Many adult children can recall childhood acts of abuse, neglect, or rejection without emotion. Others will talk about the abuse or neglect as comical or unimportant. Our experience shows that the emotion is there, but it is stuck behind our ability to deny the past or to recall it without clarity. We can have the memory of the event, but we block the feeling associated with it. This is a form of dissociation. When we journal about a childhood incident, we slow down and think about how we must have felt at that time. If we struggle with this exercise, we think about how one of our children would have felt in that situation. If we have no children, we think about how a child would feel in our place as a child. We ask members to do this exercise several times over many days and to be patient.

The "picture" exercise is another proven method to help recognize and release stored loss or grief. Some counselors will ask a client to round up several childhood pictures and bring them to a session. An ACA sponsor can do this type of work as well with a sponsee. Many of these snapshots are grade-school pictures that we had forgotten. The pictures come into sharper focus when discussed in therapy. Observing ourselves in the second or third grade, we notice how shy, giggly, and sensitive we had been as children. We had feelings. We had loss.

Another form of grief recovery is known as "sculpting" or role playing. This is also known as experiential therapy. In this type of grief recall, we are usually in a counseling setting with other clients helping reenact a troublesome scene from our past. This is a profound and powerful tool to tap hidden loss and shame.

Finally, some grief work takes time. After years of recovery, we may find ourselves weeping over a movie scene that reminds us of a childhood stage of our lives. Or we find ourselves watching a child play quietly in a schoolyard. We observe how the child is focused inward and full of imagination. We think about our own childhood and innocence. We make a connection to our Inner Child. The tears come.

As a result of working Step Five, we seem to breathe easier and judge ourselves less harshly. For some, our posture changes. Our head is up, and we make eye contact with people. We feel lighter in our step and in our breathing. We feel a greater connection to our Higher Power.

## Pinpointing and Measuring Loss/Grief

We offer this exercise to help you recognize childhood loss, which is associated with the shame and abandonment exercises in Step Four. Adult children can recount the abuse or neglect of childhood, but this does not complete the understanding of childhood loss. In exercises no. 3 and no. 4 in Step Four, you identified incidents of shame and abandonment, which are loss.

We find our loss and stored grief by naming what was taken away from us as well as what we did not receive as children. We can pinpoint and measure our loss by comparing the treatment we received as children in dysfunctional families with the care we could have received if raised by loving, consistent parents. It is important to measure our loss so we can experience it and release it.

Our search for our grief/loss can begin by asking this question: "What did I receive from my dysfunctional family and what would I have received from loving parents in the same situation?'

The difference between what you got and what you could have received is the measure of loss or grief. This loss adds up over time.

For example, many dysfunctional parents scold a child when the child accidentally harms himself or herself while playing. The frightened parent lashes out in anger instead of with affection. What would a loving parent have done if you cut yourself or skinned your knee?

In another example, a dysfunctional parent will manipulate a child into taking sides against the other parent when the parents argue. What is the loss for the child in this situation? What would a loving parent do in the same situation?

## An Important Note for The Step Worker

In Step Five, we have looked at the exact nature of our wrongs in addition to the exact nature of our childhood abandonment. We have been introduced to grief work and reparenting as well. You are now ready for your Fifth Step appointment. You will take your Fourth Step worksheets and writing with you to your sponsor or the person hearing your Fifth Step. The listener should be someone you trust and who understands what you are trying to do.

You should allow at least two to three hours to do your Fifth Step. Do not hurry the process. This is your chance to tell your story and to find greater levels of freedom. Your listener will understand.

Also, be ready to immediately do Steps Six and Seven when you have completed Step Five. Step Six—were entirely ready to have our defects removed—and Step Seven—humbly asked God to remove our shortcomings—were meant to be worked together during this phase of Step work.

Steps Six and Seven will not require a lot of writing, but there are some instructions to be read on the removal of defects of character. In Step Six, you will also read about integrating The Laundry List traits. Here are instructions on how to proceed with Steps Five, Six, and Seven.

## Summary for Steps Five, Six, and Seven

- Take your completed Fourth Step worksheets with you to your Fifth Step appointment.
- Say the Fifth Step Prayer in this section before doing your Fifth Step.
- After completing your Fifth Step, return home and read all of the section on Step Six in this book. There will be information on becoming entirely ready to have God remove your character defects and to integrate Laundry List traits (survival traits). There will be information here on how to proceed with Step Seven as well.

## Fifth Step Prayer

*Divine creator. Thank you for this chance to speak honestly with another person about the events of my life. Help me accept responsibility for my actions. Let me show compassion for myself and my family as I revisit my thinking and actions that have blocked me from your love. Restore my child within. Restore my feelings. Restore my trust in myself. Amen.*

## STEP FIVE SPIRITUAL PRINCIPLES:

### Honesty and Trust

# STEP SIX

*Were entirely ready to have God remove all these defects of character.*

## Making Myself Ready

*Part of the process of becoming entirely ready is to feel the painful consequence from my character defects. This naturally follows from admitting my wrongs, which I did in Step Five. As long as I was rationalizing and blaming others for my problems, I had no motivation to change. Once I quit rationalizing and took responsibility for my own behavior, I saw how letting go of my character defects can be of benefit to me. Change can be painful and scary. The process of becoming entirely ready in Step Six means I get uncomfortable enough to allow change to happen.*

## At Some Point I Just Stopped Fighting

*I thought I was a positive, happy, fun-loving person who laughed a lot. In ACA I discovered quite a few defects of character. I am negative, self-critical, self-sabotaging, self-rejecting, afraid of being abandoned, and unfeeling. I never realized my penchant for negativity. I criticized myself unmercifully. I heard people in program say, "Erase the critical parent tapes and replace them with nurturing tapes." I just couldn't do it.*

*I put myself in the position of my critical parent. I realized that if I had done an excellent job for thirty five years and then someone decided I was no longer necessary, I'd be furious. My critical parent, in fact, worked very hard to sabotage my efforts in recovery. I decided the only way to overcome this self-sabotage was to integrate my critical parent into my recovery process. Using self-guided imagery, I pictured my critical parent and complimented her on keeping me alive. I asked her to reallocate her energies from hiding family secrets and suppressing our Inner Child into releasing the secrets and caring for, loving, and nurturing our Inner Child. My critical parent has become my cheerleader. When I say, "That was really stupid," a voice in my head retorts, "It was human, not stupid."*

*I've learned in ACA that when I turn things over to my Higher Power, He takes care of me. So it is with my defects of character. I am no longer negative, self-critical, self-sabotaging, self-rejecting, afraid of being abandoned, or unfeeling. At some point I just stopped fighting and gave God my shortcomings. In ACA, I was able to see things about myself I didn't like and modify them. I don't think we ever change who we are, but we can change how we react.*

## Integration Led To Freedom

*When I first arrived at ACA, I thought I was a defective character instead of having defects of character. Because of my all-or-nothing thinking, I did not give Step Six a serious try at first because I thought the Step meant literally removing all my defects of character. Since I did not think this was possible, I ignored the Step for the most part. What I have learned, for me, is that Step Six is about how willing I can be to have my defects of selfishness, lust, or pettiness lessened. I am sure some people have their defects removed. I have had mine significantly lessened. I remain willing to have them totally removed.*

*Today I look at Step Six from the standpoint of integrating behaviors I developed to survive my violent alcoholic upbringing. I was a people-pleaser without an opinion. I was never a good friend. I never stood for anything because it might mean I could be challenged or criticized. I used drugs addictively to avoid my childhood abandonment. I was full of hurt, but I unknowingly blamed others until I could find help. Getting clean and sober and going to ACA did not change that overnight.*

*For years, in meetings, I struggled with my survival behavior thinking it was a defect of character. In reality my survival traits were deeply rooted friends. They are the Laundry List traits. They were no longer useful, but they had protected me. The harder I pushed against them, the harder they seemed to push back. I felt hopeless trying to let some of them go. But then I heard about integration. I heard about an exercise in which I could visualize meeting these traits and making friends with them. I could thank them for their work in protecting me, but I could also ask them to step aside. I got results and remained willing to give up these traits on a daily basis.*

*By viewing my survival traits as part of me rather than something that was awful or defective, I took a softer approach. I humbly asked God to allow me to lay down these survival behaviors and replace them with trust, forgiveness, and self-love. The results have been awesome. I integrated most of the traits into my life, and I feel the most freedom ever.*

## Step Six Summary

In Step Six we realize that we have defects of character like most of the population in the world. However, our defects of character tend to be entrenched and trap us in unfulfilling relationships and block us from receiving the love of a Higher Power. Our defects can include procrastination, lust, envy, greed, selfishness, and judgmentalness. We also have survival traits or common behaviors. The survival traits are the 14 characteristics of The Laundry List (Problem). These common behaviors represent the effects of growing up in a dysfunctional home. They are in a different category than defects of character.

Our survival traits include people-pleasing, addictiveness, hypervigilance, and stuffing our feelings to avoid conflict or arguments. We often confuse love with pity and tend to "love" those we can rescue. Even though we have identified such traits in Step Four, we are still new at this. We need focus to find our best course of action for release. Many adult children take the path of removal for character defects and take the path of integration for the survival traits.

There is a key distinction between defects of character and the survival traits of The Laundry List. Adult children readily identify with the survival traits; however, they struggle with claiming defects of character. Most adult children willingly admit to being people-pleasers or fearing authority figures but balk at claims of being judgmental, dishonest, or jealous. Adult children tend to feel relief when reading The Laundry List traits because they realize they are not unique in actions or thought. They often feel shame or dread when hearing a list of defects of character. These are the distinguishing points between defects of character and survival traits developed as children.

Admitting defects of character can be terrifying for adult children who have grown up in perfectionistic homes. To admit an error or to appear less than perfect is equated with extreme fear or a feeling of being unduly vulnerable. Some of us experience a plummeting feeling in our stomachs when it is suggested that we have defects of character. Admitting defects had no real value in most dysfunctional homes so we see no value in it before coming to ACA. We must remember that we are recovering in ACA. Admitting our defects of character does not make us inferior or inadequate. In fact, it means we are human.

The key to becoming free of character defects while making peace with our survival traits involves a three-prong approach with willingness, prayer, and time. In some cases we have seen defects of character removed completely in a short time, but for most of us it takes prayer and patience to mark progress. But progress is possible.

We were introduced to willingness in Step Three when we made a decision to turn our will and lives over to the care of God, as we understand God. We also showed willingness in Step Four by inventorying our behavior and thinking.

We will be the most willing to have our character defects removed by a Higher Power after we have completed Step Five. However, we can concentrate on willingness each time we meditate on Step Six or any of the Twelve Steps. As long as we make a sincere effort, we make progress on removing our defects of character with God's help. Willingness is our most powerful ally because it means we are teachable when it comes to addressing our defects of character. By being teachable, we learn to discern how much effort to put into changing our defects and when to get out of the way and let God handle it.

Many times we have seen an ACA member fraught with frustration over repeating a defect of character. We have seen the member work diligently to change only to return to old thinking or behaving. Finally, the adult child gives up and God moves in, and the behavior is changed or at least made tolerable.

Most newcomers in ACA can be overwhelmed at Step Six since it is hard for them to believe that God would remove their defects of character. To the new member, we urge you to make a start and keep trying. This is a good use of the will. With the help of ACA, we make progress and avoid perfectionism in Step Six.

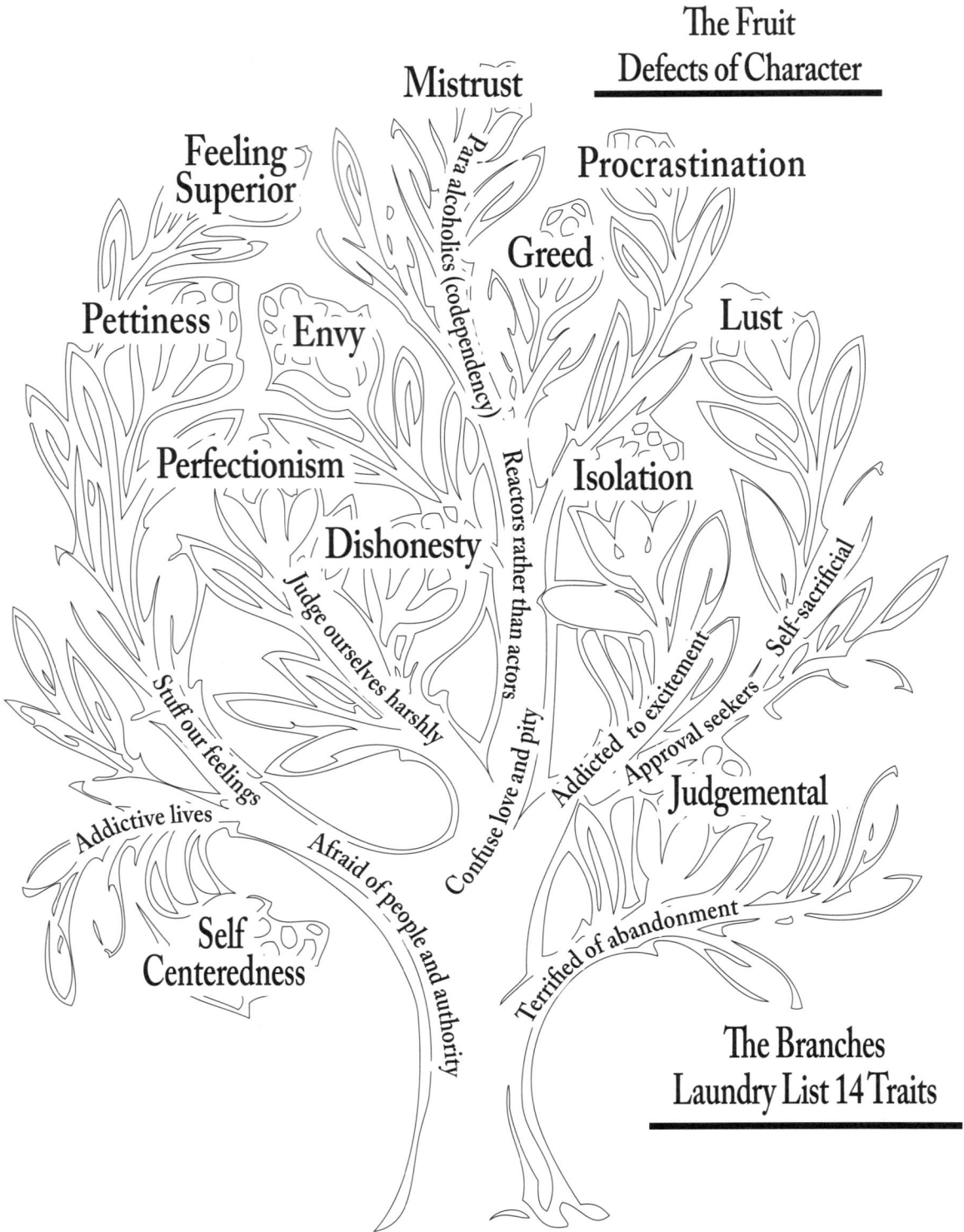

The Fruit
Defects of Character

Mistrust

Feeling Superior

Procrastination

Greed

Pettiness    Envy

Lust

Para alcoholics (codependency)

Perfectionism

Isolation

Dishonesty

Reactors rather than actors

Judge ourselves harshly

Self-sacrificial

Stuff our feelings

Addicted to excitement

Approval seekers

Confuse love and pity

Judgemental

Addictive lives

Afraid of people and authority

Self Centeredness

Terrified of abandonment

The Branches
Laundry List 14 Traits

## The Value of Healthy Pain

Becoming willing to have a Higher Power remove our defects of character can range from being painless, to moments of discomfort to agony. Some character defects such as gossiping and judgmentalness can be stopped painlessly. In ACA we learn to focus on ourselves, which cures a lot of gossip and the judging of others.

We face moments of discomfort and emerging pain with our ACA support group and a sponsor or counselor. Adult children dread emotional pain because we rarely had anyone to stand with us as we experienced anguish as children. Growing up in a dysfunctional home, we often endured unspeakable suffering in silence. We became hypervigilant to emotional pain and sought addiction, work, sex, or drugs to stay "pain" free. Many of us have writhed on the floor with codependent pain; however, pain is different in ACA. We now have friends and a Higher Power to rely on. We are not alone.

Our experience reveals that there is value in emotional pain. With support, and with gentleness, we can find our healthy pain and its healing release, just as we reclaimed our tears. Before we arrived at ACA, our tears seemed unproductive so many of us stopped crying. Through Step work or counseling we reclaim our tears and their value.

Emotional pain is a similar gift. Many of us had a preview of this pain in Step One or Step Four as we detailed the abuse of our lives or the abuse we visited upon others. We realized that we were not alone or unique in our pain. We realized that the pain we will feel in ACA is different than the unproductive pain of growing up in a family wrought with abandonment. In our homes, we learned to seek unhealthy pain that served no real solution and which fed our addictiveness. With the support of ACA, we experience healthy pain and find release.

We have seen adult children struggle in isolation and sorrow when such a solo struggle is not necessary. The emotional pain will end, but it can be prolonged if we fail to ask for help. During these times, we muster all the humility we can and ask someone we trust to listen to us. We become willing to share our fears and doubts about ourselves with another person. We find that ACA members really will help out. We find out that emotional pain can be the gateway to a closer connection with God as we understand God. We learn that the denouement of pain—the winding down of pain—is often where the integration of survival traits occur. After making it through, we feel changed. We embrace the inner strength we have always had, and we see emotional pain in a new light. We see it as one instrument which can temper our diamond hard survival traits.

By facing our pain, we learn that we really are not alone in our suffering. When we find ourselves in this kind of pain in Step Six, we stay close to meetings and keep our faces turned toward God as we understand God.

## Entirely Ready

Upon completing Step Five, we return home and find a quiet place to reflect upon what we are doing with our lives. We are on a path of self-honesty and self-forgiveness that will lead us to a new way of life. We are also moving away from our victim, perpetrator, and authority figure roles. We learned in Step Four that our survival traits have an opposite that we have practiced as well. If we feared authority figures, we often became an authority figure who was feared either as a parent, supervisor, or other position in life. If we judged ourselves without mercy, we also judged others just as harshly. We have been victims, but many of us have also been perpetrators. If we have gossiped maliciously, we stop. We become willing to ask our Higher Power to help us forgive ourselves and to change.

We are seeking a life in which we can feel our feelings and talk honestly about what is going on in our lives with the support of our ACA friends. Some of us will reconnect with our family of origin and have the best relationship we can have with them. We will be less judgmental of our family, but we also will know when to disengage if necessary. We are reparenting ourselves as we grieve a lost childhood. We are on a path to the Inner Child or the True Self.

After completing Step Five, we sit quietly and reflect upon our inventory. We notice our breathing and remember to breathe deeply. We have looked at shame, abandonment, sexual issues, and a praise deficit. We have also looked at stored trauma and frozen feelings and our spiritual beliefs. We sense that we have an inner courage that has always been there and which in now emerging. We may have had notions of spiritual beliefs or universal truths before, but we now begin to believe more deeply. With Step Five, we have focused on ourselves. We have done something for ourselves that matters and which has spiritual weight. We have inventoried our lives and taken a risk by telling our story to another person. We have broken the family rule of remaining silent. We realize we are among true friends. We are reparenting ourselves. We are not alone anymore.

With Step Six, you are taking the time to become entirely ready. You are about to humbly ask God to remove your shortcomings with a Seventh Step prayer. Step Seven states: "Humbly asked God to remove our shortcomings."

We have a list of our defects of character. We prepared our list by reviewing our Fourth Step inventory. We also understand our survival traits and their function in our life. These are The Laundry List traits that we respect but which now must be further lessened or integrated.

Our defects of character usually include self-centeredness, judgmentalness, envy, greed, lust, jealousy, feeling superior, dishonesty, and pettiness. As we sit and think about our shortcomings, we do not judge ourselves. Our character defects and survival traits are old friends we are beginning to bid farewell. Some will leave us immediately. Others will fade gradually. Still others will be integrated into our personality to enrich our lives and character. We are seeking our wholeness with what we are about to do.

By now, we have stopped punishing ourselves. We are asking God, as we understand God, to help us become entirely ready to have these defects of character removed. We must realize that good intentions do not work in removing our defects of character. Likewise, will power or self-determination is no match for these flaws in our thinking and reacting. We need help from a power greater than ourselves to achieve Step Six results.

We sit in a relaxed position, but we concentrate on becoming entirely willing to have our character defects removed. When we are ready, we repeat the Seventh Step prayer for each defect or survival trait we wish to have removed or integrated. As we prepare to say the Seventh Step prayer, we review our possible defects of character and survival traits.

## Possible Defects of Character:

Self-centeredness, judgmentalness, procrastination, perfectionism, envy, greed, lust, feeling superior, dishonesty, and pettiness.

## Laundry List Survival Traits or Common Behaviors:

People-pleasing, fear of authority figures, stuffing our feelings, addiction, and confusing love with pity (The complete list is at the front of the workbook).

## Options for the Removal of Defects of Character and Integration of Laundry List Traits.

Option 1—Read all of the section on Step Seven. Then say the Seventh Step prayer for the removal of each of your defects of character, and for the integration of each of your Laundry List traits. For example, we might integrate our trait of fearing authority figures into a belief that authority figures are human beings instead of possible abusers or adversaries.

Option 2—In Step Seven, turn to the heading on "Removal of Defects of Character" and read the information there. Say the Seventh Step prayer for your defects of character and Laundry List traits. Read the remainder of Step Seven the following day.

### STEP SIX SPIRITUAL PRINCIPLE:

### Willingness

# STEP SEVEN

*Humbly asked God to remove our shortcomings.*

## He Finally Gave Up

*I can remember how I fussed with a defect of character of jealousy for weeks. I would seem to make progress by talking about it and attending meetings, but I would see this person again and be burned up inside. I also felt helpless and abandoned. I wanted to do harm to this person. I wanted to act out like a little child. I was hurt so I wanted to hurt someone else.*

*I cared enough about ACA that I did not act on my urge to harm anyone. In recovery, I have learned that my first thought is on God. He takes it no matter how wild the thinking is. My second thought is on me. I am responsible for my actions.*

*I continued to pray and attend meetings. I called my sponsor and another person regularly. I avoided this person when I could, but I could still be upset when I thought about her. One day, I was struggling with this defect and feeling weary of the effort. I was tired of it, but I did not think I could be free of jealously. I finally felt tired enough and sat down. I was whipped. I settled back into my chair alone. I raised my head to stare at the ceiling. A simple prayer formed in my mind: "God. Please help me let go."*

*During the next few days I felt more peace inside. I still had to work at it, but I gave less energy to jealousy and this person. I found out I was giving away my power to someone else.*

## We Can Take Ourselves Back To God

*My aunt once told me, "Humility is truth." For me, Step Seven could be rephrased, "Truthfully asked God to remove our shortcomings." A humble spirit means I've been through my Fourth, Fifth, and Sixth Steps so I know the truth about myself. The truth is that I am a good and loving person who has some flaws. Those flaws are like small cracks in a beautiful vase.*

*I heard someone ask at a meeting the other day, "What do you do when something gets broken?" Then that person said, "You take it to the manufacturer to be fixed. When we are broken, we can take ourselves back to God."*

## All I Had to Do Was Ask

*I didn't have any defects of character until I came into this program. I thought! The hardest part for me was to admit I had any shortcomings. To survive, I had to believe I was sane, in control, and lucid. Recognizing my defects and then admitting them nearly killed me. Humbly asking God to remove them was easy in comparison.*

*I wasn't aware of the family secret until I came into ACA. Once I recognized the secret affected both my family and me, I didn't want the character flaws anymore. I had been molested, and in an effort to keep my children safe, I had hurt them. I kept my son at arm's length, but embraced my daughter. My son grew up believing something was wrong with him. I was afraid to get close to him because I did not know what a healthy relationship was between a parent and a child of the opposite sex.*

*At the same time, my daughter said, "You told me you loved me, Mom. I heard it, but I didn't feel it." With my Higher Power's help I accepted my basic personality and character defects and integrated the ones I could. I made amends to my children knowing they might walk away hating me. God gave me the courage to make amends anyway. When I was done, God removed my defects of character. They just fell away. There were no more barriers between my children and me. The energy and love flowed freely between all of us at last.*

*Because I was able to ask God to remove my shortcomings, and He did, my children did not have to carry the family dysfunction into their lives like I did. They were young enough to assimilate the information, ask their questions, accept honest answers, and ask for what they needed.*

## Step Seven Summary

As we approach Step Seven, we take time to notice that we have taken a fearless and thorough look at ourselves and our family of origin. In the First Step, we admitted our powerlessness over the effects of family dysfunction. That powerlessness includes the development of our survival traits that blocked us from a meaningful relationship with God. The traits also caused us to recreate our family of origin in our adult relationships. We focused outwardly on others, trying to control them or to fix our families through them. We developed an over-powering obsession or compulsion for another person. This obsession brought us to "hitting bottom" and asking for help in ACA.

In Steps Two and Three, we revisited our concept of a Higher Power, learning that many of us transferred the traits of our parents onto God. We projected our abandoning parents onto a Higher Power, believing that God was vengeful or indifferent. Even if we thought God was love, many of us secretly wondered if God truly cared or listened.

We also learned that our compulsion to control ourselves or others was a major stumbling block in our ability to let God help us. Many of us exposed our facade of self-sufficiency for what it was: a camouflaged isolation in which we were terrified of asking for help. We were hiding in plain sight from ourselves and others. We chose a sponsor—a fellow traveler—and took the first step to move beyond isolation.

In Steps Four and Five, we made a searching and fearless moral inventory and told someone our story for the first time. While we reviewed our parents' behavior in a "blameless" fashion, we also faced our behavior. We take responsibility for our actions. These are some of the first steps to reparenting ourselves and truly focusing on ourselves and what we can change in our lives.

In Step Six, we learned that willingness is the key to removing our character defects. We also learned that our survival traits from childhood could look like character defects; however, they had much deeper anchors and responded better to integration. We made peace with the traits and asked them to step aside so that we could live our lives in freedom. In Step Six, we learned the value of healthy emotional pain.

In Step Seven, we realize we cannot remove our shortcomings without the help of a Higher Power. We may have had moments of freedom from our defects, but they seem to return or take on a new form if we fail to ask for God's intervention. To our horror, we see a defect reappear in a new obsession or new twist that is torturous to face alone. In Step Seven, we muster all the trust or faith that we can. We rely upon God to remove our defects of character. We humbly ask God, as we understand God, to remove our shortcomings.

## Removal of Defects of Character

For the removal of our defects of character, we sit in a relaxed position and concentrate on becoming entirely willing. We also become willing to integrate our survival traits. We may meditate and pray. When we are ready, we repeat the Seventh Step prayer for each defect or survival trait we wish to have removed or integrated. Do not be concerned if you are not clear if you are addressing a defect or survival trait. God will understand. Humbly ask God, as you understand God, to remove your defects of character.

## Seventh Step Prayer—Character Defects

*God. I am now ready that you should remove from me all my defects of character, which block me from accepting your divine love and living with true humility toward others. Renew my strength so that I might help myself and others along this path of recovery."*

Possible defects of character are: self-centeredness, judgmentalness, procrastination, perfectionism, envy, greed, lust, feeling superior, dishonesty, and pettiness.

*"I humbly ask you to:*

*"Remove my defect of* _____.

*"Remove my defect of* _____.

*"Remove my defect of* _____.

*"Remove my defect of* _____.

*Amen."*

## Seventh Step Prayer—Laundry List Traits

*God. I am now ready that you should integrate my survival traits, which block me from accepting your divine love. Grant me wholeness.*

Laundry List survival traits or common behaviors: people-pleasing, fear of authority figures, stuffing our feelings, addiction, and confusing love with pity. (See the complete Laundry List in the front of the book).

*"I humbly ask you to:*

*"Integrate my trait of*_____.

*"Integrate my trait of*_____.

*"Integrate my trait of*_____.

*"Integrate my trait of*_____.

*Amen."*

With our character defects and survival traits addressed, we rely upon our Step Seven humility to prepare us for the amends process in Steps Eight and Nine. Humility will lead us as we find our path of self-forgiveness while making things right for those we have harmed.

Additionally, we realize our humility leads us to creativity and exploration. We realize we have more energy because we are focusing on ourselves instead of others. We have more mental energy available for new interests. Our Inner Child can begin to play and to create during this stage of recovery. This creativity, and accompanying intuitiveness, marks the growth of our real identity.

## Working Step Seven: A Step of Action

Step Seven is an ongoing process. We can work this Step almost anywhere and anytime we feel the need to have a character defect removed. If we slip into judging another ACA member wrongfully, we can say "God. Please remove my shortcoming of judgmentalness."

If we are impatient at the grocery market, waiting to check out, again we can pray. "God. Please give me patience. Help me live in the moment without impatience."

Prayers that address our shortcomings should be simple but sincere. Typically, the fewest number of words uttered in humility seem to resonate best with God. A sincere desire to change coupled with heartfelt humility seem to go further with God than breathy and lengthy prayers of woe.

The sincere adult child working an ACA program of meeting attendance and selfless service gets results with Step Seven. This is the sure path when we struggle with a troublesome shortcoming.

We have seen adult children struggle for weeks, if not months, with a particular defect of character. The person prays, writes in a journal, shares at meetings, and gets involved in service work, but still the defect persists and appears to be gaining strength. However, the Higher Power is at work.

During these times, the adult child continues to attend meetings. He or she stands on the program foundation built thus far. The person keeps working the program and doing the things that have worked in the past. The adult child remains focused on being free of the shortcoming while sharing about the effort to bring about change. The days pass. The adult child continues to pray, journal, and seek the help of a Higher Power. Frustration and exhaustion may occur as the person stays focused on being free. This is healthy pain and a good use of the will. At some point the adult child realizes that he or she must seek a Higher Power with all earnestness. The meetings and prayer, have been necessary, but the person must seek God with urgency and intent. With this attitude a moment arises when all the program work, meetings, prayer, and worry have an effect and the shortcoming budges. A sense of calmness comes over the person. The shoulders ease down in a relaxed position, and the person breathes deeply and says: "God. Help me." Relief follows.

## True Humility

Humility is not humiliation; however, some adult children have humiliated themselves and found humility. Humiliation tends to come from our need to harm ourselves by reenacting the shame from our childhood. Without help, our toxic shame from the past will find a way to express itself in our adult lives no matter how perfect we act and no matter how hard we try to control ourselves or others. The shame finds a way to well up. We are horrified by its expression in relationships or events and our participation in it.

Humility comes from God and is a sibling of anonymity, a foundational principle of the Twelve Steps and the Twelve Traditions. Through anonymity, we practice service with love. We seek to be of maximum service to our Higher Power and others.

With humility we find that our will aligns with God's will on a more frequent basis. True humility is the willingness to seek and do God's will with our best effort. We know that we are not perfect and know we could fall short. Yet, we try our best to live this Step and obtain its spiritual intent of removing our shortcomings through humility.

With humility, we become more thoughtful in our decisions, and we are slower to anger. We begin to become actors rather than reactors to life's situations. We begin to have greater freedom of choice and feel more comfortable asking for help. In addition to asking for spiritual help with our defects, we begin to pray with a quiet patience for a Divine Spirit to temper our most glaring survival traits. We pray for integration of these characteristics which served us well, but which now must fade. We fear authority figures less. We back away from being people-pleasers. We stop confusing love with pity. We get sober and clean as well.

With humility, we also learn to recognize when we feel "full" in our relationships and in our wants and needs. Because of our core abandonment issue we are not sure when we have had enough attention or praise. With humility we are less restless and know how to be at peace with what we have. We also learn how to ask for what we need, instead of manipulating people for something we don't need. Humility helps us choose between what we really need, and the wants that can be placed on hold.

Without humility, we have seen some adult children place wants ahead of needs with troubling outcomes. Feeling empty inside, they chase after their wants constantly through spending, debting, and comparing their lives to others. Many adult children spend hours looking for bargains or chatting online with little nurturing effect. Other adult children run from store to store craving the latest fashion or technological advancement, but it is never enough. We have no problem with having luxury items after our emotional and spiritual needs are met. We have no problem with online chatting if the chatting is not a diversion to focus on someone else with unhealthy dependence. We tend to give away our personal power by placing our wants first. Humility gives us personal power that can help us feel "full" in our lives and less frantic to chase wants.

In addition to an inner peace and a glimpse of God's will, humility also brings an unexpected burst of creative energy for many adult children. Since we have backed away from trying to control others, we suddenly realize we have more energy to do things for ourselves. We have more time to attend concerts, go hiking, or begin a book of poems or finish one. Many adult children take their Inner Children to the circus, or buy watercolors and spend afternoons painting and mixing colors to see what happens.

## Balancing Our Remaining Defects With Our Attributes

Most adult children have a few lingering defects of character after completing Steps Six and Seven. We cannot use this as an excuse to remain in problematic situations or old ways of thinking.

During the next few days, create a list of your remaining defects of character and compare them with your positive behaviors. During Step Five, we identified many of our problematic behaviors. As we told our story, our sponsor or listener helped us identify our defects of character and our positive qualities. We reparent ourselves by listing any problematic thinking or behavior that might linger after completing Step Seven. We strive to be free of these defects of character, but we also remind ourselves that we have positive qualities. Through humility, we can ask our Higher Power to help us avoid picking up and using a defect of character. We humbly ask our Higher Power to help us address our remaining defects. In this exercise we seek balance in our lives. We avoid focusing only on our problematic behavior. List your positive qualities across from problematic behavior that continues to affect your life. We reparent ourselves with the positive qualities.

## Example:

| Continued defects | Balance/Reparent with |
| --- | --- |
| Self-centered | Selflessness |
| Not always honest | Rigorous honesty |
| Manipulative | Sincerity |
| Perfectionist | Compromise |

## STEP SEVEN SPIRITUAL PRINCIPLE:

## Humility

# STEP EIGHT

*Made a list of all persons we had harmed and became willing to make amends to them all.*

## I Loved My Father

*When I made my first Eighth Step list, I put my alcoholic father on the list even though he had perpetrated violent and shaming abuse upon me as a child. At the time, I was in another program that told me to avoid looking at his behavior and to focus on mine. I did what I was told and made my amends to him in a letter. I never mailed the letter.*

*When I worked the Eighth Step in ACA, it was a different story. I had discussion before I considered forgiving my father. I recalled how he once sat me on his knee when I was a child. He was cussing at my mother across the room. He was very drunk and I could smell his three-week-old whisky breath. When drinking, my father would get very drunk and sit for hours cussing or picking fights with my mother, who tried to ignore him.*

*On this night, my father sat me on his knee and pointed to my mother across the room and bellowed, "Son. Your mother is a whore." It was a lie, but I can remember my mother looking away as my father made me agree with him. After that, I remember my mother's hugs felt different. I felt like a coward for the next 20 years. I thought I should have fought my dangerous dad. I met a counselor, who walked me back through the episode 20 years later. The counselor asked me how much I weighed when this happened. I must have been 10 years old so I weighed about 100 pounds. She then asked how much my drunken father weighed. He was 6-feet 5-inches and 230 pounds. I understood.*

*I chose to forgive my father after I was able to get angry about what happened and to talk about his sick behavior. I found out I really loved him deep down inside. I thought I didn't, but I did. I loved him, but I could never admit it because everyone knew he was a drunk. I forgave him to move him out of my head. I want to live in peace. I have also forgiven myself. I placed my name at the top of the Eighth Step in ACA.*

## I Read My List Daily

*Like Step Six, Step Eight requires an investment of time to become willing. There's a world of difference between wanting to do something and being willing to do it. I do not want to use a needle to remove a sliver from my finger, but I am willing to do so because it will relieve my pain and suffering.*

*I made a list. I was willing to make amends to some people as soon as I wrote down their names. For others, it took longer. I used to keep the list in my daily meditation book and tried to remember each person each day during my prayer and meditation time. I was seeking willingness to make amends.*

## She Became Willing

*There were many people I had harmed. I hurt the men in my relationships. I hurt my son and my daughter as well. I hurt myself, too. I remembered my old boyfriends and how I treated them. My way of ending a relationship without having to confront the person was to push his buttons until he left me. That way I didn't have to be the "bad guy."*

*With my children, I remembered the harm I committed and sought self-forgiveness in Step Eight. I recalled how I made my daughter doubt trusting me. One day when I was trying to change the sheets on the bed, my daughter stood on the sheets. I picked her up gently and moved her so I could get on with my chores. As soon as I moved her, she jumped back onto the pile thinking this was a wonderful game. After two or three repetitions of this I gave the sheets a little yank assuming she would fall on her bottom and that would end the game. Instead she bit through her tongue. The look on her face said, "How could you!" This was her loss of innocence. She knew it was no accident.*

*Writing out a list of all the wrongs I had done to other people was like taking a stick and beating myself up with it. I felt awful about the pain I had inflicted. It hurt me deeply to keep my silence when I was a child. It hurt me to confront my mother to tell her all the things I felt about her but didn't say when I was growing up. It was devastating to me to know I had passed the family dysfunction on to my children just as my father had passed it on to me. I was a victim of my own dysfunction, too.*

*It was not difficult to become willing to make amends when I became aware of the havoc I had wreaked, especially upon my children. The weight on my shoulders was immense. I was so grateful to be able to recognize and repair some of that damage early enough so my own children were not permanently scarred.*

## Step Eight Revealed Inner Courage

*I approached my Eighth Step list with willingness, wanting to do what the program asked. I surrendered and put down all the names of the people I needed to make amends to. Even a person I hated. I stopped fighting and blaming. The Step required a list of those I had harmed and willingness to make amends. I did both and found my inner courage when I wasn't looking for it. Serendipity.*

*Making out that Eighth Step list meant a lot. I knew I was doing something important for me. It was a continuation of Step Four and the actions I took there. That's what all the Steps have meant to me. I finally found a way to do something concrete that was not necessarily easy but meaningful. I had support as well.*

# Step Eight Summary

In Step Eight we make a list of the people we have harmed and become willing to make amends to them all. While making such a list, we are also mindful of our Inner Child and the need to protect the child within from harm during the amends process. While we will concentrate here on willingness and making the list, we must realize that many adult children have families that remain in denial about family addiction or dysfunction. Walking into your home and announcing that you are an adult child might bring an unintended effect. We urge caution for some circumstances; however, we do not let fear or being uncomfortable stop us from making this important list of our wrongs.

With Step Eight and Step Nine we are strengthening our commitment to changing our lives. We are doing something that is not easy but which will build confidence and set us free. We are moving past our comfort zone. We are moving further away from our dependent, people-pleasing selves toward our new home. We are improving a real connection with our Higher Power.

With new clarity, we see where we want to go, and we believe we can get there. We realize we can change. That feeling that we could never change our lives has been faced by the time we reach Step Eight. The feeling of being unique or defective has been addressed as well. We realize we are human beings and that we make mistakes like the next person. We also realize that our life experiences place us in a unique position. We can be helpful to suffering adult children yet to find a way out. Our stories and our knowledge of the ACA program are golden to a confused adult child feeling alone and often imbalanced.

In Step Eight, we are facing our lives, and we are claiming our future, one day at a time. We know what we are doing. We know it is okay to talk, trust, and feel. We know that we have greater choice instead of decorated control. We know that we are moving forward with the help of our ACA group. We can trust ourselves. We know it is okay to know who we are.

# Letting Our Parents Go

Step Eight is where we begin to place a tighter grip on our part in the harm visited upon friends and within our closest relationships. In Steps One and Four, we inventoried our parents or relatives in addition to inventorying ourselves. We saw how our selfish, manipulative, or destructive behavior as adults originated from our parents. We took responsibility for our behavior without blaming others.

In Steps Five through Seven, we began to place more weight on our own responsibility and to separate from our parents and our dysfunctional family role. In Step Eight, we will scrutinize our behavior more than our parents' behavior. We are not forgetting our abusive past, but we are now more ready to face what we have done to others. We are not alone here. We have our sponsors, ACA friends, and a Higher Power who will not abandon us.

Step Eight is where we begin to release our parents to God as we understand God. The ACA Solution states: "When we release our parents from responsibility for our actions today, we become free to make healthful decisions as actors, not reactors."

Making an Eighth Step list of those we have harmed and facing our past is an act of courage. This outward courage is a reflection of our inward strength that has been there all along. How could we have survived and arrived at ACA without this inner courage and without a Higher Power? While we once thought we survived by coincidence, we are now beginning to believe in divine intervention at some level. Not all of us can put our finger on it, but many of us know we should not be here. We should not have survived, but we did. We certainly should not have made it to ACA where we now sit contemplating a list of people we have harmed and feeling confident enough to follow through with amends. Some of us know that we should be institutionalized or worse. Many of us who have been locked up or locked down, realize we are lucky as well to have this chance. We want to be sincere. We want to follow through and contribute to society in a meaningful manner. We also want to be the best we can be for our immediate families. We want to finally be emotionally, spiritually, and physically present with them.

Many of us prepare our Eighth Step list based on our Fourth Step worksheets. There should be names there that we have looked at in our personal inventory. We will want to work with our sponsor or counselor as we prepare this list. One of the spiritual principles of Step Eight is willingness. We need not look ahead to Step Nine just yet. We are simply making a list of people we have harmed and becoming willing to make amends. Some names will include our children, employers, relatives, friends, and parents. We realize our parents were often the perpetrators of our abuse; however, many of us have acted inappropriately toward them. Some of us have been calculating and have acted with malice of forethought. We have attempted to get even with our parents in one way or another. We hurt them and hurt ourselves emotionally in the long run. Some incest victims have extracted money and gifts as part of the compensatory guilt they use against an offending parent or relative. These are difficult claims to listen to, but we must face them if we are to be different in our dealings with other people. For if we have abused our parents in retaliation, we more than likely have abused others. The abuse started with our parents, and we will start there to change our behavior.

In many cases we have crossed the line, and we must look at that behavior for our own benefit, not our parents' benefit. This is our Eighth Step list, and this is our chance to change. We are the ones seeking change, and therefore we are the ones doing the heavy spiritual lifting. We are sweeping off our side of the street regardless of what another has done or not done. We are giving our parents to God, as we understand God. We are freeing them to their choices and their desires. We are separate from them. They have no power over us just as we have no power over them.

That said, some parents are so dangerous or perverted that the adult child must avoid them to remain safe and sane. Surely we would think twice about asking an incest victim to make amends to a perpetrator. Any amends would obviously involve harmful behavior we have engaged in after growing up and leaving the home. The actual amends may be to protect ourselves and to know that we did nothing to cause the sexual abuse in childhood. Forgiveness of a sexually abusive relative without a face-to-face meeting has been the choice of some ACA members in this situation. We gain personal power by realizing that the dysfunction did not start with us. We release the shame we have carried surrounding the sexual abuse. We know that we can have healthy love in our lives.

At the same time, some incest victims in ACA have made direct amends to a sexually abusive relative. These members report the amends, or a frank discussion with the offending relative, allows real honesty to be introduced into the family. In these cases, the incest victim forgave the offending relative and made direct amends for harmful behavior toward the relative. These adult children say the amends produced a powerful sense of resolution. Resentment and shame were removed.

We leave decisions on these types of amends to the adult child and his or her sponsor or counselor.

## Willingness and Self-Forgiveness

If we stumble in placing a name on our Eighth Step list, we ask God for willingness to at least write down the name. This is Step Eight so the amends has not occurred yet. We can at least put the name to paper and show willingness. We will trust our Higher Power to show us the time and place to make the amends. Many of us have been astonished when we watch how God works in creating the situation for an amends.

This type of willingness goes for the person we hate as well. Most adult children, if they get honest, have a person he or she hates. Given our experiences, we would not be human if we did not. Simply thinking about this person can bring great discomfort for some, but we at least consider writing down the name.

In addition to willingness, a key concept of Step Eight is self-forgiveness. We cannot forgive another until we forgive ourselves. This is a spiritual axiom. Many adult children struggle with self-forgiveness because we were oriented to doubt ourselves or to be hypercritical of ourselves as children. In most situations, we instinctively doubted, judged, or blamed ourselves for any problem that might arise. We judged ourselves without mercy even as we appeared to be fighters or debaters on the issues of life. We judged ourselves as we projected blame onto others.

Forgiving ourselves is foreign to most of us because self-forgiveness is nurturing and affirming. In most of our homes, we never heard of such talk. We must seriously consider the concept of self-forgiveness and practice it if we are to make progress in ACA. Without self-forgiveness, we tend to avoid embracing our successes in life, and we feel unworthy of loving relationships. In ACA, we learn to forgive ourselves by degrees until we become comfortable with this spiritual concept. This is a key moment for us and for reparenting ourselves.

In Step Eight, we are still learning to trust ourselves and to stand with ourselves without fading. If we balk at forgiving ourselves, we face this doubt and affirm ourselves. We get back to the business of self-forgiveness. We show self-forgiveness when we place our name at the top of the Eighth Step list. We also show self-forgiveness by listening to the words we use to describe ourselves. Where we once described ourselves as "lazy," "mean," or "incapable of love," we now describe ourselves in a gentler tone and with language that reflects the growing love inside of us. We begin to hear ourselves say: "I thought I was unlovable, but in fact I am a precious child of God. I am a miracle."

Such thoughts or words are the markers of self-forgiveness and true self-love.


## STEP EIGHT SPIRITUAL PRINCIPLES:
### Willingness and Self-forgiveness

# STEP NINE

*Made direct amends to such people wherever possible, except when to do so would injure them or others.*

## I Must Make Peace with Myself to Right the Wrongs

*Making amends sometimes means an apology. Sometimes it involves changing my behavior toward a certain person. Sometimes it means telling the truth. For me, making amends always seems to involve forgiveness. I need to forgive the other person for their part before I can make amends. Of course I must make peace with myself in order to have the strength and courage to right the wrongs I've done to others.*

## Cleaning Up the Wreckage of My Past

*The behavior I make amends for in childhood I can name here. I picked my mother's beautiful roses to give to a nice lady down the street for talking to me or in the hope she'd give me some candy. I took money from my mother's purse to pay off a bet I lost to my brother's friend. At the time I justified the act because I'd been tricked into making a wager that I couldn't win. I spent some silver dollars from the collection my parents gave to me and crossed a major highway just to buy candy. I dated two boys at the same time, being faithful to neither. The list goes on and on.*

*I told my mother that I stole her rosebuds, apologizing, giving her flowers to take their place, and never stealing flowers again. For the one dollar of dimes I stole to pay off the bet, I told my mother and returned the money one thousand fold. I never stole a dime from anyone again. I told my mother about the silver dollars and crossing the busy road. I replaced the silver dollars in the collection, safeguarded the family antiques from that day forward, and kept myself out of unsafe situations thereafter. I never told either boy I dated about the other one, but from that experience I dated only one boy at a time.*

*That was ancient history. In my adult life, I have done a few things I shouldn't have as well. I broke the moral rule, adultery. I learned my motivation for having broken it, built some self-worth, and apologized in Twelve Step meetings. This is one of those situations where it would have been wrong to contact the people I hurt by my behavior. At least one marriage ended and lives were torn apart. There was far too much pain suffered by too many to open those wounds after the fact so that I could play out my act of contrition.*

*I wrote a letter to my lover admitting my distorted ideas about love, loving, caring, and relationships. In it I apologized for the grief I had caused him, his family, and me. I burned the letter. I considered suicide, but realized that while it would stop my pain, it would never change the pain I had caused. Only in living and never engaging in this soap opera again could I hope to right this wrong before God and myself.*

## There Is Always A Way To Make An Amends

*As a recovering adult child, I still have a high tolerance for inappropriate behavior, so it is likely that another person had done serious damage to me before I noticed I was being attacked and then defended myself reactively. In recovery, however, I need to make my amends for each and every act of inappropriate behavior of my own. I do this regardless of what the other person did. Whenever possible I make my amends directly and learn a lesson in humility.*

*When the damage to me would negate the benefit, however, I do indirect amends. Putting myself in harm's way is not required of me to do this Step. I do not have to set up an appointment to make amends with someone who promised to kill me if they ever saw me again. I don't have to apologize directly to drinking alcoholics, people high on drugs, or people wallowing in any form of dysfunction because they won't hear me anyway. In these cases I do have to make indirect amends such as writing a letter that I later burn, volunteering my time to a soup kitchen, alcohol rehabilitation center, or senior center. I can send money to some community or charitable organization as it appropriately fits my misbehavior.*

## Step Nine Summary

Step Nine can be one of the greatest recovery moments that we will ever experience in ACA. While the Step can appear daunting, Step Nine is one of the fellowship's best kept secrets. The emotional and spiritual rewards of this Step are like a great hidden treasure. We cannot tell you how the amends process will turn out for you, but we can promise fulfillment and growth that will exceed your expectations if this Step is faced with honesty, sincerity, and thoroughness.

We liken the Steps leading up to Step Nine as a spiritual ropes course. The challenge course has involved risk, group support, and the realization of inner courage.

The ropes course began in Step One when we detailed the effects of growing up in an unhealthy family. Our Step One admission of the family dysfunction showed us the layout of the course that we would be encountering. In Steps Two and Three we strapped on the safety belt of a Higher Power for the hurdles and challenges ahead. In Steps Four and Five, we got a taste of trusting ourselves and others as we fell backwards off a high porch into the arms of ACA members. These members had been through these Steps and said we could make it. We felt like we were blindfolded. Many of us could not see the reasoning for inventorying our past and telling someone our story. We could not see to the other side, but we trusted our friends and God to catch us, and they did. In Steps Six and Seven, we sat around a group campfire, listening to stories and relating. We realized we are human and have defects of character like the next person.

In Step Eight, we stand at the base of a 30-foot challenge pole, tilting our heads back to see a narrow but stable perch on top. With our Eighth Step list in hand, we begin climbing the sturdy pole toward freedom and God. As we ascend, we see into the upper branches of trees around us. We stop climbing momentarily to check the "safety harness," which represents Step Three and our decision to trust a Higher Power. We glance downward into the smiling faces of friends. They know what we are trying to do with our lives. We hear their encouraging words rising from below. We climb higher now above the treetops. Reaching the pole's perch, we carefully stand up, a little wobbly at first, but we soon steady ourselves.

As we stand there with our Eighth Step list, we are astonished by a perspective we never imagined possible. We have finally gotten above it all with clarity. We can see that our parent's dysfunction was not our fault. On the horizon, we see the preceding generations of our family lined up in single file, stretching back for miles. There must be 100 generations or more. At the front of the line, we see our parents as children with their parents. We recognize our grandparents, but visualizing our parents as vulnerable children is a new experience for us.

We notice the generations of our family passing forward a bundle. They move the bundle along by handing it off from one generation to the next. We watch as the bundle moves closer to our grandparents and to our parents. The bundle is heavy and gripped tightly as one generation hands it off to the next. The bundle is held at the stomach level as it is passed forward. We concentrate on the bundle and begin to recognize it. Our eyesight has been improved by our Step work. We can see more clearly. We see our grandparents kneel down to give the bundle to our parents. As our parents receive the bundle as children, we understand what they have taken possession of. It is shame, abandonment, and loss from the ages. We think about what we have seen. We realize we don't have to take possession of the bundle. It is not ours. We are free. We look behind us, over a shoulder, to a clear horizon. There are no families there yet. We realize we have a chance to interrupt the passing on of family dysfunction.

We see no blame for anyone for what we are about to do in Step Nine. We are not blaming our parents or ourselves. We are willing to make amends to those we have harmed so that we can be free to serve God and society. During the amends process, we will protect ourselves and our Inner Child, but we will not shrink from this important Step. We feel as if we are closer to God, and we want to live and let live. We are learning to reparent ourselves with love and gentleness. The sky is clear. We step off into Step Nine.

## Moving Forward With Prudence and Courage

Step Nine is about mending relationships with others and ourselves. The Step also involves cleaning up the wreckage of our past and being willing to release resentments. In some cases, an amends will help restore a relationship. In other cases, an amends will bring closure to a past relationship or association.

With our Eighth Step list in hand, we have a good assessment of who we have harmed and who we will be approaching with our amends. While we will make the amends on our own, we realize that we are not alone.

The emotional and spiritual rewards for making our amends are awesome. Many such benefits are intangible, but they assure us that we are finally making greater progress in our lives. We are truly involved in real behaviors that are bringing change into our lives. In Step Nine, we are bringing together the pieces of our spiritual blueprint created by the preceding Steps. We are building our new home. We are turning on switches and opening windows installed by the hands of the Spirit of the Universe. There is still work to be done, but we are on our way. We have our foundation in place.

We approach Step Nine with humility and with a sense that we are about to make a significant shift in our lives. We are breaking the shackles of unhealthy dependence and carried shame. With the support of ACA, we understand we can lay down the guilt and shame we have carried from past behavior. We realize that this is a chance to address behavior that we thought was unforgivable. For years, many of us have carried guilt about some thoughts and actions. Many of these behaviors are a reenactment of what was done to us as children. Some of us have struggled horribly with these behaviors, believing we were evil or hopeless. We may have even tried to change but failed. We thought we were unique. Some of our behavior has been disturbing and perhaps outside the bounds of law. With Step Nine, we are naming what we have done and making amends for what we have done. With the help of ACA, our worst acts become forgivable if we are humble and seek help from a Higher Power. Honesty is a must as well.

With sincerity and effort, we begin to no longer feel ashamed of our past. We gradually release our carried guilt and our carried shame. We feel free. With such freedom, our behavior changes for the better. We know it is okay to trust ourselves. We realize that shame and fear of abandonment drove our harmful behavior. With help, we can stop reenacting what was done to us.

We want all of our freedom. We want to be free of food addiction, sex addiction, gambling addiction, drug addiction, and compulsive spending. We want to sleep well, enjoy our jobs, and contribute to the betterment of the world. We are reclaiming our personal power and taking our place in the world as individuals with something to offer. We have greater choice in our lives. We desire wisdom and discernment. We realize that the ACA way of life is comprehensive, practical, and spiritual. The program is a way of life that works in all areas of our lives. With it, we can face career choices, relationship challenges, and questions of God, in addition to facing our past and recovering from abuse and neglect.

We approach our amends list with an attitude of neutrality. We are not judging ourselves or others for their wrongdoings. We want to focus on our own missteps and not on the other person.

While amends is the primary objective of Step Nine, we want to be clear that we are also taking an important step to change our self-harming behavior. We harmed others in our relationships, but we also harmed ourselves because we were oriented toward abandonment and neglect as children. There was perfectionism, rudeness, and manipulation, which we learned to respond to as children and seek out as adults. As alarming as it sounds, we tended to choose people who abused us or were abusively controlled by us. In Step Nine, we are now approaching some of these people with an attitude of neutrality instead of morbid self-guilt or chipper confidence. There is a strong possibility that many of these people are still in denial. Some will not understand what we are trying to do, but that is not the point. We understand our purpose and our intent.

Sincerity, brevity, and humility are the ideas we keep in mind as we make our amends. We must remember that we are making amends for our benefit. We are not making amends to heal or fix another person. If the person gets benefits from our amends, we are grateful, but that is not our goal. Our goal is to honor our commitment to ourselves and to right our wrongs and continue our spiritual path.

During our amends, we don't attempt to educate people about ACA unless they ask. Even then we keep it brief unless they sincerely want to hear more. We don't recruit people to ACA in our amends process. We also don't bring up our newfound spirituality unless the moment is appropriate. It is not wise to meet someone we have harmed and announce our new or renewed focus on God. To do so places us at risk of being branded a religious crank.

Amends vary in type and form, but keep in mind that amends means making things right. Our first amends should be to ourselves. We have harmed ourselves with codependency, drugs, sex, work, gambling, and food like no other people on the planet. We have abandoned ourselves and judged ourselves without mercy countless times. We have stayed in abusive relationships long past the point of sanity because we were terrified of being alone. We have acted insane. Our behavior has equaled slamming our hand in a car door repeatedly or placing our hand on a hot stove believing we had no other way to live. Many of us have been a berated and castigated person, pushing ourselves far away from God, as we understand God. But no more. We are claiming our spot in ACA. We matter. We can forgive ourselves.

We use our inner courage to make a start. With our amends, we make no excuses for our behaviors, but we promise to do our best to change. We make practical statements about change instead of uttering grand resolutions or windy claims to be different. We want our actions, rather than our words, to show that we have changed.

In making an amends, we keep it simple, but we avoid being dismissive. We also avoid arguments or verbal jousting. We do not want to create additional harm during the amends process. We should have an attitude of humility and a sincere desire to repair what we have done or to restore what we have taken from another person.

During an amends, we might say: "I am involved in a program in which I am learning to change my behavior and to live more honestly and openly. Part of the process involves making amends to people I have harmed with my behavior. I am making amends to you for _____ (name the behavior, action, or other). I want to make it right. I am not making excuses, but I have harmed people based on my lack of knowledge about living. I am changing my behavior."

If we owe money, we need to make every effort to pay it back. If we have shamed someone publicly, we make amends publicly. If we have cheated a governmental agency or an employer, we find a way to make an amends either by working late or donating to a worthy cause. Carrying the ACA message of hope into a prison or treatment center is a good way of paying society back for harms against the greater public. This benefits our personal recovery as well. We get out of ourselves and help create a better society by helping the suffering adult child.

In making amends to our parents, we realize we are returning to the place where our abuse or neglect occurred. If we have retaliated against our parents, abused our parents, or used their grandchildren against them to harm them, we need to consider making amends for such behavior. At the same time, we need to be mindful that our Inner Child is with us as we walk into this amends scenario. Many of our parents have been batterers, blamers, manipulators, vindictive, self pitying, judgmental, silent, petty, aggressive, poor listeners, bossy, bullies, detached, or unloving. Others have been overly sweet, wishy-washy, inconsistent, vague, doomsayers, worriers, hypochondriacs, martyrs, and predictors of great catastrophe of the world or our lives. These are the souls we are leaving in God's hands. We are no longer responsible for them. We did not fail in fixing them. We are powerless over them and their choices.

With parental amends, we have to balance protecting our True Self with our need to fulfill the spiritual requirement of Step Nine. The Step calls us to be honest and to make our best effort to right our wrongs. We remember that our parents are spiritually sick people who repeated what was done to them. We are not minimizing what they have done to us, but we are not judging them. We are giving them to God with our amends, and we are protecting ourselves during the process.

Forgiveness is the key here. We seek forgiveness for ourselves and give forgiveness to our parents. Forgiveness does not mean that we are forgetting or minimizing our parents' behavior. We are forgiving them so that we can move forward with greater freedom in our souls. There is spiritual power in forgiveness. Cultures of all times and places have recorded the inner and spiritual value of forgiving another. ACA is no different.

Our experience shows that some parents will respond with a sincere desire to change. Others will be indignant and attempt to place blame elsewhere. For potentially violent parents, we need to gauge our safety and consider whether or not we can meet with them for amends. Whatever the situation, we make the amends for ourselves regardless of an anticipated response. We want to do all we can to clear up the wreckage of the past so that we can live in the present with honesty, hope, and spirituality. We are living our own lives. We are gaining greater freedom from the effects of growing up in a dysfunctional home.

## Amends to Our Children

If we make amends to our children, we need to keep it simple and make sure the language we use is age appropriate. We should have the agreement of our sponsor or counselor on what we will say. Children do not always need all the details about our abuse or neglect. They have lived it and need a demonstration of changed behavior more than psychological or wordy explanations.

We are truly concerned and remorseful for what we have done to our children, but we avoid feeling overly guilty. Such guilt can lead to overcompensating with even poorer parenting skills. Because we feel guilty, many recovering parents allow their children to act out with greater frequency or run over them until the parent explodes in anger. We must remember that we are still parents, and we have some skills. We also have a genuine desire to love our children and help them have a better life than we had growing up. We face our children and their behavior by attending meetings, working the Steps, and seeking help from a sponsor, counselor, or spiritual advisor.

When we focus on ourselves and ask for help, we are more ready when our children want to talk about their feelings and emotions. This is a key point. We try to avoid prodding or prompting our children into talking unless we are clear about our motives. Parents who cajole their children into talking too soon are usually trying to relieve their own uncomfortable feelings of being a dysfunctional parent. Under the disguise of wanting to listen to the child, the parent is actually gathering information about how the child thinks and feels about the parent. If the child opens up, the parent may invalidate the child's thoughts and feelings. In other cases, a child's honesty about unhealthy parenting can overwhelm the parent who can shift into a mode of overcompensation and lose more ground. We need to attend meetings and be on a solid foundation to listen to our children and to take the best course.

Similar experience is offered to grandparents recovering in ACA. These adult children can feel doubly guilty for passing on dysfunction to their children and grandchildren. If this is our situation, we must remember an important distinction about our lives. We are courageous. We are facing our behavior and actions instead of denying them. Adult children with grandchildren bear the brunt of being a pioneer for the family. They are often the first in a dysfunctional family to recover. They can be criticized or not understood by their family of origin, yet they stay focused and remain in recovery.

We must make a focused effort on self-forgiveness to avoid drifting into morbid guilt. If we feel paralyzed by the past, we stay focused on our program and know that we are doing God's will. We must attend meetings, pray, ask for help, and be ready if children or grandchildren want to talk.

## Except When To Do So Would Injure Them Or Others

In making amends, we avoid bringing harm to another person by disclosing something that might be unnecessary and off the mark.

For instance, if we are making amends to an ex-wife, we need not bring up the infidelity we might have had with her sister. To do so serves no purpose in the moment. We need to admit our cheating to our sponsor or counselor and know in our hearts that the behavior was wrong. We change such behavior in the future and stay out of the lives of our ex-wife and her sister.

If we have been sexually promiscuous in our current marriage, we need to proceed with caution unless we have contracted a sexually transmitted disease that could affect our spouse or partner. If that is the case, our spouse or partner should know immediately about our sexual activity so they can seek medical care.

A fair number of marriages have been destroyed by disclosing details about extramarital affairs. While it appears noble to tell everything about an affair, we have seen such disclosures cause jealousy that destroys the relationship.

There are at least two options here that meet the rigorous honesty required by Step Nine. Many unfaithful wives and husbands have confessed their infidelity to a sponsor or counselor and changed their behavior without having the spouse involved. Others believe that telling everything to the spouse or partner is the best course. We leave the method of handling infidelity up to the Step worker; however, the key is honesty and a willingness to tell someone about the cheating followed up with a commitment to stop the behavior.

Many adult children owe money and have difficulty handling money. Some of us have absconded money or plunged ourselves so far into debt that we cannot possibly repay all that we have squandered, stolen, or manipulated out of people, employers, or relatives. It is not the purpose of Step Nine for you to live in poverty in a noble effort to pay off an impossible debt. However, we cannot use this as an excuse to avoid paying back reasonable amounts of money we have borrowed or accepted. If we can cut back on spending and make payments, we need to do so. We want to change our attitude about spending. Step Nine can help us live within our means and grow spiritually.

If the debt is so large to force bankruptcy or a similar situation, we need to know in our hearts that we would pay back such bills if we had the resources. We also change our behavior by avoiding building up more debt while we still have this large deficit in our lives. To say we would pay off a huge financial burden if we had the money and then continue to spend recklessly or charge up debt is dishonest. This behavior is contrary to the Step Nine amends process.

If you have stolen money or manipulated people for money, gifts, or other items, this must cease as well. To continue such behavior is a relapse of sorts and a sure disconnection from God. To steal or manipulate for money is self-harming behavior in the long run since it shuts down our connection to the Divine.

If we have committed a crime that has been undetected, we need to visit with our sponsor or get legal advice about how to proceed. We need to be willing to go to the authorities and turn ourselves in if that is the course that we choose to take.

There is always a way to make an amends if we are sincere and patient. We can make amends to a deceased person by writing a letter and reading it aloud. If we are unable to locate someone on our amends list, we wait for God's timing to show us how to make the amends. We are astonished how our program works when we become willing and leave the results to the Divine Creator. One of the keys to the amends process involves our attitude and our willingness to make amends when the opportunity presents itself.

## Sexual Compulsivity

Many adult children have struggled with sexual compulsivity that has brought great sorrow and a hellish isolation from society. However, the isolation does not stop here. Sexual compulsivity separates the adult child within. The sexually compulsive self is at odds with the True Self, and this serves as a battleground of compulsion versus doing the right thing. In this person, you have the self divided against the self. This conflict is common among all adult children but is highlighted by sexual compulsivity. Sex addicts live in a state of toxic shame fueled by despair. They live and breathe and walk in hell each day. They are driven by compulsions and obsessive thinking that over powers their rational mind. These adult children are deeply hurt individuals, who can get better if they can find absolute honesty and hang on while God acts.

When an adult child progresses into sexual addiction, they become two people. They can be hard-working and creative people on the job and an obsessive sex addict when they are cruising restrooms, parking lots, or bars looking for sex "dope." We are not moralizing on sexual preference here. We are talking about selfish, predatory adult children, who place themselves and others in danger with unsafe or illegal sex. This behavior can occur by gay or straight adult children. Sex addiction does not respect sexual preference. We cannot rule out innocents being harmed by a perpetrating adult child as well.

After acting out sexually, many of these adult children reel in horror with what they have done; however, they return to the same acting out behavior or worse unless help is sought and sought earnestly. These adult children live out a cycle of work, ritualistic thinking, acting out, and remorse. Then the cycle begins again. Some adult children will spend the rest of their lives in prison for a sex crime they felt powerless to avoid.

Most, if not all, sexually addicted adult children were victims of sexual abuse as children. We are not making excuses for their wrongful acts as adults. But they were once children without a choice. They are whole but fragmented just like the next adult child seeking help. Adults with this kind of compulsivity are members of the adult child family. ACA is their program.

If we have been a sexual predator or sexually compulsive, we must know in our hearts that we were wrong. We cannot minimize our behavior. There are people we can never approach in making amends by the very nature of our acting out with them. Some of us have victims that we cannot approach for legal reasons. God understands what we have done and what we are facing. For support, we talk with our sponsor or a trusted friend and take our forgiveness needs to a Higher Power. We pray and pray hard for forgiveness and the ability to change.

Some of us have progressed to disturbing levels with pornography, multiple partners, dominance, bestiality, compulsive masturbation, and forms of sexual abuse. But we can change. We were not born this way. We are still children of God no matter what we have done. We must remember that God loves us always. This is a matter of grace for adult children facing this kind of agony.

Our experience shows that these adult children typically have good intentions and want to change. They need God's grace and professional help to deal with the sexual compulsion. We must remember that God's grace is limitless for those who truly want to change. The Higher Power is there whether we have failed one time or 1,000 times. Always we are loved by God as we understand God. This is difficult for an adult child raised in a punishing or judgmental home to understand. We think we have limited chances or only one chance. After acting out we want to be punished, but a loving God waits for the right moment of surrender. We must surely try and surely be willing. A Higher Power loves us the same whether we have failed or succeeded. A loving God never abandons an adult child truly wanting change and making an effort.

Surely we need a miracle if we are facing this in our lives. Adult children in this category have had such miracles when they sought God with their heart's desire. Certainly, meeting attendance, prayer, and association with other recovering adult children are important to relieve this compulsion. We pray and pray unceasingly in this situation.

## STEP NINE SPIRITUAL PRINCIPLES:

### Forgiveness and Courage

# STEP TEN

*Continued to take personal inventory and when we were wrong, promptly admitted it.*

## Step Ten Helped Him Find Boundaries

*Step Ten taught me more about boundaries than I could imagine. When I first came into the program, I would apologize to everyone and everything at the drop of a hat. One time, I had judgmental thoughts about someone. I began talking about him behind his back. Due to the program I felt guilty, but I was not prepared to take appropriate action on my healthy guilt. In my confused thinking of the Steps, I called this person out of the blue and made amends. It was awkward because he had no idea what I had been doing behind his back. I felt embarrassed as I talked. I realized I crossed someone's boundary even though I meant well. I tried to work the program without a sponsor and it backfired.*

*With the help of Step Ten and my sponsor, I learned that I don't have to tell everyone what I am thinking all the time to be honest. I can inventory my thoughts and actions at the end of the day and call my sponsor if anything is lingering or troublesome. I have learned that thoughts are just thoughts and not necessarily actions I will take. That was a huge relief for me to know. After reviewing my day, I make amends immediately if I have wronged someone. I understand boundaries. I got one.*

## Step Ten Pays Big Dividends

*Learning to promptly admit when I'm wrong has paid big dividends for me in peace of mind. Learning that the response from others is almost always positive has also made it easier. When I admit I am wrong quickly, I prevent possible grudges from building up. I don't have to expend huge amounts of energy blaming, rationalizing, and covering up. I don't get bogged down with guilt or shame. Being able to admit that I'm wrong when I am wrong makes me feel free. I am very grateful for this wonderful sense of freedom.*

## He Is Doing Things Right As Well

*Step Ten taught me a lot about self-acceptance. It also taught me to stop being so hard on myself. I was hypervigilant in looking for ways to beat myself up or always make myself wrong. By inventorying my behavior regularly, I could see where I was doing a lot of things right. I began to inventory those things as well. In fact, my Tenth Step includes what I do right. I need that. It's a great balance.*

## Keeping Step Ten Simple

*I keep Step Ten simple. It does not have to be a big ordeal at the end of the day. I have a few simple questions that I ask myself at bed time. Was I judgmental today? Did I criticize another or myself today? Am I keeping something to myself I should talk about? Am I loving myself and being good to myself? Did I see how similar I am to others today?*

*I answer these questions and make amends if an amends is necessary. I keep Step Ten simple. I have received immense spiritual rewards from it. I am more honest and I feel like I can talk about my feelings and behaviors so they don't get bottled up. I am so grateful for ACA.*

## Every Night I Review My Day

*Each night before I go to sleep I read. I also take an inventory of what I have done during the day. When I pray, I plan how I will behave tomorrow.*

## Step Ten Summary

Step Ten is where we continue to inventory our behavior and thinking. With this Step we continue to let go of control and expose our denial about the effects of being raised in a dysfunctional home. We learn to take a balanced view of our behavior, avoiding the tendency to take too much responsibility for the actions of others. At the same time, we also curb our tendency to blame others when we are obviously wrong, yet are too afraid or ashamed to admit it. In these cases, we keep it simple. There is no need for long analyses of our behavior. We know that we come from wounded childhoods and we are addressing that in the Steps. We don't have to cast every amends or apology in the light of how we were raised or how we reacted before recovery. We know what the issues are for us. We make an amends with briefness in mind but with a sincere desire to change. Keeping it simple is the best course in some matters. Other amends might require background information about our past and a longer explanation. We will discern those situations as they arise.

Step Ten helps us apply what we are learning in meetings and to gauge our daily progress. In Step Ten, we are making a statement to hang onto the hard-won changes we are employing in our lives. We are living with more honesty and affirmation of ourselves. We realize we don't have to act perfect or flawless to be loved or accepted. We can make errors and laugh at ourselves without feeling shame. We are less fearful of people and their opinions of us.

We are trying out new ways of thinking and acting, but we must be diligent if we are to follow through with our recovery process. We will not change overnight, and the tendency to pick up old habits is tempting at times. ACA is not an easy program to work, but the rewards are great for those who try with sincerity.

Step Ten helps us polish the spiritual principles we are learning and using in our daily lives. To remain spiritually fit, we must continue to attend meetings, share our feelings, and help others. By helping others on their path of recovery, we help ourselves and learn to break our isolation. We get out of ourselves and contribute to the well-being of our ACA support group. With Step Ten, our personal and spiritual lives improve gradually.

Step Ten calls us to inventory our use of the ACA program to improve our marriages, jobs, and choices. We must practice the ACA program in the home and in our jobs if we are to be true to ourselves. The home or office is not an easy place to practice the principles of ACA, but we must. We do not preach about ACA or invade boundaries with our program. Yet we stand ready to apply the principles of honesty, humility, and forgiveness outside ACA meetings as well as within the meetings. We also ask for what we need and keep our word. This is not easy, but neither was living with our addictiveness. It took effort to support addictive choices. Practicing spiritual principles and inventorying our lives takes effort as well, but this is the labor of self-love.

We have more courage and inner strength than we think. It is essential that we practice ACA in every area of our lives to continue to grow emotionally and spiritually. We cannot let another person's behavior divert us from our program or give us cause to wander and live unfocused lives.

We learn to spot red flags, which once served as excuses to run from our problems. With Step Ten, we learn to recognize the cues that lead to fantasizing or dissociation. Many adult children use fantasy, daydreaming and "splitting off" to avoid being in the moment. We also learn to recognize when we are obsessing on another person or activity to avoid our feelings or staying in the moment. With Step Ten, and with help from our sponsor or counselor, we can disrupt a fantasy or dissociation episode. When these dissociative moments happen, we relax and think about what might have happened leading up to the moment. Sometimes the triggering activity occurred days before or hours before. We stop and breathe and get in touch with what is happening. We give our program a chance to work and to meet this challenge. We can make it. We can do this. We can survive our feelings and memories and heal.

We often cannot avoid triggers, but we can change the way we deal with them. We stop dealing with them in isolation. We have help now. We are not alone. We can talk to another person about our fears and thoughts regardless of what they are.

A daily or weekly inventory is different than the hypervigilance we have practiced before recovery. In our Step Ten inventory we judge ourselves less harshly because we know we are human and will make mistakes. We know we can talk about our feelings and our missteps without being judged when we share in ACA meetings. We have shaken hands with our critical inner parent. We are beginning to listen to the Actual Parent, whom many of us choose to call God.

There are two suggestions for a daily or weekly inventory: Keep it simple, and look at what you are doing right as well as reviewing your shortcomings. Look at what your ACA group is doing right. This is critical in reparenting ourselves with gentleness and patience. When we discover we have harmed someone with our behavior, we promptly admit it and move on. If we have apologized repeatedly in the past, we need to stop apologizing and change our behavior. During these times, we avoid condemning ourselves for making mistakes or acting in a manner that might offend or harm another. We are not perfect and never will be. We are involved in a fellowship of people trying to learn to live decent lives while also addressing troublesome behaviors. ACA is a fellowship of some of the most abused and fractured people in the world; however, we accept each other and focus on helping one another. We give each other support as we try to repair our lives. We do not have any place else to go. We must stick together and love one another and help one another while realizing there will be bumps. We are not complaining about our station in life. We are facing it and taking responsibility for it in Step Ten and the rest of the Steps. What we are doing is not easy, but we accept where we are individually and as a fellowship. We can make a commitment to live life by spiritual principles and to be fair to others and ourselves.

## One Day At a Time

Step Ten reminds us to focus on the present and live in the moment. We live one day at a time in ACA. By living one day at a time, we are free to focus on ourselves and handle the challenges of life as they come. Step Ten helps us avoid feeling overwhelmed by staring too long at the past or obsessing on the future. One day at a time we make progress in our emotional, physical, and spiritual lives. Our past can be our greatest asset, but we remember to focus on the present. We begin to actively participate in our lives and in the lives of others seeking fulfilling relationships. As the Twelve Promises of ACA state, we learn how to have fun and play. We fear authority figures less, and we discover our real identities. We feel more connected to ourselves, and we believe that a God of our understanding is available to us. We are learning how to set boundaries and how to keep them. In relationships, we are learning to choose people who love themselves and can be responsible for themselves. Gradually and slowly we are releasing our dysfunctional behaviors with the help of our ACA group and a Higher Power. These are ACA's great promises, which are being fulfilled among us daily.

With a Step Ten inventory, we are learning that we have choices. When we arrived at ACA, many of us used control disguised as choice. In reality, we had no choice before working Step One or the remaining Steps of ACA. Before finding ACA, many of us had control usually followed by loss of control and self-blaming despair that left us confused and lost. Our denial locked us into believing we must reapply ourselves. Before recovery, we did try again—countless times—and we failed again. We repeated the same mistakes expecting different results. We blamed others for the results and failed to change our own behavior. We repeatedly picked people who could not love themselves and attempted to extract love from them. Some of us developed a compulsion so strong for another person that we could not easily break away from that person even when we were clearly involved in a relationship that duplicated the abuse of our neglectful homes. Many of us needed intervention to move on and focus on ourselves.

Real choice means that we give up control and trust our Higher Power to provide the love and help we need to live with flexibility. Real choice is a spiritual continuum beginning at denial and leading to self-honesty, humility, wisdom, and finally discernment. Step Ten is part of that continuum of spiritual discernment. When we inventory our motives and trust our Higher Power, answers seem to emerge. Solutions seem to appear. By practicing Step Ten and all the ACA Steps, we intuitively learn how to address problems which once baffled us. We learn to avoid being enmeshed in the unhealthy dependent problems of others. Gossip is less appealing because we don't have the need to become transfixed on the problems of others to avoid looking at ourselves. We trust ourselves to stand steady and to be patient. We recognize manipulation—our own and others'—more quickly and take a different path. We learn to inventory our motives before taking action. Sometimes we take no action which is the best action. These are the elements of choice and discernment found in Step Ten.

Step Ten is about using the new tools of recovery we have discovered in ACA. In addition to the Twelve Steps, the tools of recovery include attending ACA meetings regularly, getting a sponsor, and associating with recovering adult children. Other tools of recovery include sponsoring new members and getting involved in service work. We volunteer to share our recovery at prisons or the treatment setting. We answer the Intergroup helpline if we have an active Intergroup. We seek to become a trusted servant.

## Integration

Step Ten is where we can continue to integrate any left over character defects or survival skills into our emerging identity. As we learned in Step Seven, there will be residual defects and Laundry List survival traits that won't recede easily. This does not mean we have failed in previous Steps. Step Ten is where we can acknowledge and embrace these lingering but less useful traits. We use humility and consistent effort to integrate these aspects of our personality.

Some adult children describe integration as walking into a dark room, closing the door, and talking to each lingering trait. We visualize such traits as people-pleasing, addictive thinking, confusing love with pity, and judging ourselves harshly. In the darkness, we speak to these traits. We thank them and others for their protection in our lives. We ask them to retire or step back. Some we bid farewell, and some we integrate. We make peace with those parts of ourselves that kept us alive as kids but which now no longer serve a useful purpose. This exercise is called walking into the darkness to find the light. Coming out of the dark room, we stand in the light, knowing we have faced our most disturbing traits again and survived. Facing our "shadow" helps us live in the moment and feel hopeful about the future.

## What Does Integration of the Laundry List Look Like?

With this exercise we take a closer look at integration and what it means to transform the Laundry List traits into helpful tools of recovery.

In summary, ACA experience shows that the Laundry List traits are somewhat distinguished from character defects. We believe the traits are a normal response to being brought up in a dysfunctional family. While many of these traits are troublesome, we recognize them as survival tools that we are now willing to surrender. These 14 traits are the effects of family dysfunction mentioned in Step One of the Twelve Steps. That means the traits have their roots in Step One whereas character defects seem to emerge from the Fourth Step process and are addressed through removal in Steps Six and Seven.

The Laundry List traits have deeper roots and are addressed beginning in Step One and throughout the Twelve Steps. We believe these characteristics serve as the branches that create our character defects or ineffective behaviors. While we seek to remove defects of character, we focus on integrating the Laundry List traits. Integration means that we blend, fade or soften these traits, which served as our protectors in the past but which now must be laid down. With the help of our Higher Power, we transform these traits into useful tools for reparenting ourselves.

In this exercise, we offer examples of what integration looks like for a few of the Laundry List traits. Integration does not mean that we revert to relying upon these characteristics to avoid feeling or to control others. Relying upon the Laundry List traits in this manner equates to "emotional intoxication." This is an ACA relapse. A relapse always involves a return to dishonesty, fear, resentment and a sense of feeling lost. In relapse, we revert to one of our childhood roles.

With integration there is honesty, attendance at ACA meetings and a sincere desire to change even as we occasionally find ourselves using one of the traits in our relationships or daily living. If we are fearing authority figures or judging ourselves harshly, we recognize the trait and take steps to lay it down. This is a process that can take many attempts, but progress is possible. We must be sincere and committed to our ACA program for integration to work and to move toward emotional sobriety.

The following exercise offers an example of an integrated trait and a blank line for you to fill in your own example or experience.

### Trait 1—We became isolated and afraid of people and authority figures.

**Example of integrating Trait 1:** We couple our ability to spot authority figures with our recovery work thus far. By using the principles of the Twelve Steps, we begin to see authority figures such as an employer or policeman as someone to be respected rather than a potential abuser or perpetrator.

Your experience with integration of this trait _____

_____

_____

_____

_____

_____.

## Trait 2—We became approval seekers and lost our identity in the process.

**Example of integrating Trait 2:** To transform this trait, we integrate all that we have learned from the previous Steps about separating from our family. Through the Steps, we realize that the thoughts, feelings and actions of others are separate from our own. We are not responsible for the codependent feelings or thoughts of another person. By claiming our own identity, approval-seeking behavior becomes unappealing.

Your experience with integration of this trait _____

_____

_____

_____

_____

_____

_____

_____

_____

_____.

## Trait 3—We are frightened by angry people and any personal criticism.

**Example of integrating Trait 3:** By converting Trait 3, we realize that courage is not the absence of fear and that all criticism is not personal. If we are triggered into fear by an angry person, we use our program to trace that trigger to its origin. With our Higher Power's help, we find our triggers and disarm them. We reparent our fear with self-love and by talking about what we are feeling and thinking.

Your experience with integration of this trait _____

_____

_____

_____

_____

_____

_____

_____.

## Trait 4—We either become alcoholics, marry them or both, or find another compulsive personality such as a workaholic to fulfill our sick abandonment needs.

**Example of integrating Trait 4:** We use Trait 4 to expose our addiction to alcohol or other drugs. We also use it to see how we have selected people for relationships. We integrate this trait by becoming sober from alcohol and drugs and by becoming willing to steer away from drug users, workaholics and other addictive types who usually take without giving back to the relationship.

Your experience with integration of this trait _____

_____

_____

_____

_____

_____.

## Trait 5—We live life from the viewpoint of victims and are attracted by that weakness in our love and friendship relationships.

**Example of integrating Trait 5:** We integrate Trait 5 by realizing we can be a persecutor and rescuer in addition to being a victim. We recognize this as the triangle of the three selves—victim, rescuer and persecutor. We avoid using these roles in relationships and at work by relying upon our program. If we find ourselves engaged in one of these roles, we can talk with our sponsor, go to an ACA meeting or take a program action that steers us toward change.

Your experience with integration of this trait _____

_____

_____

_____

_____

_____.

Beginning with Trait 6, detail how each trait might be integrated into a useful tool of recovery. Integration can involve an attitude, changed behavior or an awareness of how we used one of the traits in the past and how we want to change.

**Trait 6—We have an overdeveloped sense of responsibility and it is easier for us to be concerned with others rather than ourselves; this enables us not to look too closely at our own faults, etc.**

Your experience with integration of this trait _____

_____

_____

_____

_____

_____

_____.

**Trait 7—We get guilt feelings when we stand up for ourselves instead of giving in to others.**

Your experience with integration of this trait _____

_____

_____

_____

_____

_____

_____.

**Trait 8—We became addicted to excitement.**

Your experience with integration of this trait _____

_____

_____

_____

_____

_____

_____.

## Trait 9—We confuse love and pity and tend to "love" people we can "pity" and "rescue."

Your experience with integration of this trait _____

_____

_____

_____

_____

_____

_____.

## Trait 10—We have "stuffed" our feelings from our traumatic childhoods and have lost the ability to feel or express our feelings because it hurts so much (Denial).

Your experience with integration of this trait _____

_____

_____

_____

_____

_____.

## Trait 11—We judge ourselves harshly and have a very low sense of self-esteem.

Your experience with integration of this trait _____

_____

_____

_____

_____

_____.

Trait 12—We are dependent personalities who are terrified of abandonment and will do anything to hold on to a relationship in order not to experience painful abandonment feelings, which we received from living with sick people who were never there emotionally for us.

Your experience with integration of this trait _____

_____

_____

_____

_____

_____

_____ .

Trait 13—Alcoholism is a family disease; and we became para-alcoholics and took on the characteristics of that disease even though we did not pick up the drink.

Your experience with integration of this trait _____

_____

_____

_____

_____

_____

_____

Trait 14—Para-alcoholics are reactors rather than actors.

Your experience with integration of this trait _____

_____

_____

_____

_____

_____ .

# Step Ten Guide

## Exercise 1—Personal Inventory

Here are a few Step Ten questions we ask ourselves daily or weekly. These questions help us live the ACA program in all areas of our lives. Step Ten keeps us mindful of our program.

- Am I isolating and not talking about what is really going on with me?

- Did I view anyone as an authority figure today and feel frightened or rebellious?

- Did I dissociate, fantasize, or become involved in self-harm today?

- Am I keeping secrets and feeling unique? Am I talking about my feelings?

- Am I being honest in my relationships or am I seeking approval over honesty?

- Am I acting "perfect" and obsessing over making mistakes?

- Do I overreact or isolate from others when I perceive that I have been criticized?

- Am I attending ACA meetings to nurture myself and to give back what was given to me?

- Have I acted helpful recently to manipulate others?

- Am I secretly angry at someone, but I am avoiding talking about it?

- Have I listened to my Inner Child or True Self today?

- Did I judge myself or someone else without mercy today?

- Am I listening to the Critical Parent or Loving Parent?

- Am I remembering that I can ask for help today and that I can call someone?

## Exercise 2—Choice Exercise

In Step Three we realized that our need or compulsion to control others is a major stumbling block in allowing a loving God or Divine Presence to work in our lives. In Step Ten, we revisit this troublesome survival trait. We are not saying that all control is bad. We must have some order in our lives or risk chaos; however, rigid control can mean death for some ACAs and their loving relationships. If we think about it, we know the difference between compulsive control and practical order in our lives. There is room for spontaneity and imagination in the latter.

With Step Ten, we also realize we have released more of our control, and we are learning the difference between control and discernment. Discernment comes from inside and is the breath of God guiding us to do the right thing. We know what to do in a given situation when our breathing matches God's breathing. In comparison, with control our breathing is often unnatural and short. There is constriction in the body. We feel driven and fixed without a sense of having real choices when we operate from rigid control. We speak without thinking, and we feel embarrassed. We then punish ourselves harshly and apologize to others a lot. We hold unpurged resentments.

With discernment, we refrain from saying something off color or acting impulsively on a given situation. Discernment means we know who we are. We trust ourselves at last. We can relax and be an actor in life rather than a reactor.

In the following exercise, create a continuum of choice ranging from denial to discernment. Place this simple continuum on your refrigerator or at your work station. Each day, pencil in where you think you are in having real choice in your life. Move the mark around throughout the day if necessary because we can change our level of control at any time. That is the beautiful nature of choice. We can have choice at any time and back away from rigid control. There are no waiting lines for choice. You are first in line always.

**Choice Continuum**

| Denial | Some Choice | Greater Choice | Discernment |

⸻⸻⸻⸻⸻⸻⸻⸻⸻⸻⟶

## Exercise 3—One Day at a Time Exercise

Step Ten reminds the recovering adult child to live in the moment to enjoy life's gifts and to feel connected to life. List the tools of recovery you are using to help you live in the moment.

_____

_____

_____

_____

_____

_____

_____.

## Exercise 4—Feelings And Journaling Exercise

We were introduced to the feelings exercises in Step Four. In ACA, we believe that feelings are one method by which we know ourselves and God as we understand God. Feelings expressed in the safeness of ACA give us a second chance to experience imagination, creativity, and love. We can also experience anger, frustration, and fear in healthy degrees. These once troublesome feelings—anger and fear—lose some of their power over us in ACA. We learn how to express them with the knowledge that they will pass. Experiencing fear and anger in ACA is different than when we were children and saw no end to such feelings or had to repress them. Feelings come and go. We survive them, and we grow emotionally and spiritually.

Because of the important nature of learning to identify how we feel and think, we are including the feelings exercise in Step Ten for regular use or practice. Many adult children are unsure of their feelings or cannot distinguish feelings. This exercise is a simple tool to help you get started identifying feelings and becoming more comfortable with using feelings words.

Talking about our feelings is a risk; however, this is a risk worth taking because the rewards are great. When we let others know about our feelings, we connect with people on a spiritual and equal level instead of a dependent and manipulative level.

Many adult children learn how to identify and distinguish between their emotions by practicing the feelings sentence. Select one of the feeling words and complete the sentence. Complete a sentence each day or every other day to become comfortable with talking about your feelings.

**Feelings practice sentence**

I feel _____ when _____
because _____ .

**Example:**

"I feel hopeful when I attend an ACA meeting because I know I am being heard."

| | | | | |
|---|---|---|---|---|
| loved | joyful | ashamed | humorous | irritated |
| angry | embarrassed | trusted | betrayed | pleased |
| satisfied | ambivalent | hopeful | inspired | loving |
| frustrated | disappointed | grief | accepted | excited |
| grateful | confident | humiliated | guilty | serene |
| rested | shame | abandoned | pleasure | safe |
| tenacious | thoughtful | playful | fascinated | enthralled |

## Exercise 5—Praise Exercise

We were also introduced to a praise exercise in Step Four. We include this exercise here to remind adult children to celebrate their good qualities as we also inventory our mistakes and missteps. We urge them to note what they do right or how they are thoughtful, caring, and unselfish. We are breaking out of our people-pleasing role and learning to affirm ourselves through self-love.

Following is a list of 25 assets, which will help balance positive and spiritual qualities for your Step Ten inventory. Circle at least 10 attributes. Include those you are unsure of or those you would like to have in your life. Because we operate from a praise deficit, we often do not realize the assets we have in our lives.

| | | | | |
|---|---|---|---|---|
| strong | compassionate | spontaneous | trustworthy | prompt |
| humorous | courteous | creative | tenacious | kind |
| sensitive | talented | loving | judicious | hard working |
| willing | honest | a listener | accepting | a friend |
| intelligent | organized | spiritual | modest | an ACA member |

After circling your assets, sit quietly and acknowledge each one by repeating:

"I am _____ (fill in the affirmation)."

## STEP TEN SPIRITUAL PRINCIPLES:

### Honesty and Discernment

# STEP ELEVEN

*Sought through prayer and meditation to improve our conscious contact with God, as we understand God, praying only for knowledge of God's will for us and the power to carry that out.*

## Meditation Brought Meaning to the Closing Prayer

*When I was introduced to meditation years ago, I was skeptical. I come from a religious affiliation in which meditation was not discussed much less an option for spiritual growth.*

*I was willing to do what the program asked. I tried it, but nothing seemed to happen for months. I would meditate and become drowsy or be distracted by a buzzing fly or a passing airplane. I continued because I wanted to get the emotional sobriety I heard about in meetings. I liked reading my meditation book, and I thought my daily meditation was relaxing but not too productive.*

*The first inkling I got that meditation was working occurred at the end of a meeting. It was during the closing prayer. Before I began meditation, I was usually distracted during the prayer. I would shift from foot to foot or keep my eyes open thinking about what I would do after the meeting. Typically, I never listened to the closing prayer.*

*I don't know which night it was, but it happened during the prayer. As I was standing in the circle after the meeting, I realized that I was motionless. I was present in the moment and listening to the prayer. I was relaxed and allowing the words to enter my mind. I felt at peace the moment I closed my eyes for the prayer. I later recognized this as the relaxed state from my meditation. However, the quickness of the calmness is what struck me. It came immediately as I stood with friends and closed my eyes. I was "in" my body and in the moment, which had not been possible as a child.*

*The next time I meditated I began with the closing prayer and again felt relaxed. I was making conscious contact with my Higher Power. I was in the moment and "in" my body. I once doubted the value of meditation, but I cannot live without it.*

## Meditation and Motives Lead to Solutions

*My meditation and styles have changed during the years, but I have always meditated and gotten great results. I began with simply sitting in a chair and taking slow, deep breaths with my eyes closed. This worked great for years. I could find peacefulness or make conscious contact with my God regularly. I even meditated on problems and relationships and found solutions. The answers or direction I got usually involved me looking at my motives and wants and needs. Meditation could lead me to a direct thought that produced a solution. Sometimes it would lead me to ask myself questions about my motives. A solution or answer would emerge, or I would talk to my sponsor and find a path to take. I feel more emotionally mature when I use prayer and meditation to live my life.*

## How I Keep a Conscious Contact

*I work a spiritual program. I go to God for all the tools and information I need. God, to me, is a higher level of consciousness. Everyday in prayer and meditation I go deep within myself to a quiet place where there's peace, love, light, hope, and joy. I honestly take my daily inventory, I release all my self-will, I turn over my will, and I ask God to lessen my nonfunctional character traits. I commit myself to correcting my previous mistakes. This gives me a conscious contact with my Higher Power.*

## How Do You Know If It Is God's Will?

*I have two channels to God: my Inner Child and my prayers. My Inner Child lets me know what she wants to do. When I pray to my Higher Power, I ask Him to let me know how I should proceed. I get God's answers by looking for opportunities that excite my Inner Child and by observing what happens when I use all my God-given talents.*

*My Inner Child gets very excited and animated when she has something to say to me. She's the one who feels the feelings, who is closest to God. She insists I stop and watch God's glory in a sunset, a flower bud, and a child chasing a butterfly. She stares in utter fascination and reverence at God's hand at work as an artist paints or a carpenter builds. She is magnetically drawn to the languages, customs, clothing, foods, and crafts of people from all ethnicities, races, countries, and classes. She is amazed at how a bee makes honey or how an engineer harnesses the power of a river. She is amazed at how a 10,000 pound jet lifts itself off the ground. She is connected to the great force that created the wonders all around me, and she touches the hand of God.*

## Step Eleven Summary

Step Eleven is where we travel often to find greater levels of maturity through prayer and meditation. Through meditation, we begin to visualize emotional sobriety. We find out what ACA recovery looks like. We begin to see that recovery is a noticeable freedom from the damaging affects of The Laundry List traits. We realize our Step work has brought some measure of healing from the trauma and neglect of our childhood. We intuitively rely on the Steps and ACA meetings to face every situation in our lives. We rely upon God as we understand God for sure footing. With emotional sobriety, reparenting ourselves becomes a reality in our lives. We love ourselves. The proof of emotional sobriety can be found in our relationships with others and with God, as we understand God. If our relationships are still controlling and without feelings or trust, we must reconsider the strength of our emotional sobriety. True emotional sobriety brings a connectedness to ourselves and to others. This connectedness in relationships is characterized by expressed feelings, trust, mutual respect, and an acknowledgment that a Higher Power is real. We realize we don't need to chase after others to soothe our childhood fear of abandonment. We begin to see that we can bring our True Selves to a relationship. We have something to offer that is different than unhealthy dependence. This is what ACA recovery looks like. It addresses our rupture from our primary relationship with our family. This is the relationship template that has colored every relationship going forward. A demonstration of ACA recovery and emotional sobriety must show that we have changed the pattern of our lives. We live with feelings, spirituality, and with our true identity.

Step Eleven is also where we further address our addiction to excitement. This is the eighth trait of The Laundry List. Through meditation we learn to quiet our minds and to relax. With meditative techniques, we let go of racing thoughts. We learn to be in the moment and to be present in our bodies. We learn that our thoughts can end. This was new to many of us who have been troubled by images and thoughts all of our lives. We learn that thoughts are born, live, and die. We can let troublesome thoughts die a natural death in meditation.

In Step Eleven, we take time out of the day to focus on our spiritual path. We connect with God through our True Self when we find stillness and listen for God's footstep. Our True Self knows God's call. The True Self knows the path that our Higher Power takes to the heart. It is the path of love.

Through Step Eleven, we find God's will and a personal power that we did not know existed. There is real power. We can have it if we make the effort and let our Higher Power lead the way.

Adult children approaching Step Eleven, arrive at the Step with varying attitudes. Some adult children approach meditation with skepticism or disinterest born from the newness of this suggested practice. Many of us were raised with suspicions about meditation or without information about its spiritual qualities. Some may think they can skip this Step or brush by it. Ignoring meditation is not wise if we are to get the greatest gifts of inner peace from ACA.

Some adult children may still be holding onto notions of a Higher Power having the traits of their parents. They tend to wonder if God is indifferent, punishing, or really there at all. Some adult children secretly believe that meditation is reserved for the clergy or for serious spiritual seekers. But aren't we all serious about finding relief and acceptance within ourselves? Is that not spiritual? Can only the clergy want freedom and conscious contact with God?

Some of us have attempted meditation half-heartedly and found it lacking. Others have used drugs to enhance the experience and found that lacking as well. In ACA, we do not need drugs to connect to a Higher Power or the Divine. We are whole. We have all the energy centers, spiritual gifts, and cosmic powers within us. We are spiritual beings opening ourselves up to the Higher Power of the heavens. Through prayer and meditation we find out that we are more than our abuse and neglect. We are miracles asking and praying for an opening. The seekers understand this path.

Each adult child has been a spiritual seeker from childhood without knowing it. We are now realizing it as recovering adult children. When we look back at our lives and see the choices we made leading to this path, we are often astonished. What once appeared as disconnected decisions that may have turned out poorly were actually choices that steered us to our "true north" in ACA.

Some of us took the long route, but the steering was there. The seeking was there. The intuition was there. We had a magnetic pull towards ACA that we are now realizing. We had an inner spiritual compass that cannot be denied any longer.

Our primary founder, Tony A., said: "The adult child personality is a personality which doubts God or cannot believe the unseen, but which seeks God who is unseen."[4] We cannot stop ourselves from seeking contact with a Higher Power. It is part of being an adult child, and we must accept this great fact. We are called to God and cannot resist. Acting distracted or indifferent no longer works. The True Parent calls.

Looking at our pathway leading to ACA, we realize the miracle of it. Many of us are adults who should not be here, but we are. Many of us should be dead, institutionalized, or lost at sea. Instead, we are here with our faces turned toward the Creator of Light. We are seekers, and we have always been. We cannot deny it, so why not seek further with one of God's favorite tools—meditation?

History tells us that all great spiritual seekers used meditation and prayer to gain the greatest quality time with a Higher Power or the Divine Presence. The Vedics and Buddhists of the East came this way and received great rewards. Through focused meditation, they were transported into a new dimension and received mystical and spiritual gifts hard to describe yet real. These bodhisattvas and yogis know that the cosmos is endless and blissful. They have experienced consciousness as a different dimension, yet they remain here helping others find it for themselves.

The West also had its share of meditators and seekers. Their dramatic transformations or glimpses of the eternal are well documented. With meditation and prayer, they have received power to focus their talents and to make a better world. These opportunities are open to ACA members as well through Step Eleven.

## Getting "In" Our Bodies

Many adult children are disconnected from their bodies without realizing it. Step Eleven is one method to reconnect with our bodies. Our disconnection can occur in the form of frozen feelings, which is also known as "psychic numbing." We become numb to feelings and sensations. This is a symptom of being disconnected from our True Self, which expresses itself in the body through feelings and imagination. That means our disconnection from our body represents a disconnection from our real identity.

Some of us have been so traumatized that we shut down our emotions and cut ourselves off from our bodies. While we still function in our jobs and relationships, we are not totally present in our own bodies. We look at others and wonder what it is like to feel "normal" because we are sure that we don't feel normal. In reality, we are not feeling much of anything. Wondering if we are normal or being confused about feelings are clues to being disconnected from our own body.

[4]Tony A conversation 2004

Another form of not being in the body involves dissociation or "leaving the body." Many sexual abuse victims describe leaving their bodies during the abuse. Part of the healing process for these adult children involves getting back into the body and reclaiming wholeness.

Many young boys and girls who have been cursed harshly, brow-beaten, cowed, and threatened undergo a similar separation from the body. They experience stuffed feelings, psychic numbing, and dissociation all together. They usually complicate the dissociation with drugs, sex, or another compulsive behavior. Once the addiction is addressed the numbing and dissociation must be addressed in ACA and usually with professional help.

We know of an adult child who sought help for his dysfunctional upbringing. He was sober and clean, but he sensed that something was not right. He compulsively acted out in other areas of his life, but he maintained his drug free lifestyle. His acting out caused him great shame. His issues of frozen feelings and dissociating from his body came up during an early counseling session. During the session, his therapist asked a simple question: "How does it feel to feel loved?"

The adult child struggled with an answer and tried to offer a definition of love; however the counselor gently interrupted and said: "No. I am not looking for a definition of love. I want to know what it feels like in your body to feel loved. When I feel loved, my breathing is easier, and there is a warmth in my face below the skin. I feel like smiling a lot."

The counselor repeated her question: "What does it feel like to feel loved?"

The adult child said he stared at her. He could not answer. He later realized he was 26 years old and could not recall feeling loved. He had never stopped to think about it until that day. He knew his parents had cared for him and provided food and shelter. They had said they loved him, but he could not remember feeling safe or loved as a child. His alcoholic father threatened the family and cursed his children.

This simple question about feeling loved raised the question of whether the adult child had truly been loved at all. He was so shut down emotionally that he could not recall the physical reaction—bodily reaction—of feeling loved. He recalled being an object of infatuation in a relationship, but that never seemed to last. He had never felt warmth in his face, and his breathing had not been made easier by the infatuation.

Becoming sober and clean improved his life, but it also allowed his original sense of feeling inferior and defective to emerge. In sobriety, he remained disconnected from his body and struggled with accepting love because of a deep sense of feeling flawed. He thought he could recognize love in others, but inwardly he resigned himself to believing he could never feel it. He had a definition of love from books and movies, but he did not feel loved. Outside observers saw a helpful man who held a job and had friends and a purpose in life. He was a stellar Twelve Step member who helped others. He could be counted on to help out his home group. After this counseling session, he said he understood what it meant when his counselor said: "You are not in your body. You are not feeling your feelings. You are up in your head."

Step Eleven is a point where adult children can get "in" their bodies and into the moment. By getting "in" our bodies we can then go out into the world and make our best contributions. This is important work and should be taken seriously. Taking the time to sit quietly and do simple meditative breathing and concentration is a proven way to accomplish this soul healing exercise. By returning to our bodies or becoming aware of our bodies, we find another piece of the puzzle to reconstruct our wholeness. We have all the parts within us, and we are finding them with God's help.

## God Within

In meditation, there are no hard and fast rules that we present here. Typically, a person who meditates finds a room or location free of noise and distraction. The person may sit in a chair with both feet on the floor. Some adult children sit on the floor in the cross-leg, yoga position.

The person usually begins a meditation by taking several deliberate and extended breaths. The breathing is important to slow down our thoughts and prepare us for seeking conscious contact with ourselves and God, as we understand God. As we breathe in deeply and slowly exhale, we listen to the air traveling in and going out of our lungs. This breathing is the language of the Higher Power for many of us. It is the signal to draw the Higher Power from within out. Many ACA members believe this is where the Higher Power dwells and has always dwelt—within. Meditation gives us a chance to find that out.

During meditation, some adult children close their eyes and concentrate on a simple prayer or meditative reading. Others meditate with their eyes open, concentrating on a focal point.

The straightforward purpose of Step Eleven is to improve our conscious contact with God, as we understand God. In meditation, we pray for knowledge of God's will and the power to carry that out.

Some adult children pray for wholeness during meditation, asking the Higher Power for clarity. We were introduced to wholeness in Step Three. In ACA we believe we are whole and have been fragmented by our upbringing. We have all the pieces within us for our spiritual awakening to occur. We are seeking God's will and the power to carry out the process of wholeness. We are asking God for what we need. We want wholeness and our miracle restored.

As we meditate, we let our thoughts come and go. We let them fade. We concentrate on our breathing, but we don't over concentrate. We breathe naturally and relax the tension in our bodies. At some point in the meditation, many adult children become very still inside. This is the point of being aware of our bodies and being "in" our bodies. It is also our initial contact with God, but there is more. There is much more if we meditate regularly.

During meditation our breathing is calm, and we feel rested. Our shoulders are relaxed, and our legs feel firmly grounded. We are connected to the earth. We realize we are fully in our bodies. We also feel full spiritually and emotionally. We feel loved by our True Parent. During this state of being, we can lose track of time because we have slipped the bounds of physics. We are physically sitting in a chair, but our conscious contact is with God. Some of us glimpse bliss and an ocean of acceptance, forgiveness, and self-love. There is another dimension. This is the God we went searching for without knowing it but knew at some point would be here. This is the Higher Power who formed ACA from the prayers of children and adult children across the world. This is the God who arrests shame.

If we believe we are not reaching a meditative state after many tries, we do not worry about it. We keep trying, knowing we will make it. There is no right or wrong way to meditate. God will not leave us behind. The Higher Power is within. It is our True Self. We cannot be abandoned or left behind.

Whatever meditative style we choose, the goal is to seek God's will and the power to carry that out. With continued meditation, we return to our everyday activities, feeling more emotionally sober. We feel more energy to get involved in life and to contribute in making a better world. By traveling inward in meditation, we find strength to go farther outward than we could have imagined.

As we greet co-workers or friends, we feel that we are changing inside. We begin to recognize a power inside we had not known before. We are less frightened of authority figures, and we see the strengths in people as well as their weaknesses. We are not easily stirred into frantic action when things don't go our way. We begin to back away from situations that once compelled us to argue without cause or do the bidding of another. We are less harsh on ourselves and our mistakes. We want to attend ACA meetings and help others with their journey.

In addition to meditation, Step Eleven also encourages prayer in our search for seeking God's will and the power to carry that out. In ACA, we examine our prayer life and our thought life. Our thought life is the place in our head once dominated with all the negative and minimizing messages from our childhood. This thought life was invisible to others, yet it was real to us because it contained the experiences and beliefs that drove our compulsions and unhealthy dependence. We became addicted to excitement or to our thoughts. While we appeared orderly in the public eye before arriving in ACA, we always had a "script" in our minds. No one else could see or hear the script, but we could hear it and we acted on it. We developed odd obsessions and compulsive behaviors based on this script or thought life. We sometimes felt powerless to change, but we now believe we have found a power to address our destructive thinking. With the help of a Higher Power, we work at freeing ourselves from obsessive and compulsive behaviors. The preceding Steps have gone far to modifying our thought life. We have changed the negative messages, and we are changing our behaviors—slowly and gradually.

Prayer and meditation will take us further. We pray to put into action the principles and concepts we are finding in ACA. We pray for strength and power to work the ACA program and to stay focused. We pray for God to enter our thought life and take out what blocks us from accepting ourselves. We pray to connect with our Inner Child.

While there are few rules on prayer, many ACAs believe prayer is reserved for the end of the day and usually practiced in the home or at a religious facility. We suggest that prayer can be done almost anywhere and any time. We are not confined to praying in one location or at any particular time. Like meditation, prayer has been used through the ages for worship, guidance, intervention, salvation, and to find comfort from aloneness. There is no standard length for a prayer, but some of the most powerful prayers have the fewest words. The Serenity Prayer comes to mind and represents a concentrated measure of serenity, humility, courage, wisdom, and spirituality in 25 words. It is a prayer that has anchored Twelve Step meetings and the development of Twelve Step fellowships for decades across the world. It is a proven prayer which causes anyone hearing it to pause. It has that kind of power.

Some ACA members recall prayers from childhood that served them well and brought comfort on some level. In recovery, they speak of how these prayers were little lights pointing the way to help. One adult child learned a short prayer as a third grader and now sees that prayer as a plea for clarity to decipher the contradictory messages of her severely enmeshed home. She now recognizes ACA wisdom in the prayer.

*"God,*
*When I look let me truly see.*
*When I listen let me truly hear."*

When she found the prayer as a 9-year-old, it resonated with her and brought a measure of comfort in her young life. When she hit bottom at age 33, the prayer rose in her consciousness like an old friend. She believes her prayer for clarity and understanding led her to ACA and guides her in the program.

The simple prayer is an example of seeking and listening, which is the heart of ACA's Eleventh Step. Many ACA members describe prayer as seeking God's guidance and meditation as listening for it. We pray and listen in Step Eleven.

There are no limits on prayer length. Longer prayers have their purpose and serve the seekers well.

With prayer and meditation we find our true inner power. This is the inner strength that we have always had but used limitedly. God has been holding onto it until we were ready to claim it in Step Eleven. This is the power which changes our life and our course of thinking and behaving. This is the power which keeps us going when we lapse into judging ourselves or feel discouraged about making progress in ACA. This is the power that we find when we ask humbly to be used for the greater good of the world.

We feel more alive than ever before with Step Eleven. We are more imaginative and hopeful. A return to prayer and creativity are two of the gifts of Step Eleven in addition to making conscious contact with the God within.

While we have spoken much of God and God's guidance, ACA is not a religious program nor does it represent any religious belief. However, the disease of family dysfunction is a cunning, baffling, and powerful disease. It requires a spiritual solution in addition to our practical efforts to work the Twelve Steps and share our stories in meetings. We believe the disease of family dysfunction is a spiritual dilemma. We need a connection to the God of our understanding for our best hope.

## Grief Work Revisited: Connecting With Our Inner Child

In Step Eleven, we will revisit grief work. We recommend guided meditation for this type of grief work. In this exercise, you will travel back into your childhood to connect with your child within. While grief can stir the emotions, it is not always sad or unpleasant. Many times we recognize the measure of our loss and that is enough. At other times there are tears and a sense of lament and then we feel release. With grief, we are properly labeling a loss or a key event in our childhood. For the best results, we suggest that you tape record the script below and play it back to serve as a guided meditation.

## Meditation Exercise

Read and record the script here in your voice, or have a friend record it on tape or a CD. When you have recorded the script, play it back to begin the guided meditation.

### (Begin recording here)

*To begin the guided meditation, find a quiet and comfortable room without distraction. You may sit in a chair or sit on the floor. An outdoor location is acceptable as well. Sit upright but be comfortable. Begin the exercise by closing your eyes and taking a deep breath and releasing it slowly.*

*As you take four or five slow breaths, let any thoughts you might have fade away. Be aware of being present in your body. If your mind is wandering, gently focus on yourself and be present in the moment and in your body. Continue breathing naturally.*

*(Let 10 to 20 seconds of the tape lapse here without talking. This will create silence for you to relax and breathe several times before the script continues. Begin recording the script again after the silent delay.)*

*Imagine that you are sitting on a warm beach. The weather is pleasant and not too hot. The beach is secluded but safe. You can feel the warm sand beneath your feet as you stand up and look out upon a calm, blue ocean. White sea gulls are diving for fish and the smell of seawater is refreshing. You are wearing a T-shirt, loose trousers, and a floppy hat to block the sun.*

*In front of you, near the shoreline, you see an image of yourself when you were six or eight years old. Your Inner Child is bent at the waist picking up starfish and sea shells. The child notices you and waves you over. You walk up to the child and the child reaches out and places a starfish in one of your hands. You smile and feel the bristles of the tiny starfish tickling you. Your Inner Child smiles and squints to block the friendly sun.*

*The child reaches out and grips your hand. The child's skin has been warmed by sun rays. You both begin walking along the beach. You notice the child's soft hair and sensitive touch as you walk. The child trusts you and giggles softly each time a wave washes up the shore almost touching your feet.*

*You walk for many moments, chatting softly, but paying attention to the child's innocence and imagination. You want to protect the child.*

*You notice two people ahead, and they seem familiar so you keep walking toward them. Your Inner Child squeezes your hand and moves slightly behind you as you move closer to the couple. The child becomes shy, pushing into your leg from behind. You keep walking.*

*You recognize the couple before you reach them. They are your parents, waiting for you to walk up. They grin at you and your Inner Child. They ask if they can walk with the child.*

*You feel your stomach tighten, and you look down at your Inner Child to find the child pressed into your legs from the back. The child won't look at you and won't let go of your hand.*

*You smile at your parents but ask them to wait for another day to walk the child. You and your Inner Child walk up the beach away from your parents and sit down. The child looks over a shoulder, climbs into your lap, and sits down. You hold your Inner Child. You both watch your parents walk away.*

*The sun is lower now but still warm. Your Inner Child naps. You are safe. Your Inner Child is safe. You are going to make it. You know what you are doing. You can trust yourself to take care of your Inner Child. You can trust yourself to love.*

*Continue to meditate and hold your Inner Child. When you are ready to stop, gently wake the child, walk the child to your cottage, and tuck it into bed. After putting the child to bed, back out of the room, counting slowly backward from ten. Open your eyes.*

**(Stop recording)**

The recording is complete. You now have a recording to transport you on a guided meditation to the child within. The exercise represents the loss or grief of our childhoods. Our families were not always safe or nurturing. This is loss. The exercise also represents our reparenting choice today. We can take care of ourselves and our Inner Child.

You can use this exercise to revisit your childhood. Upon occasion you can ask the Inner Child how the child feels or what the child is experiencing. Listen and then journal or write about what you hear from the child.

## Creativity Exercise: Wallet Card

Create your own Eleventh Step prayer and place it on a wallet card to carry to work or to meetings. Keep it simple, but create a prayer that is specific to you and your relationship with the Divine, Higher Power, or God. This is your own prayer.

## STEP ELEVEN SPIRITUAL PRINCIPLES:

### Seeking and Listening

# STEP TWELVE

*Having had a spiritual awakening as the result of these Steps, we tried to carry this message to others who still suffer, and to practice these principles in all our affairs.*

## Our Story Is Our Greatest Asset

*I remember how skeptical I felt when someone said my abusive upbringing would be my most valued asset. I did not see how my experience could help anyone, but I also did not know about ACA either. In ACA, I am not a victim. I have come to believe that my childhood places me in a position to help others when no one else can. I don't live in the past, but I can help myself by helping others. I know this is true because I have been helped by listening to others share about their lives in meetings. It creates identity and unity. I share my ACA story for identity and to help others.*

*I have seen the results of adult children helping adult children in prison meetings and in treatment as well as regular meetings. I don't have anything against doctors or psychiatrists but sometimes they cannot help. They often don't understand that the adult child needs contact with other recovering ACAs and meetings instead of setting goals and merely changing behavior. Goals and changed behavior are important, but you can't beat the help that comes from relating to others in an ACA meeting. You can see a new person's eyes change when The Laundry List (Problem) is read. This is powerful stuff.*

## Apply The Wisdom And Share It

*The Twelfth Step means I have come so far from the original pain that brought me into the program. I have awareness, strength, and the power to apply this program in every area of my life, not just a specific compulsion or addiction. I can be of service to others, both within and outside the program. I volunteer my time by listening and being supportive. I strive to be an example of a peaceful and happy way of living.*

*As it says in The Solution, "We progress from hurting to healing to helping." Thank God.*

## I Give It Away To Keep It

*There's a piece of table literature we have, which groups the Twelve Steps into stages. The stages are listed as: Steps One through Three as "Giving Up," Steps Four and Five as "Fessing Up," Steps Six through Nine as "Cleaning Up", and Steps Ten through Twelve as "Stepping Up."*

*I see Step Twelve as the Step where I begin taking responsibility for this program by sponsoring others, doing service, and serving on outreach committees, and giving talks when asked.*

*This is the program that saved my life. I owe this program and the people in it my life, my success, my money, and my joy. Because of my love for ACA, I have delivered meeting directories to every library, therapist's office, Twelve Step recovery center, college and university health facility, counseling office, psychology department, business and government personnel office, and church in my city.*

*The people in my family of origin now communicate and show their love and respect for me. I know others who feel the way I do; they're all giving service in ACA. They're all serving on service boards, putting on special events, sponsoring others, or doing ACA outreach. It goes beyond gratitude. It's the essence of the program.*

## Keep Coming Back

*The program does not end with Step Twelve. I work the Steps to maintain my emotional sobriety and to stay out of unhealthy situations. I don't have to be hypervigilant, but I stay alert to my people-pleasing and rescuing ways. After 20 years, I still attend meetings for myself and to give back what was given to me freely. That's what I heard early on: "Keep coming back no matter what." I did, and I found a new way of life. I continue to get what I need from the meetings and by sponsoring others and being sponsored. I can't tell you how many times I have gone to a meeting and the topic was about a situation or incident in my life. This program continues to amaze me.*

## When It Counted, My Spiritual Awakening Was There

*I remember the first time I read Step Twelve. I was attracted to carrying the message and practicing ACA principles, but I was skeptical of my chances of having a spiritual awakening. Looking back, I can see how I decided that spiritual experiences were for other people. Doing the best I could with my limited faith, I worked all of the Twelve Steps, but I focused on carrying the message in Step Twelve. I mostly ignored talk of spiritual matters. I was willing to settle for earnest Step work, giving service, and helping others. I hoped this would be enough to get me through life. With this approach, my life improved dramatically. I finished college and started a career. I remained active in meetings and sponsoring others. I got honest about my people-pleasing and controlling ways. I could honestly share in meetings about turning my will and life over to the care of God, but I still wondered if I was truly letting go. I hoped God was hearing my prayers, but I was unsure. Looking back, I realize I was bringing my Laundry List "self" to Step Twelve. I was trying to have an intellectual relationship with a Higher Power without actually letting go. This was my pathway to a spiritual awakening that has been dramatic and unanticipated.*

*I never thought my decision to enter a relationship that turned abusive would lead me to the part of Step Twelve I had been ignoring, but it did. This relationship almost drove me to insanity with its pain and abandonment. I was losing my soul, and I knew it. I was faced with throwing away ACA or breaking free. When I made my decision to leave, I faced panic, obsession, and fear at levels that I never imagined possible. I prayed night and day and stayed close to my sponsor and meetings. For weeks it was touch and go, but I turned the corner. I faced my terror of abandonment from childhood. I knew I could survive my feelings. I continued to pray and stay close to my Higher Power. A few months later my spiritual experience came in a dramatic vision and with synchronicities that prove to me that God is there, and God is loving. This happened in my 20th year of recovery. I was not looking for it, but it happened. I have had a spiritual awakening as the result of facing my fear of abandonment.*

## Step Twelve Summary

In Step Twelve we claim our program of recovery for ourselves by putting into practice the spiritual principles we have used and continue to use to reparent ourselves. The principles include surrender, hope, honesty, self-forgiveness, humility, and many more from the Twelve Steps.

Step Twelve calls ACA members to carry the message to other suffering adult children in addition to practicing these principles in all our affairs. We can also expect a spiritual awakening as promised in Step Twelve.

There is possibly no greater act of reparenting ourselves than carrying the message of hope to another suffering adult child yet to know of a new way of life. By doing so, we grow emotionally and spiritually. We learn to love ourselves more surely.

Through reparenting, we learn to use spiritual principles in our daily lives to replace old ways of thinking and reacting. The Solution states: "By gradually releasing the burden of unexpressed grief, we slowly move out of the past. We learn to reparent ourselves with gentleness, humor, love, and respect."

In carrying the ACA message of hope to another, we use gentleness, humor, love, and respect in the same manner that we do these things for ourselves. There are other points to consider when carrying the ACA message to those who still suffer, but we begin with this attitude.

We progress from hurting to helping. We awaken to a sense of wholeness we never knew was possible. By working the ACA Steps, we learn that our past can be one of our most important assets in our effort to help others and ourselves. We don't live in the past, but we can help another adult child when no one else can or when sincere attempts by professionals have failed. We use our stories to build identity with the person we are sponsoring or carrying the message to in treatment or elsewhere. Adult children new to the program can be skeptical without showing it. Many are experts at disbelief. They can only be reached by someone who can share about his own family dysfunction in terms that the new person understands. When we talk of being a people-pleaser or confusing love with pity, we see the connection we make with the person seeking help. Before long, the person usually opens up and begins relating similar experiences. That is the power of our story when we tell it with humility and hope for helping others.

The Twelfth Step is our stage where we become actors instead of reactors without solutions. Acting from a foundation of self-love and respect, we offer our spiritual solutions to adult children seeking a better way of life. We also help ourselves.

## God Exists

One of the results of a spiritual awakening involves the understanding that God is real. With a spiritual awakening, we move from theories about God to the belief that a Higher Power is accessible and hears our prayers. We know that a loving God or a Spirit of the Universe exists. We have come to believe that God, as we understand God, is the Actual Parent.

Many of us approached Step Twelve realizing there is a general standard for a spiritual awakening. The AA Big Book outlines two types of spiritual awakenings, yet there are many others across cultures and across continents. In AA, there is the dramatic spiritual awakening or "bright light" experience. AA cofounder Bill Wilson had such an experience in 1934 as he faced near insanity brought on by an alcoholic binge.[†] This experience is not the norm, but it does occur. The dramatic experience can bring about a profound change in attitude and belief in a Higher Power. There is also a spiritual awakening of the "educational variety." This gradual awakening emerges as the person comes to a greater understanding of a Higher Power through Step work, meditation, prayer, and helping others find ACA. A gradual spiritual awakening holds just as much meaning and brings just as much lasting serenity as a dramatic awakening can bring.

ACA members have experienced these types of awakenings. Our experience reveals a third type as well. This third awakening has features of the dramatic awakening and educational variety combined. This "dramatic educational" awakening can involve profound visions and indisputable evidence that God is among us. We know a freedom from dependent thinking and actions that we have not known before. We realize that we are loved and can love others.

Occasionally, the person having the dramatic educational awakening is not sure what has happened. He must educate himself about the event.[†] We avoid analyzing the experience or over-thinking it, but we do seek information from a reputable source about our spiritual vision or episode.

Education alone is not enough to gain the greatest benefit from our spiritual experience. We also learn that spiritual experiences have greater meaning when matched with a dedication to work the ACA program. Spiritual experiences can be thrilling and consciousness expanding. They become a sustained spiritual awakening through Step work and by relating with the Inner Child. This is the True Self and a conduit to the God within.

With a spiritual experience, we usually realize that we are transformed in some manner. We know something has changed inside of us even though we do not yet fully understand it. For some of us, our spiritual focus seems sharper. We know a peace that we could not imagine previously. We can still have moments of being affected by life, but these moments seem milder and are handled more quickly. We know there is something greater than ourselves at work in the universe. We let go and let God work in these matters with greater ease. For others, there may be an intuitiveness not previously known. There can be a new creativity or energy that flows freely.

The dramatic element of this awakening can come at any time, yet it tends to come when the adult child is faced with a crisis of some sort. Intense emotional pain or an extreme sense of hopelessness can be the gateway to a dramatic spiritual experience. The intensive desperation usually lasts for several hours or several days. This gift of desperation can set the stage for a dramatic spiritual experience if we are humble enough to ask our Higher Power for help. During these moments, this acute feeling of hopelessness represents an abandonment crisis. This is our childhood terror of abandonment welling up in our adult lives. This sense of fear and pending doom reaches back to our deepest fears of being alone. Some of us have dealt with this creature in previous Steps and found relief. For others, a final showdown is necessary to face our fear of abandonment once and for all. If we are willing and sincere, we learn we can survive our feelings and our worst fear. To get through, we pray often, and we pray hard. We call our sponsor, go to meetings, and talk about how we feel. Eventually, we release our terror of abandonment and embrace our Higher Power. We may experience significant dreams or unexplainable events during these times. We come out of this experience knowing we are changed. We feel the difference in our body and our mind.

For many of us, our spiritual awakening began in Step One when we realized that we were not alone or insane with the thoughts we had. We attended our first meeting, believing we were unique or that our family was the only family of its breed or pattern. What an amazing sense of relief washed over us as we heard The Laundry List (Problem) read. The traits of an adult child seemed to crack decades of hardened denial that had built up in our heart and soul. Many of us wept at hearing the traits of an adult child being read. Our awakening at our first meeting continued as we listened to adult children share their experiences as children and adults. As they talked we heard clarity, hope, and the ACA solution. We also heard honesty, openmindedness, and willingness. This is "HOW" the program works. By the end of the meeting, we were changed. We could not be the same again after hearing the message of recovery. There would be tough days ahead, but we were subtly different after that first meeting.

Others experienced an awakening in writing a Fourth Step and telling their story in Step Five. With these Steps, we finally got to see the patterns of our family and to finally talk about what matters in our lives. Many of us trusted ourselves and another person for the first time in Step Five. We bravely broke the family rule of secrecy by telling our story to another person. Who would have thought that talking, trusting, and feeling would equal a spiritual experience, but it does for adult children. We felt this new spirituality in our breathing and in the sense that we could face life on life's terms. Many of us felt a stronger connection to a Higher Power after Step Five.

There are many more examples of spiritual experiences and awakenings from the Twelve Steps. They all add up to the spiritual awakening we are seeking in ACA. Such spiritual awakenings are necessary for the long haul. We need a spiritual awakening, which creates a personality change that breaks the grip of family dysfunction on the soul. Only God, as we understand God, can bring about this change. Without this personality change, we can be subject to setbacks into people-pleasing, judging ourselves harshly, or remaining in abusive relationships. The preceding Steps made us aware of these survival traits, but in Step Twelve they become unbearable with our newfound awareness. The knowledge we gain in Step Twelve forces us to take action if we feel ourselves drifting into unhealthy behavior.

While spiritual awakenings can take different avenues to emerge, most awakenings tend to have some common characteristics. In addition to knowing that a Loving God exists, a spiritual awakening typically brings an end to the aching sense of being different and alone. Shame, abandonment, and control have been dealt with as well. If they resurface, they are handled in a more efficient manner once we become spiritually awake.

A spiritual awakening simplifies our lives. We intuitively know what we need and what we can live without. We are no longer reacting to people, places, and things. We live and let live.

Spiritual awakenings, regardless of the variety, do not signal an end to personal growth. The awakening is the beginning of new growth for many. We are transformed, but we still can have behavioral and relationship challenges ahead; however, there is new energy and creativity to help us grow. There is the effortless effort that opens up for many of us. By serving others, we tap into an outflow of love and light that attracts others. We give away what was given to us. We know how to use the spiritual principles of the Twelve Steps. We want to mentor that experience for others.

## Avoiding a Spiritual Bypass

While some spiritual experiences are miraculous, breathtaking, and bring a sense of awe, they do not equal recovery by themselves. ACA members have had spiritual experiences that bring dramatic visions and powerful dreams. In some instances, the experience transports the person to another dimension of timelessness and pure love. The body ceases to exist in this place of higher consciousness and bliss. Spiritual experiences of this nature help us to confirm our belief in a Divine Creator, but the experience does not exempt us from doing the work of recovery. We must still work all of the Twelve Steps to address the effects of growing up in an unhealthy family. We must attend ACA meetings and give back what was given to us. We must be willing to give service and to help out at our ACA support group. We can know that we have experienced something dramatic and otherworldly while we keep our feet on the ground and live one day at a time.

ACA members who focus primarily on seeking a spiritual awakening without working on the effects of family dysfunction are often involved in a spiritual bypass.[†] A spiritual bypass means that the person is attempting to avoid the pain that can come with working through the trauma and neglect from childhood. In some cases, the person attempts to jump ahead in the recovery process without going through the entire process. This path invariably fails or leads to dissatisfying results. If one does succeed in having a spiritual experience, but avoids program work, the person can still remain mired in addictiveness or problematic relationships. The spiritual experience may bring some forms of enlightenment; however, the person can cling to old ways of living without embracing ACA recovery. Through arrogance and fear, the person appears to work a program that has little resemblance to the ACA program. At the same time, compulsions and addictiveness continue. A spiritual experience without grounded program work can produce an unhealthy ego. With an inflated ego, the person can use the spiritual experience as a shield against suggestions to work a full program.

Spiritual experiences, if handled properly, can lead to a spiritual awakening that brings creativity and serenity. With a spiritual awakening we are willing to practice ACA principles in all our affairs and to carry the message to others.

## Service is Love Grounded in Self-Love

Spiritually awake adult children understand the spiritual axiom which states: "We must give away what we have to keep it." This is one of the most selfless acts of love we can offer a confused world; however, we must love ourselves first to have something to give away. Without self-love, the Twelfth Step merely becomes another goal we achieve or a mark we pass on our way to pleasing others or abandoning ourselves. Without self-love, we tend to use service to others as a camouflage to hide in plain sight. Self-love is a result of working the Twelve Steps, being vulnerable, asking for help, and being aware of our bodies through meditation and proper breathing. We love ourselves when we find our pain. We sit with it without acting out on drugs or some other compulsive activity. We go after our stored grief and greet it and feel it. We find our True Selves and sit beside the Divine Light.

In his final days, in the Twelfth Step of his life, our founder, Tony A., focused on self-love. He boiled down his 30 years of recovery into the simple but powerful concept of self-love and self-forgiveness. In his last days, he continued to encourage adult children to love themselves.

Because of his own violent upbringing before World War II, Tony knew that adult children carry inherent shame and abandonment. Without help, we can abandon ourselves in a heartbeat. He believed we can only be healed by self-love and the hand of God called upon by the willing adult child. He knew adult children spend a lifetime running from abandonment or shame disguised as a variety of compulsions and self-harming acts. He knew we never stopped loving our parents even though we thought we had. Through his recovery, Tony realized his parents were the biological couple who brought him into the world. However, the actual parent is a Higher Power who never abandons.

We meet the actual parent through the Twelve Steps. With spiritual help, we stop resisting the idea of loving ourselves unconditionally. In self-love, Tony was not speaking of narcissistic self-centeredness or navel gazing. He was speaking of embracing our wounded inner self and turning to our Higher Power for breath, life, and healing. He knew that when adult children go inside and find their wholeness they can serve God and the world as Trusted Servants. We go outward by going inward. We become inwardly illuminated.

By loving ourselves, we can begin to take down our final wall and let love in. This is the core of the onion—self-love. Letting someone in takes courage because we have been hurt deeply by rejection as children. We loved our parents naturally, but our parents could not accept our gift. They did not love themselves. They could not recognize what we were trying to give them. As children, we were confused by our parents' rejection. We quickly learned to retract our love and bury it deep inside. We created a false self, who chased people and things so we could feel in control but never whole. We thought we had buried our love permanently, but it is there. No matter what we have done in the false self, our love is there. This means we can love others. This means we can be a friend.

By loving ourselves, we see there is more love in the world than we realized. There is still much dependency and addiction, but there is love and we can see it. We recognize it because it is in us. By recognizing love, our false self dissolves. We realize we are not our addictions. We are not drugs, food, spending, gambling, sex, or compulsions. We are love.

As children of God, we want to carry the ACA message to the adult child who still suffers so that we might continue to grow spiritually ourselves. We attend ACA meetings for ourselves, but we also do it to be available to new people making a start in the program. We know what our story is, and we know our loss. We also know hope and forgiveness. We have progressed from hurting to helping.

Meanwhile, those who are spiritually awake accept Twelve Step work with an attitude of service rather than sacrifice. By the time we reach this Step, we know the difference between being a rescuer and giving service with love.

The difference between reacting like a caretaker and lending a hand involves the fact that we are helping ourselves. We are not people-pleasing or fearing authority figures. We do not seek titles or power in ACA. We sincerely want to help out in the spirit of anonymity. We are moving out of isolation by attending meetings and getting involved. We see service work as giving love rather than enabling or manipulation. We also know when to step back or ask for help. We also know that we are going to be all right no matter what happens. We have God and our friends in ACA. We are going to make it.

## Step Twelve is a Beginning

Reaching Step Twelve is the beginning not the end. It is a beginning of a new way of life that we can take into our work place, relationships, and on our spiritual journey. We have been applying ACA in all three areas in the preceding Steps; however, in Step Twelve we are making a more formal statement that we have adopted a life of surrender, hope, honesty, humility, and forgiveness.

With the Twelve Steps we have a design for living that we believe will help us face life's challenges and joys. There are no guarantees that the Twelve Steps will straighten out life's meandering path; however, with the Steps, we believe we can take the curves more gently. We believe we have an edge in whatever life deals us. In addition to having a proven program to rely on, we also realize we are not alone. We have ACA friends we can count on. We have meetings we can attend. We have our feelings, and we have prayer. We also know we don't have to be perfect or in control all the time. We keep it simple in matters of living and relating to people. We live one day at a time and handle what is in front of us. What a great relief as we face the future.

Some of us will face relationship challenges, health issues, and death as part of life. ACA members tend to meet these challenges in good form due to their support group and spiritual life. We have seen adult children use the principles of the Twelve Steps to handle family illness, despair, and death with amazing serenity and faith. We have marveled at some ACA members and their ability to stay focused without falling into blame or destructive behavior when faced with an unfairness of life.

These adult children realize the importance of staying active in ACA and remaining spiritually fit to face the vicissitudes of life. Many will say it is easier to stay spiritually fit by taking daily program action than attempting to catch up once a crisis hits. Regular attendance at ACA meetings helps us stay spiritually fit.

Many recovering adult children will need the Twelve Steps to face children who may have been affected by their dysfunction. Many of our members fit into this category. They have children or adult children who are acting out in addiction, dependency, and other forms of self-harm. Some of their children or grandchildren live in another state or area and are rarely seen. All of these circumstances bring great emotional pain to an adult child who has inventoried his life and realizes the generational nature of family dysfunction. It aches to know that he or she is powerless and cannot fix anyone.

These adult children continue to attend meetings and talk about their feelings of guilt and powerlessness. They pray. They do service work or sponsor a new member and stay involved. They avoid isolation. They forgive themselves. Their emotional pain is lessened. Many have positive outcomes over time. They reconnect with their children or see a child find help.

Practicing ACA principles in our relationships with our children and others is possibly one of the most challenging areas of our lives. Relationships are where our survival traits attempt to reemerge. We must remain open to steer our lives away from stifling control. With honesty and kindness, we allow God to work in our relationships. We talk about our feelings in the relationship, and we listen to the feelings of others as well. We check our motives with a trusted friend or with a sponsor. We remember we can talk, trust, and feel instead of control, isolate, and fume. Relationships can be different in recovery. It is never too late to have a happy childhood or relationship.

## Get Out of Yourself

While much of ACA's program involves the inward journey, Step Twelve reminds us to journey outward as well. We carry the message to other adult children in our meetings, on the telephone, and through service work. We get out of ourselves by sponsoring others, giving rides to meetings, and by getting involved at an ACA event or fund raiser. There are many opportunities if we only look. Most of this activity falls under the title of Twelfth Step work, and it means that we are answering the call to carry the message to others. We cannot use old excuses of feeling ill, not good enough, or unique to continue sitting on the sideline of life. To avoid helping others is to avoid helping ourselves. We can do this. We have our Higher Power and our friends to help us participate in life. We learn how to have fun in addition to contributing to our own recovery. The gratitude we feel is limitless.

In ACA, we carry the message of hope to adult children across the world. There are ACA groups in Denmark, Germany, Italy, Turkey, Russia, Hungary, and Japan, as well as North and South America, Australia, and the Pacific Islands. There could easily be 300 million adult children across the world who qualify for ACA. We doubt there will ever be a shortage of people who could use the ACA way of life. However, we typically carry the message to people who want it and not to people who need it. We have learned that you cannot give ACA to someone who does not want it. But at the same time, you cannot stop someone who wants it from having it. We know of adult children in some of the poorest countries in the world, with minimal amounts of ACA literature, living the ACA way of life. Their willingness, openness, and courage are amazing.

Additionally, we try to answer calls to carry ACA's message of hope into prisons, treatment centers, or mental health care facilities. Adult children are sent to prison every day for harming themselves or others. Still others have psychiatric problems so severe that they require hospitalization. Both the prisoner and the psychiatric patient are adult children and deserve to hear ACA's message. Our program is mature enough, and our members are strong enough, to do this work within the guidelines we have established for these facilities. No one should put themselves in harms way by carrying the message into these facilities; however, there are opportunities to carry the message here. The program has had success in these facilities.

Carrying the ACA message gets us out of ourselves and builds confidence. We see that we can help others as a sponsor or mentor. There is great joy awaiting you to watch a frightened or foggy newcomer attend his or her first meeting and watch that person open up. This is something you do not want to miss. To watch a new person realize that he or she is not alone is heart warming. To hear a new member sharing about finding clarity about his childhood is equally joyous. We really feel like we are a part of life during these moments. We believe we are living the life we always wanted to live. We are finally home. We have found a fellowship of people we have always sought.

In carrying the ACA message to another, we keep it simple. Our stories are sufficient. There is no need to embellish or minimize what we have been through. When carrying the message, we follow a simple formula of building identity, describing the ACA program, and then inviting the person to a meeting. To build identity, we offer a few examples of what our life was like before finding ACA. We talk about our feelings of isolation and uniqueness even as we worked hard at trying to fit in with others. We talk about hitting a bottom in relationships or at work.

Next, we let the person we are trying to help read a copy of The Laundry List (Problem). At this point, the person will usually begin to share some of his or her own story if the person is wanting help. We ask the person to attend an ACA meeting as soon as possible.

As ACA members trying to help another person, we know that the program works and what the Steps can do for a person. They offer another way to live for the person wanting to live differently. The message of ACA states that ACA works, and it will work for anyone who can hit a bottom, surrender, and ask for and accept help. That's the tricky part. Most ACA's are self-sufficient. They attend meetings and learn the language but fail to ask for help. They suffer with an entrenched feeling of being different or frightened. But there is hope with willingness and with time.

Our promise is this: Any adult child seeking help from the effects of growing up in a dysfunctional home can find acceptance, honesty, and self-love in ACA. We are the fellowship who reaches out to the self-sufficient adult child winning employee awards and to the adult child in the institutional setting. We judge neither. We love both. We see them as the same because we know what they did not receive and what they seek. We also know what we have to offer. We know what we are doing. We are arresting the disease of family dysfunction at its generational nature. We focus on ourselves in ACA. To each adult child seeking this way of life, we say: "God will be there when you need God."

## STEP TWELVE SPIRITUAL PRINCIPLES:

### Love and Self-love

END NOTES

†ON PAGE 74: Read Tony's Fourth Step on Page 57 in The Laundry List: The ACoA Experience, by Tony A. with Dan F., 1991, HCI Publications.

†ON PAGE 82: Alcoholics Anonymous "Big Book," Step Four, p. 64, Fifth Edition.

†ON PAGE 176: Bill's Story, Alcoholics Anonymous "Big Book," p. 1, Fifth Edition.

†ON PAGE 176: Tony A. spent much of his life experiencing spiritual and mystical moments that he investigated and used to understand his life journey. One of the most powerful experiences occurred in 1978 when he wrote the 14 traits of The Laundry List. In his book, Tony wrote: "I felt that I was receiving inner guidance and direction as I wrote the words. It was a strange feeling." (The Laundry List: The ACoA Experience by Tony A. with Dan F., Page 12, 1991, HCI publications).

†ON PAGE 178: The concept of a spiritual bypass is attributed to Dr. Charles Whitfield and Barbara Whitfield. The Whitfields have written extensively on spiritual experiences and practical mysticism in addition to adult child recovery.

# APPENDIX
## Hearing a Fifth Step

*"Admitted to God, to ourselves, and to another human being the exact nature of our wrongs."*

Hearing or listening to another person's Fifth Step is an ultimate act of service coming from love. To hear a person's story, you should have completed your own Fifth Step and the remaining Twelve Steps. You should be working an active ACA program by attending meetings and changing your behavior in workable relationships.

The following guidelines are one method of listening to a Fifth Step given by an ACA member. These guidelines are consistent with the Fellow Traveler method of sponsorship. This guide is designed to match the exercises in the ACA basic text. In addition to offering tips on hearing a Fifth Step, this guide will help you assist the person with Steps Six through Eight as well.

This guide is designed for a sponsor and sponsee working the Twelve Steps of ACA. Typically, the Fifth Step is heard by the sponsor of the sponsee working the Steps. However, there are others who can hear a Fifth Step. These people can include counselors, spiritual advisors, and members of other Twelve Step fellowships. A person should not ask a spouse, parents, relatives, friends, or old lovers to hear his or her Fifth Step. The person hearing the Fifth Step should have an understanding of the design and focus of the Twelve Steps of ACA. While ACA is similar to other Twelve Step fellowships, we have expanded the Fourth Step to include an inventory of the family system in addition to an inventory of one's self. That means ACA looks at the effects of parental behavior and some sibling behavior in addition to the behavior of the individual. The sponsee needs a listener who understands what he or she is trying to accomplish with the ACA Steps.

Step Five represents the courage of an individual to admit the exact nature of his or her wrongs without embellishing or minimizing the events. The person is telling his or her story to another person and to God. In Step Five, the ACA member trusts another to hear his or her life story without judgment. For many, this is the first time the adult child has told the most intimate details of his or her life to another. Trust of another person is one of the spiritual principles of Step Five. There is also the principle of self-honesty.

Your sponsee should have worked Steps One through Four before beginning Step Five. Ideally, you and the sponsee should work the first four Steps together. This workbook is designed to help an ACA member work all of the Steps with a sponsor or counselor. The workbook is an excellent Twelve Step guide for these purposes. There are no timelines on completing the first four Steps of ACA, but usually a person should be making progress in finishing Steps One through Four within the first year of recovery. Some members will complete these Steps more quickly while others will take longer. There should be no rush to complete these early Steps; however, we should not procrastinate with the Steps.

## Hearing Someone's Fifth Step Involves Three Basic Elements:

1. Understanding the sequence of the Steps and what the person is trying to achieve by working Steps Four and Five.

2. Listening with empathy and without judging the person.

3. Helping the person move onto Steps Six, Seven, and Eight, and the rest of the Steps after Step Five.

**No. 1—Understanding the sequence of the Steps and what the person is trying to achieve by working Steps Four and Five.**

There is a specific sequence of the Twelve Steps that begins with the person hitting a bottom, asking for help, and admitting denial. The person doing his or her Fifth Step should have admitted powerlessness over the effects of family dysfunction in Step One followed by an equal admission of unmanageability. There should be a willingness to seek spiritual solutions in Step Two and Step Three. In Step Four and Step Five, there should be self-honesty and a willingness to speak openly with another person about one's life. These are the undercurrents of attitudes that we listen for as we listen to the main details of someone's Fifth Step.

The result the sponsee is trying to achieve in Step Four involves a searching and fearless inventory of himself or herself. The sponsee is exposing secrets, abuse, and false loyalty to a dysfunctional family system. The person is seeking clarity and a fair look at parental behavior that affected him or her as a child and continues to affect the person as an adult. The sponsee is also addressing his or her own selfish or harmful behavior.

As you listen to a Fifth Step, you should not overly identify with the victim or victimizer aspect of the sponsee. Most adult children have been victims, and they have victimized others. As a listener you seek neutrality. In Step Five, we avoid the urge to rescue the sponsee as he or she relates some of the harrowing events of childhood. We can feel empathy and compassion for the sponsee while maintaining our neutrality.

In Step Five, we encourage our sponsee to tell everything, holding back nothing, so that the person can be free of secrets and carried shame. As the Fifth Step progresses, we may briefly share some of our own story to create identification, but we do not dominate the time. The Fifth Step is for the sponsee to talk and to share his or her story.

### No. 2—Listening with empathy and without judging the person.

Most adult children have never been listened to, so listening to another adult child without judgment is possibly one of the greatest gifts we can give another person. Listening with empathy adds spirituality to the gift.

At the same time, listening with empathy does not mean that we suspend our duty to point out problematic behavior. We can gently highlight where a person has wronged others. We can help the sponsee see the exact nature of the wrong. As a sponsor, we can listen to others without judgement but still offer our experience on where amends should be made. We can point out problematic behavior that could be inventoried in the future. We do not do this during the Fifth Step. We wait until the Fifth Step is done. At the end of Step Five, we offer the person a balanced assessment of his or her strong points and points that can be improved.

As the person shares his or her Fifth Step, we listen to the story with complete attention. We also listen for clues that the person has admitted powerlessness over the effects of family dysfunction in Step One. For example, do we hear the person still holding onto notions that he or she can control outcomes? Or is the person truly seeking to let go and focus on himself or herself? Is the person being honest? Is the person seeking help from a Higher Power?

### No. 3—Helping the person move onto Steps Six, Seven, and Eight, and the rest of the Steps after Step Five.

To hear a Fifth Step you will need a pen and paper and a quiet, comfortable place. On the day of the Fifth Step, the sponsee should arrive with numerous lists and worksheets from the Fourth Step guide in this book. The ACA Fourth Step contains 12 exercises. The lists need to be complete enough to present a searching and fearless inventory of the person's life. Listen to all the lists. Information about character defects and making amends will typically come from exercises No. 5, No. 7, and No. 9. Exercise No. 12 has a list of positive traits that will help you balance the problematic behaviors.

1. Inventory of Laundry List Traits (How traits developed)
2. Family Secrets
3. Shame List
4. Abandonment List
5. Harms Inventory
6. Stored Anger (Resentment)
7. Relationships (Romance, sexual, or friendships)
8. Sexual Abuse Inventory
9. Denial Inventory (Parent's behavior; Sponsee's behavior)
10. Post-Traumatic Stress Disorder worksheet
11. Feelings Exercise
12. Praise Work

These exercises represent a comprehensive Fourth Step that includes an inventory of the dysfunctional family system in addition to an inventory of the sponsee.

To begin, you should allow plenty of time for the Fifth Step to be completed. Before the Fifth Step begins, you may tell the sponsee that you will listen to him or her without judgment. You may also assure the person that you will treat his or her story with confidentiality. Everything that is said during the Fifth Step will remain between you and the sponsee. You can tell the sponsee that you will take brief notes while he or she talks. The notes will be used to help create a Sixth Step List and Eighth Step Amends List when Step Five is done. (Do not take a lot of notes since this can be distracting as the person talks out his or her Fifth Step.) Keep it simple.

**Sixth Step List (defects of character)**

On a piece of paper, before the Fifth Step begins, write "Sixth Step List" at the top of the page. Then write "assets" on the left-hand side of the page. On the right-hand side, write "defects of character" or "ineffectual behaviors." As the sponsee talks during the Fifth Step, write down positive behaviors and problematic behaviors that could be addressed by attending meetings, journaling, prayer, and further Step work. Helping a sponsee identify his or her character defects based on your own experience with the Steps, is well within the Fellow Traveler method of sponsorship. Think about your own Step work and how you addressed assets and defects of character. Help the sponsee identify his or her attributes as well. Most adult children can identify negative thoughts and behaviors but struggle with seeing their good traits. As a sponsor and fellow traveler, you can help the sponsee see positive qualities that the person possesses. You can simplify this list by limiting it to three or four examples.

**For Example:**
**Sixth Step List**

| Assets: | Defects of Character or Ineffectual Behaviors: |
|---|---|
| Selflessness | Selfishness |
| Caring | Judgmental |
| Creative | Jealousy |
| Hard worker | Procrastinates |

When the Fifth Step is done, you will use this list to help the person move on to Step Six and Step Seven (removal of defects of character). The key is to balance the behaviors. Each adult child has strong qualities and qualities that can be improved.

## Eighth Step Amends List

Also, before the Fifth Step begins, use a separate piece of paper to create an Eighth Step Amends List. At the top of the page write "Eighth Step Amends List." As the sponsee talks, list names and incidents that should be addressed in Step Eight—"Made a list of all persons we had harmed and became willing to make amends to them all." Place the sponsee's name at the top of the list. We must make amends to ourselves and forgive ourselves before we can take action to do the same for others.

To keep it simple and to avoid distractions during the Fifth Step, just write down the name of the person who will receive an amends in the left-hand column. Fill in the "incident" and "amends type" after the Fifth Step is completed.

For Example:
Eighth Step Amends List

| Name of Person receiving amends (fill in during Fifth Step) | Incident (fill in later) | Amends type (fill in later) |
|---|---|---|
|  |  |  |

An Example of a Completed Eighth Step Amends List

| Name | Incident | Amends |
|---|---|---|
| John (Sponsee) | self-hate, inner critic | learn to love myself |
| Sue | damaged her car in a fit of rage | pay to have car fixed |
| Mike | gossiped about him | stop gossiping |
| Father | cursed him in public | apologize for cursing him |
| Boss | stole from him | pay it back |
| My daughter | blamed her for my temper, my rage | living amends, ask for forgiveness |

When the Fifth Step is done, you will use this list to help the person move onto Step Eight. You might set up time on another day to fill in the Step Eight list. In Step Eight we become willing to make amends. The actual amends are made in Step Nine. Have the sponsee read Step Eight for insight into willingness. Along with willingness, the key to making amends is making things right for harms we have done. Some amends are monetary amends in which we pay back money, while other amends are living amends in which we change our behavior one day at a time. Other amends can involve naming our behavior and asking for forgiveness from the person we have harmed. We usually say "I am making amends for my behavior and for harming you. It was wrong/selfish/hurtful (pick one or a combination of these). I am learning how to live differently. I am not making excuses for my behavior. I will try to not repeat my behavior. In the meantime, here is what I am doing to make it right."

We must back up this statement with program action such as attending meetings and helping others. We also change our behavior.

If there is a question about an amends, the weight of responsibility should lean toward the sponsee. We want to grow up, and that involves being responsible. We want to be free of harmful behavior that brings isolation and regret. Making amends with the support of ACA, even if the direction of harm is unsure, is better than living with open questions about the past. We make these amends and leave the results up to God, as we understand God.

## Recap on Hearing a Fifth Step

1. Set a date to hear the Fifth Step.

2. Prepare for hearing the Fifth Step by reviewing the exercises in Step Four in the ACA Twelve Step Workbook or the ACA Fellowship Text. These are the lists and worksheets the sponsee will be bringing to the Fifth Step.

3. On the day of the Fifth Step, before the sponsee arrives, get a notepad and make a Sixth Step List and Eighth Step List. Avoid taking a lot of notes during the Fifth Step, but take enough notes to sketch out character defects, positive traits, and individuals to receive an amends.

4. When the sponsee arrives, explain that you will listen with empathy and fairness to the Fifth Step. Explain that Step Four and Step Five involve rigorous honesty and identifying the exact nature of his or her wrongs. Explain that you will help the sponsee identify positive traits and problematic traits as part of balancing the personal inventory and as part of preparing for Step Six and Step Seven.

5. Begin Step Five.

6. When the Fifth Step ends, review the Sixth Step List. Share your experience with identifying your own character defects and positive traits. Keep it simple when helping the sponsee do the same. Give three examples of positive traits and

three examples of character defects that the sponsee possesses. This helps the sponsee avoid focusing only on defects, and he or she will not be overwhelmed by a lengthy list. (The list of character defects and positive traits at the end of these instructions will help you and the sponsee select items for the Sixth Step list.)

7.  Make plans to discuss the Eighth Step Amends List on another day.

8.  Instruct the sponsee to return home and read all of the section on Step Six in this workbook. He or she will find directions on how to proceed with Step Six and Step Seven in the reading. There will also be directions on integrating Laundry List traits.

## For Use In Helping the Sponsee Determine Positive Traits and Defects of Character

**Possible Defects of Character are:**

Self-centeredness, judgmentalness, procrastination, perfectionism, envy, greed, lust, feeling superior, dishonesty, gossiping, and pettiness.

**Positive Traits include:**

| strong | compassionate | spontaneous | trustworthy | prompt |
|--------|---------------|-------------|-------------|--------|
| humorous | courteous | creative | tenacious | kind |
| sensitive | talented | loving | judicious | hard working |
| willing | honest | a listener | accepting | a friend |
| intelligent | organized | spiritual | modest | an ACA member |

## A Discussion About Step Eight and Step Nine

Step Eight involves becoming willing to make amends to those we have harmed while Step Nine puts that willingness into action. As you help a sponsee create an Eighth Step Amends List, family situations must be considered. By their nature, some dysfunctional families can be violent or potentially violent. In other cases there can be demeaning remarks and hurtful denial. We try to not project how an amends will proceed, but the Steps do not require us to place ourselves in harm's way. We also do not use an amends to have a showdown with our parents or relatives. The amends involves our effort to repair harm we have caused and to forgive ourselves and others. We want to make amends to our family to the best of our ability while also protecting ourselves from potential harm.

We don't grovel or plead while making amends. We can feel good about what we are doing for ourselves. Our attitude is one of humility and a sincere desire to make amends for harms done. Some people may accept our sincerity, and others may not, but we remain committed to our recovery. We have usually harmed other family members with remarks, judgments, and physical abuse in some cases. We may have struck someone, and we may have been struck back. Yet, we are focusing on our behavior so that we can go forward. We cannot make excuses for our behavior to avoid making amends.

At the same time, there can be incest, emotional abuse, and physical trauma perpetrated by the parents or other family members upon the sponsee. The sponsee is obviously not responsible for this behavior since he or she was a child. The child did not cause it and cannot cure it. However, the Twelve Steps require us to make amends for our selfish and destructive behavior as adults so that we can change from within and contribute to ACA and to society. There will be behavior by the sponsee that is clearly abusive to his or her family. In some cases it is retaliatory abuse in which the sponsee has actively sought to hurt the parents or family since the family harmed him or her. There could also be matters of money in which the sponsee uses guilt to get money from a perpetrating family member. It is an understood pay-off for secretive behavior. None of this is healthy, but it can be dealt with through honesty and a willingness to live life without secrets or dependence.

Asking an incest survivor to make amends to his or her perpetrating relative for harms the incest survivor has done after leaving the home must be discussed in greater detail. (Read Step Eight for more details.) We seek discernment in these circumstances since each one is different. We also seek fellowship experience. Some ACA members will not make amends to a violent or perpetrating family member for reasons that involve personal safety and retaining self-dignity. Some of these parents or family members remain unrepentant and sick. There is lust and perverseness and a complete rejection of the truth. The sponsee must protect himself or herself from such family members. Under these extreme conditions, a direct amends to the family is usually not appropriate; however, the sponsee can find freedom from the shame that surrounds the sexual abuse if he or she remains focused on the Twelve Steps and seeks guidance from a Higher Power. At the same time, the sponsee must continue on with amends to other people on the Eighth Step List. The bar must remain high so that we can make things right and claim personal freedom. This is a courageous and meaningful path that fulfills Step Eight and Step Nine.

In other cases, incest survivors in ACA have made face-to-face amends to a perpetrating parent or relative. The amends involved behavior committed by the incest survivor after leaving the home. With help, the person was able to judge the situation and discern the spiritual aim of Steps Eight and Nine and to balance that with retaining self-dignity. These members knew they were making amends for adult behaviors that have roots in the abuse visited upon them by the family. In essence, they release the shame surrounding the sexual abuse while taking responsibility for their adult behaviors. In some of these cases, full forgiveness for the perpetrator usually comes later rather than sooner.

These examples are our fellowship experience that we can rely upon, in addition to prayer and a sincere desire to not back down from Step work that can bring lasting and spiritual peace.